Radical Simplicity
Transforming Computers Into Me-Centric Appliances

Dr. Frederick Hayes-Roth
Daniel Amor

PH
PTR

Prentice Hall Professional Technical Reference
Upper Saddle River, New Jersey 07458
www.phptr.com

Library of Congress Cataloging-in-Publication Data

CIP data available.

Editorial/production supervision: *Mary Sudul*
Acquisitions editor: *Jill Harry*
Manufacturing manager: *Maura Zaldivar*
Marketing manager: *Dan DePasquale*
Cover design: *Nina Scuderi*
Cover design direction: *Jerry Votta*
Editorial assistant: *Noreen Regina*

Publisher, Hewlett-Packard Books: *Patricia Pekary*

© 2003 by Hewlett-Packard Company

Published by Prentice Hall PTR
Prentice-Hall, Inc.
Upper Saddle River, New Jersey 07458

Prentice Hall books are widely used by corporations and government agencies for training, marketing, and resale.
The publisher offers discounts on this book when ordered in bulk quantities. For more information, contact Corporate Sales Department, Phone: 800-382-3419; FAX: 201-236-7141; E-mail: corpsales@prenhall.com
Or write: Prentice Hall PTR, Corporate Sales Dept., One Lake Street, Upper Saddle River, NJ 07458.

Other product or company names mentioned herein are the trademarks or registered trademarks of their respective owners.

Printed in the United States of America
10   9   8   7   6   5   4   3   2   1

ISBN 0-13-100291-0

Pearson Education LTD.
Pearson Education Australia PTY, Limited
Pearson Education Singapore, Pte. Ltd.
Pearson Education North Asia Ltd.
Pearson Education Canada, Ltd.
Pearson Educación de Mexico, S.A. de C.V.
Pearson Education — Japan
Pearson Education Malaysia, Pte. Ltd.

Radical Simplicity
Transforming Computers Into Me-Centric Appliances

ISBN 0131002910

HEWLETT-PACKARD PRESS STRATEGIC BOOKS

- ◆ *Mobilize Your Enterprise: Achieving Competitive Advantage Through Wireless Technology*
  Patrick Brans

- ◆ *The Fast Track to Profit: An Insider's Guide to Exploiting the World's Best Internet Technologies*
  Lee G. Caldwell

- ◆ *Itanium Rising: Breaking Through Moore's Second Law of Computing Power*
  Jim Carlson and Jerry Huck

- ◆ *The Business and Economics of Linux and Open Source*
  Martin Fink

- ◆ *Radical Simplicity: Transforming Computers into Me-Centric Appliances*
  Dr. Frederick Hayes-Roth and Daniel Amor

www.hp.com/hpbooks

As information technology becomes more thoroughly integrated into our lives, it also becomes like all infrastructure—indispensable, yet invisible. This means the emphasis shifts from the technology to the people, from computational devices to appliances, and from being technology-centered to being me-centered. Hayes-Roth and Amor have provided a long-needed, essential book for the technology and business strategists who will provide the new services: for everyone who does not wish to be left behind.

Donald A. Norman
Northwestern University and the Nielsen Norman group
Author of *The Invisible Computer*

Too many of today's computing tools are user-hostile gadgets that force people to adapt to them, rather than doing what people really want. Web services and wireless communication can change all that. This book shows how.

Hal Abelson
Department of Electrical Engineering and Computer Science at MIT

Contents

FOREWORD BY
IAN BROWDE

One dark night a dervish passing by a dry well heard a cry for help. "What is the matter?" he called down.

"I am a grammarian, and have fallen due to my ignorance of the path, into this deep well, where I am all but immobilized," came the response.

"Hold friend I'll fetch a ladder and rope," said the dervish.

"One moment please!" said the grammarian, "Your grammar and diction are flawed; be good enough to amend them."

"If that is so much more important than the essentials," shouted the dervish "you had best stay where you are until I have learned to speak properly."

And he went on his way.

From *Tales of the Dervishes*, Idries Shah.

Our lives are growing more and more complicated. Technology aimed to relieve our burden is increasingly difficult to use and to manage. Experts and meta-experts are required even for the apparently most simple of tasks. We have become "slaves of what our slaves create."

There are few people that I encounter these days who are not too busy, too stressed, or too pressed for time. Companies of all hues, particularly the large "successful" ones, are feeling pressure on their ability to sustain the business models that brought them to where they are. Lay-offs are commonplace, health benefits are being cut or restructured, and many employees privately view employment as a privilege not a right. All the time, executives, managers, especially IT managers, are driving harder to "do more with less." A fundamental shift is required, not only in what we do but in how we think.

Enter *Radical Simplicity* by Rick Hayes-Roth and Daniel Amor. These two technology visionaries share a perspective of why the reality we are experiencing is the way it is, and why that can change over the next decade or so. The reality this important book helps us see is that we are living in the era of computers as tools. Ironically, the better we are at using these tools, the greater the load and the stress until we are literally bursting our seams mentally, physically, and emotionally.

This forward-looking work helps us gain insight into the fact that the many tool users around the world are really the menial workers of the information age. Yet we continue to believe that another Powerpoint presentation, another MS Word memo, another Excel spreadsheet, not to mention the 20, 90, 250 emails a day of dubious value, are providing us a better life.

Hayes-Roth and Amor, in a simple, accessible way called me-centric computing, offer a view into a possible future that is ours for the taking. They share a vision of a new possibility for our relationship with these ubiquitous tools, and hence ourselves, that could be a Renaissance in how human beings work, learn, and play with computers as our support system, our agents, and our menial task performers.

This book is essential reading for any business or technology strategist who wants to ensure that her or his company will survive the next decade and be part of the emerging solution, part of the knowledge age or the age of enlivenment.

Radical Simplicity uses its own metaphor and simply tells us that most of the technology is presently available for this seemingly idyllic world where computers do the menial work and people get to take back their time and enliven their spirit.

Whether your interest is technologies and applications like SOAP, UDDI, HTTPS, and XML or whether you want a view of what is actually available like Cooltown, OnStar, Screenfridge, or Hive, it is all there.

If you want to understand how designing appliances and products must change and how to do it; or if you want to learn how software agents, mobility, and trust are fundamental building blocks for the future, this eminently readable book tells it like it is, simply and unpretentiously.

In a nutshell, *Radical Simplicity* urges us to move beyond focusing on the tools and the products and start focusing on each and every "me" out there; how we work, and what we need. The book tells us not just "why" but "how," while providing useful URLs as footnotes, a neat touch! It explains in both lay and professional terms how software agents are critical in our own evolution from tool-slaves to appliance-masters. It offers an optimistic yet balanced view of what the future can be, a most useful book; thanks Rick and Daniel.

Ian Browde
VP Business Development
Nokia Internet Communications
ian.browde@nokia.com

FOREWORD BY DEX SMITH

I am delighted to see this book. Consumers certainly want things to be simpler so they can focus more on life and less on technology. Businesses want work simplified because productivity and less rework goes directly to the bottom line.

Hayes-Roth and Amor describe a compelling vision of the future where technology serves humans. However, they pick up where other visionaries and futurists leave off and outline how it can be done. They begin to describe, in a structured and realistic way, the technical approaches and architectures that will enable simple, intelligent appliances to be conceived and built.

Making an experience simpler for a customer is good business. Making it *radically* simple could disrupt a market in your favor. Whether you are a designer, a technologist or a marketer, this book will undoubtedly become a valuable handbook for helping you realize a me-centric future for the people that use your products and services.

Dex Smith
Director, Experience Strategies & Architectures
Hewlett-Packard Company

INTRODUCTION

It's hard to make predictions—especially about the future.

Robert Storm Petersen

Disruptive New Technology

Until recently, the growth of computer usage was driven primarily by our need to easily work with numbers and text. Computers in the backroom were invisible to us. Computers on our desks and laps were powerful business tools, making us prolific tool users.

Initially, this meant our days included extra work that either wasn't necessary before computers or was done by assistants, graphic artists, and typesetters, among others. The computing trend became to use more tools more of the time, to process more information. Productivity gains were modest initially, but probably reached diminishing returns some time ago.

The world is about to be turned upside down, however. Or perhaps, more exactly, inside out. Whereas previous generations of technology built a tower of new computing tools that required a new mindset to use, the next generation is being built around the human, supporting our different roles and groups.

This technology is called *me-centric* because it fits into the individual's life in a natural way—it conforms to preferences and requirements, takes orders, and automates any number of delegated tasks. In me-centric computing, every appliance becomes part of *my* environment, *my* team, *my* extension. I get increased power and save time because the vast power of computing technology is working in concert to do my bidding.

The Fourth Wave

The first wave of computing addressed back-office transactions; it was a simple number-crunching business. The second wave provided interactive tools for office work. With the introduction of the personal computer, the architecture also shifted from a central host to the so-called client/server model. The third wave allowed everyone to access and exchange information. Three-tier architecture emerged to overcome the limitations of two-tier architecture. One of the most prominent applications of the third wave is the Internet.

The fourth wave will transfer everyday work from people to machines. It will multiply the time and reach of everyone, and initiate an explosion of machine-to-machine negotiation, problem-solving, and transactions. With the recent emergence of smart applications, it has become obvious that the computer is not a machine whose main purpose is to get a computing task done. With its attendant peripherals and networks, the computer has become a machine that allows us to explore new capacities to communicate, reaching new audiences in ways previously unthinkable.

The fourth wave will empower appliances with built-in computing and communication abilities that will make them work smarter on our behalf. Computing as we know it will transform into a computer-supported collaborative effort rather than a solitary one.

This revolution in computer usage will be unleashed by founding computing architecture around knowledge of the user, giving the user the capability to delegate work to computers; thus, computing functionality will begin in the interface the user accesses to various devices; work will be tasked from this interface to various computers, applications, and intelligent agents distributed around the world on the Internet or its successors.

This transition will exploit several technological trends already underway, including advances in Web services, communications, interfaces, information processing, and agents. Demands for computing, storage, bandwidth, and management will soar. Though the technology will be more complex, it will become increasingly invisible, as it disappears into our new communicators, problem-solvers, personal assistants, and living spaces.

Smart appliances and intelligent agents will change the way we work and live by working *for us*. Here are just a few ways it will affect the industry:

- Telecommunications and utility companies will automate location information to route the closest engineer to a customer.

- Insurance agents will download and complete forms on their PDAs and submit them via wireless connections to expedite on-scene accident assessments.

- Once privacy and security issues are resolved, mobile banking will become commonplace.

- Doctors' offices and hospitals will process forms and prescriptions using Internet appliances, to be able to treat patients more quickly.

To begin to understand where this revolution will take us, just look at TiVo[1], which records TV programs that match your interests and delivers them to you whenever you want. Using similar technology, here are a few simple examples of how agents and smart appliances will affect our homes:

- Personal assistant software will keep track of birthdays and anniversaries for you, then suggest gift purchases for people as these special dates approach.

- Automated travel agents will know what types of vacations you like and when you like to take them, and they'll find them at the best prices.

- Bots will actively manage your liquid assets, achieving 50-percent better cash management through continuous monitoring of rates across various Internet-enabled financial institutions.

- Washing machines will determine when it is cheapest to wash based on water and energy prices, initiate contracts with energy suppliers, even start your laundry at the specified time. Other appliances will suggest and prepare your dinners, drive your car—the list goes on.

This book is called *Radical Simplicity* because new technologies have the power to achieve the ultimate simplification of technology: Make it disappear into the devices and appliances that do for us what we want them to.

Moving On to a New IT-Supported Society

Society has used IT so far as a tool. With me-centric computing, IT will become more tightly integrated into society than ever before as it

---

[1]http://www.tivo.com/

takes over services and processes autonomously. The future computing ecosystem will be interwoven with society in such a manner that it may become difficult to distinguish between communicating with other people and communicating with intelligent appliances.

Today, computers are the masters, and users are the servants. In a me-centric world, this will gradually shift as the vision of computing becomes a reality. As a result, user frustration will decrease, because the devices and services will adapt to the needs of the user, as opposed to the other way around. It will be also much easier for the user to change service than it is today. Through repetitive usage, the IT products will get to know more about the user, providing shortcuts and other information based on past experience with the user.

In addition, intuitive input and output interfaces, such as voice and gesture recognition, will make communicating with devices easier than in the past. They will also be less expensive, opening the door for much broader market appeal than exists today. In Japan, for example, disposable mobile phones are available that are made out of paper.

By broadening the user base and simplifying the interaction between humans and computing devices, me-centric computing will become truly pervasive and support users in every possible situation.

Who Should Read This Book

This book should be important to technology and business strategists. It tells the technology strategists how the IT world and the end-user expectation will likely undergo a major revolution within the next ten years. Those who miss this wave likely will feel that they missed a major opportunity and were left selling or supporting anachronistic approaches. Me-centric computing is about a fundamental shift in the value proposition of IT—its value will rise as less time is spent learning to use it, leaving more time to reap the benefits.

Business strategists will need to ask how their companies can participate in this revolution. If they're IT companies, they need to rearchitect products and services around the user, not around the network and server equipment. In fact, the networks and services will be transformed greatly by the changed demands these usage patterns will create. If they're IT purchasers or customers, they need to exploit the opportunity to build up new IT assets that directly address measurable productivity goals—something that will be made easier with smarter tools.

Besides strategists, this book is also aimed at product designers, product marketers, and R&D leaders who need to get started now building the new wave of products. The book provides a clear set of steps that can help to make these products successful.

Lastly, the book should be irresistible to readers who like to see the big waves coming, far enough in advance to choose whether to ride them or get out of the water. The leading edge of this wave is already visible, but the full impact is barely perceived.

Rick is a world authority on IT and artificial intelligence, and was the CTO for Software at Hewlett-Packard, a company uniquely positioned to participate in all elements of the revolution. Daniel is a well-known author of books about e-business and is chief technologist for e-commerce for Hewlett-Packard in Europe.

The anticipated changes in daily life are exciting, provocative, and readily accessible. The historic significance of discontinuity in human-machine relationships will stimulate the imagination and provoke an active participation in future opportunities. The consequences of the transitions, the nature of the transformations, and the timing of opportunities will stay with readers long after they finish the book.

We expect many new businesses to coalesce around the vision and bring to market whole new categories of products and services in the next few years. In addition to gaining insight into the future, you will learn about the key technologies that are collectively combining to create these disruptions, how they work, and how they work together.

How This Book Is Organized

The book is organized in five parts. The first part provides an introduction to me-centric computing and its historical roots, and provides some showcases to make it easier to understand what me-centric computing is about and how it can be applied to everyone's life. In the first chapter, a historical review of computing is presented, and some of the most important trends are analyzed. Chapter 2 provides a set of scenarios that show how me-centric computing can be applied. These range from personal services to enterprise-level services using a variety of networks and devices.

The second part of the book describes the design elements of a well-defined me-centric solution. It provides an overview of the different input and output interfaces that can be used for me-centric computing and provides an introduction to the design models that make me-centric services successful. Chapter 3 provides an overview of human-computer interaction (HCI). It describes the different means of communicating with smart appliances and what needs to be considered in doing so. This chapter also provides some insight on context awareness and how it can be applied to smart applications in order to reduce the amount of input from and to the user. Chapter 4 describes in detail the different approaches for good design. Good design takes not only technology into account, but also many other areas of science.

The third part details the architectural building blocks on the technology side. It digs into the data exchange mechanisms behind me-centric computing, which is built on XML technology. It provides an introduction to agent technology and Web services, which provide the infrastructure for me-centric applications. Chapter 5 provides an overview on me-centric architectures. Chapter 6 provides an in-depth review of Web services and how they have become the infrastructure backbone for the me-centric world. It also offers a detailed description of XML and how it can transport information through different devices, processes, and applications. Chapter 7 talks about agents and how they can be made intelligent and mobile for improved interaction between applications, humans, and devices.

The fourth part is about new business opportunities that will arise as me-centric computing becomes reality. This part tries to explain the impact me-centric computing will have on the economy, IT, and the people using it. Chapter 8 explains how devices will look in the future and how they will be constructed to be competitive. Chapter 9 provides an overview of the way me-centric computing will revolutionize our lives, no matter how involved we are with it.

The fifth part of the book contains the two appendices, the bibliography and the index. The first appendix provides an extensive glossary of all terms that are connected to me-centric computing. The second appendix provides an overview of Web sites connected to me-centric computing.

Acknowledgments

Rick would like to thank the many enlightened colleagues he has worked with over the years who have contributed to the vision of intelligent agents, me-centric user interfaces, and task-oriented problem-solving. Chief among these are the visionaries Allen Newell and Raj Reddy of Carnegie-Mellon University[2] and many DARPA leaders who promoted these possibilities long before they seemed practical. It seems obvious now that AI, intelligent interfaces, and the Internet, all developed with DARPA support for decades, will combine to transform our lives in profound and positive ways. Rick's former colleague, Bob An-

---

[2]http://www.cmu.edu/

derson of Rand Corporation[3], started developing software around these ideas more than 20 years ago. Good novel things apparently take some time to ripen.

Daniel would like to thank first and foremost his wife, Sabine, who is supporting him now with his fourth book in three years. He would also like to thank his readers who provided invaluable feedback and all colleagues and customers who he has worked with and gained insight. Thanks also to Gabriel Seher of IBM[4] for his important input. Special thanks go to Jana and Mike for the trip to Lausanne.

Rick and Daniel would like to thank Pat Pekary of HP Press[5] and Jill Harry of Prentice Hall[6] for their invaluable support in getting this book completed. They would also like to thank Ralph E. Moore for his contribution in reducing the complexity of some parts of the text.

If you would like to contact the authors, you can send an e-mail to Rick at rick@radicalsimplicity.com or to Danny at danny@radical-simplicity.com. More information about the book and its topics can be found on the book's Web site at http://www.radicalsimplicity.com/.

---

[3] http://www.rand.org/
[4] http://www.ibm.com/
[5] http://www.hp.com/go/retailbooks/
[6] http://www.phptr.com/

Part I

Introduction

Chapter 1

FROM THE BACKROOM TO EVERYDAY LIFE

1.1 A Day in Your Life (ca. 2010)

You are awakened by an intelligent alarm clock that gives a brief summary of your day including a synopsis of your business appointments and domestic chores. It then asks whether you want to hear a personalized news digest or just listen to NPR. On your way to work, your car informs you that there's an accident near Exit 4 on the freeway and gives you an alternate route that is clear of traffic. It also reminds you that you need a tune-up and can schedule one for you Monday at four o'clock, if you like. Through voice-activated response, you don't even need to release your hands from the steering wheel to make the appointment. When you arrive at work, your personal assistant agent notifies you about an urgent e-mail from your boss that arrived early this morning concerning a proposal for a new project that is supposed to start next week. It then notifies you that it has not only responded to your boss with budget and status information extracted from your spreadsheets, it has also set up a conference call tomorrow at noon between you, your boss, and three qualified contractors who are available to help with the project. You assign it the task of downloading statistics that will help fill out your proposal. By ten, you are notified that the information has been downloaded, compiled, and added to your spreadsheet. When you arrive home that evening, there is a delivery of groceries waiting for you—ordered, scheduled, and paid for by your personal agent. You happily note that this time it ordered the fat-free sour cream, now that it knows you are on a diet.

1.2   History of Computing

Through rapidly evolving network and computer technology, hundreds of millions of people are able to receive fast, pervasive access to a phenomenal amount of information, through desktop machines at work, school, and home, through televisions, phones, pagers, and car dashboards, from anywhere and everywhere. As a culture, we are "mobilizing." But pervasiveness alone will not be the key success factor for companies producing computing devices. In is very important to understand the past, the present, and what needs to be changed in the future to move from the evolutionary path to the revolutionary one.

The short scenario that opened this chapter depicts a world of computing that is not yet possible. Although most of the components are available today, they are not yet as integrated as they are in the example.

Another important difference is that today computing is tool-centric as opposed to me-centric. We have devices that have become important tools for us, such as mobile phones, PDAs, laptops, television sets, refrigerators, and many other things. Over the years, we have had to learn how to use these tools and to program them to do the right things for us. In a me-centric world, the device adapts to our needs; it "knows" what we want it to do and how we would like to communicate with it.

But there are many successful examples of how the future is being formed. Off the coast of Kerala state in southern India, fishermen use mobile phones to contact the dozen-odd seafood markets, checking prices at different ports even before they land their catch. As a result, the profit on each eight-day fishing run has doubled. And they're not alone in embracing wireless technology. From garment exporters in Tiruppur in the south to farmers in Punjab in the north, rural India has discovered the convenience of doing business on mobile phones. Many areas have never had conventional fixed-line service. Half of India's 660,000 villages were never wired for fixed-line service, and those that were connected have outdated equipment and long waiting lists for new service.

To create the future, it is necessary to understand the past. Therefore, this chapter provides some historic context to make it easier to understand why we have this device-centric view today and why it cannot work in the future. The history of computing starts long before the first electronic computing device was introduced. Computing or calculating was a need for man since the early days.

Already in the early days it was necessary to account to others for individual or group actions. The operations of combining and removing were simply the operations of adding or subtracting groups of objects to the sack of counting stones or pebbles. Early counting tables, named abaci, not only formalized this counting method. The next logical step was to produce the first "personal calculator"—the abacus—which used the same concepts of one set of objects standing in for objects in another set.

From there on, it was still a long way to the first digital computers, but the concept has remained almost the same: a tool for calculations. With me-centric computing, the calculation element won't go away, but other features become more apparent to the user. The major difference is that a computer is not a tool anymore, but a partner in solving problems. A smart appliance in the me-centric world will support the person using it or even do the work on behalf of that person.

If we look at the history of digital computers, we can see easily four waves that have swept through the last fifty years.

1.2.1   First Wave

When computers first appeared a half-century ago, they were machinery for computing, nothing else. A computer could make short work of a task such as calculating ballistics trajectories or breaking codes, which previously required huge quantities of computation done by teams of human "computers."

The first wave of computing addressed mainly back-office transactions. The first thing resembling a computer network was the terminal-to-host system used on timesharing computers. First developed in the 1960s, the timesharing computer (which became known as a "host") allowed many people to access it simultaneously from terminals wired directly to the computer. In the late 1960s and early 1970s, the availability of modems allowed the terminals to be located at the far end of ordinary voice phone lines. Each host was the center of the universe without a connection to the outside world or to other hosts.

Although technologically obsolete, these machines are still in operation because it is difficult to port the applications to a new operating system and hardware platform. The data could also prove problematic to move, and some companies cannot switch off their data center to move to a newer system without having a major financial impact on the company.

1.2.2   Second Wave

The second wave of computing provided interactive tools for office work. With the introduction of the personal computer, the architecture also

Figure 1.1. Host Screen

shifted from a central host to the so-called client/server model. The term client/server was first used in the 1980s in reference to personal computers on a network. The actual client/server model started gaining acceptance in the late 1980s. The client/server software architecture is a versatile, message-based and modular infrastructure that is intended to improve usability, flexibility, interoperability, and scalability as compared to centralized, mainframe, time-sharing computing.

With two-tier client/server architectures, the user system interface is usually located in the user's desktop environment and the database management services are usually in a server that is a more powerful machine that services many clients. Processing management is split between the user system interface environment and the database management server environment. The database management server provides stored procedures and triggers. There are a number of software vendors that provide tools to simplify development of applications for the two-tier client/server architecture.

The two-tier client/server architecture is a good solution for distributed computing when work groups are defined as a dozen to 100 people interacting on a local area network (LAN) simultaneously. A limitation of the two-tier architecture is that implementation of processing management services using vendor proprietary database procedures restricts flexibility and choice of database management sys-

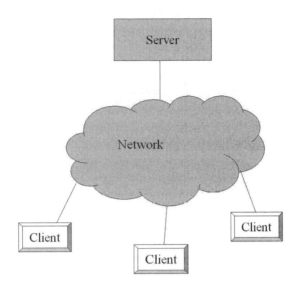

Figure 1.2. Two-tier Architecture

tems (DBMS)[1] for applications.   Finally, current implementations of
the two-tier architecture provide limited flexibility in moving program
functionality from one server to another without manually regenerat-
ing code.

Besides connecting personal computers (PCs) via the client/server
architecture to larger servers, PCs became even more popular as stand
alone computers. In this configuration, everything that was needed
to work was on the client. Office applications such as word processors or spreadsheet applications are probably the two most common
applications used on stand-alone computers. Information was entered,
processed, and outputted (to screen or printer) on the same system.

1.2.3 Third Wave

The third wave allowed everyone to access and exchange information.
The three-tier architecture emerged to overcome the limitations of the
two-tier architecture. In the three-tier architecture, a middle tier was
added between the user system interface client environment and the
database management server environment. There are a variety of ways

---

[1]A program that lets users create and access data in a database.

of implementing this middle tier, such as transaction processing monitors, message servers, or application servers. The middle tier can perform queueing, application execution, and database staging.

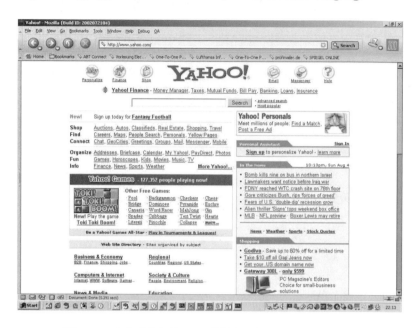

Figure 1.3. Web Page of Yahoo! on the Internet

For example, if the middle tier provides queueing, the client can deliver its request to the middle layer and disengage because the middle tier will access the data and return the answer to the client. In addition, the middle layer adds scheduling and prioritization for work in progress. The three-tier client/server architecture has been shown to improve performance for groups with a large number of users (in the thousands) and improves flexibility when compared to the two-tier approach. Flexibility in partitioning can be as simple as "dragging and dropping" application code modules onto different computers in some three-tier architectures. A limitation with three-tier architectures is that the development environment is reportedly more difficult to use than the visually-oriented development of two-tier applications. Recently, mainframes have found a new use as servers in three-tier architectures.

But the third wave did not change the model of having a single user sitting in front of a screen with a keyboard and pointing device, interacting with a collection of applications and other systems. So far, only the applications and the systems behind the keyboard and the screen have evolved.

1.2.4 Fourth Wave

The fourth wave will change this user-device model that we experienced through the third phase. Computing will move away from this model, as the "traditional" desktop/laptop becomes merely one computing device among many others. We are already experiencing a new wave of computing devices, such as information appliances (PDAs, computers integrated with cell phones, and small specialized information devices of diverse kinds), which allow for greater mobility of information and services. We experience new information environments, which occupy room-sized or building-sized spaces, making use of large display areas, sound, and environmental control. First prototypes of immersive environments, for example head-mounted, are available. Multi-user work environments, with large shared displays and multiple devices operating in an integrated information environment, have become available in big numbers. Probably even more important is the fact that deviceless interaction, in which people's normal movements, gestures, vocalizations, and even physiological parameters are observed and interpreted by the computer system, is becoming a reality very fast. Based on these new technological advances, the fourth wave is about to begin.

The fourth wave, often called pervasive or ubiquitous computing, is going to transfer everyday work from people to machines, multiply the time and reach of everyone, and initiate an explosion of machine-to-machine negotiation, problem-solving, and transactions.

With the recent emergence of smart applications, it has become obvious that the computer is not a machine whose main purpose is to get a computing task done. The computer, with its attendant peripherals and networks, is a machine that provides new ways for people to communicate with other people and directly manipulate the environment. The excitement that infuses computing today comes from the exploration of new capacities to manipulate and communicate all kinds of information in all kinds of media, reaching new audiences in ways that would have been unthinkable before the computer.

Pervasive computing has roots in many aspects of computing. One of the roots have been *The Age of Intelligent Machines: Fairy Tales* by Allen Newell.[2], which describes computer technology as "the possibility of incorporating intelligent behavior in all the nooks and crannies

---

[2]http://www.kurzweilai.net/meme/frame.html?main=/articles/art0301.html?m%3D11

of our world". In its current form, it was first articulated by Mark Weiser[3] in 1988 (even before the introduction of the World Wide Web) at the Computer Science Lab at Xerox PARC[4]. In his opinion, pervasive computing is roughly the opposite of virtual reality. Where virtual reality puts people inside a computer-generated world, pervasive computing forces the computer to live out here in the world with people. Virtual reality is primarily a horsepower problem; pervasive computing is a very difficult integration of human factors, computer science, engineering, and social sciences. Weiser also calls this invisible, everywhere computing that does not live on a personal device of any sort, but is in the woodwork everywhere. Its highest ideal is to make a computer so embedded, so fitting, so natural, that we use it without even thinking about it, you focus on the task, not the tool. A pair of eyeglasses is a good tool—you look at the world, not the eyeglasses. Pervasive computing enriches objects in the real world and makes them "smart," thereby making them better tools for the people using them. This allows these devices to assist people better. By adding information about the environment and the context, these devices become better tools for the people using them.

Pervasive computing can liberate us from the dominance of the desktop to allow computation and communication any place, any time. With a profusion of form factors, laptops will be replaced by tablet computers and they, in turn, by digital paper. Walls in our offices and homes will be reactive displays. All the digital accessories cluttering our briefcases, purses, and belts will merge into much more general-purpose communication devices with knowledge of our preferences, our context, and our geographic location. Our environment will become smarter, more responsive, and more accommodating. Sensors, actuators, even computing power will be embedded into our appliances, furniture, walls, vehicles, clothing, even—via micro-electromechanical systems (MEMS) and nanotechnology —our bodies.

But all this is only a small part of the future to come. Pervasive computing is just about inventing better tools. Me-centric computing goes a step further: The power of computing and communication will be designed into appliances that embody solutions we access and surrogates (agents) to which we delegate concerns.

This means a move from human-computer interaction to a human computing environment interaction and human-human interaction mediated by this federation of devices. Computing, today largely a solitary vice, will metamorphose into computer-supported collaboration.

---

[3]http://www.ubiq.com/weiser/
[4]http://www.xerox.com/

This revolution in computer usage will give the user the capability to delegate work to computers; thus, computing functionality will begin in the interface the user accesses to various devices, and then work will be tasked from this interface to various computers, applications, and intelligent agents distributed around the world on the Internet or its successors.

1.2.5   Countdown to Me-Centric Computing

Although the concept of me-centric computing is new, there exist some appliances now that perfectly align with this concept. In this section, we'll take a look at a few of the advances over the last twenty years or so that are leading the way toward the Me-Centric generation.

The earliest me-centric appliance we can think of is the airplane "auto-pilot" system. In the first models, pilots could set a heading or altitude, and the appliance would do the rest. Over time, these appliances got much more effective, so that some modern planes can take off and land by themselves. The auto-pilot takes away the need from the pilot to check the speed, direction, velocity, and altitude all the time, so that she can concentrate on weather forecasts and how bad weather may affect the flight route.

Similar to the auto-pilot feature in airplanes, the cruise control function in cars can help to reduce the amount of tasks a driver has to do while driving, by controlling the speed automatically. Another feature to both of these advances is that the computer can calculate the optimum fuel consumption for a given speed. Although only small improvements, they made flying and driving safer, easier, and more ecology-friendly.

Another technology designed with the user in mind is the auto-focus camera, which automatically adjusts settings for a given motive. This lets inexperienced photographers concentrate more on their shot and is much faster than manual focus. Now, with digital cameras, they can even view the result without having to wait for processing.

In the financial world, the Merrill Lynch[5] cash management account (CMA) system, which sweeps money into higher interest money marketing accounts, was considered a big improvement. The CMA is a comprehensive financial management tool designed to respond to all investing, borrowing, spending, saving, and asset-allocation needs. It is a combination brokerage account, money market account, Visa card, and checking account that gives access to a vast array of resources and services. Merrill Lynch was awarded a patent for this innovation.

---

[5]http://www.merrilllynch.com/

Over the last few years, GPS-based navigation systems have become affordable in cars. Most car manufacturers offer a GPS navigation system as an add-on for new cars. You just enter the destination address and the system calculates the optimal route, even considering weather and road conditions. Most systems are now also connected to the Internet via the built-in mobile phone for updates and/or to receive specially encoded data over the radio networks. To make sure that the driver can concentrate on the road, navigation systems use speech synthesis (to tell the driver what to do next) and speech recognition (to receive commands from the driver).

These speech technologies have been playing an important role in automated speech recognition (ASR) systems that have been in place for years now in telephone services. While ASR-based telephone directories have become common, Victor Zue's lab at MIT[6] has implemented a more complex system, called the Spoken Language System (SLS). Some of their projects include, among others, Jupiter, a weather forecast system; Voyager, a traffic and navigational assistance system; and Pegasus, a flight status system. All of these systems are accessed via telephone, and users can interact with them in English, Spanish, Chinese, Japanese, or all four, interchangeably in the same dialog. The system responds automatically in the right language.

Speech-to-text dictation products are also based on the same technologies and have improved greatly over the last few years. Products from Dragon[7] and IBM[8] have enabled speech as a viable input technique for computing. Another application of speech to text and then text to speech is the speech-controlled stock system used by Schwab[9]. It enables users to get stock quotes and take other actions simply by speaking the ticker symbol or company name."

On the Internet, new technologies have made it possible to shorten existing processes dramatically. Two things have dramatically changed the way we shop: For example, Amazon.com one-click purchasing enables you to fill your shopping cart with your items and then just click one button to automatically process your order. Shopping bots, too, have changed the way we shop. Instead of spending hours manually comparing prices from various vendors, bots can search and compare products and prices for you automatically in just a few seconds, such as CNET Shopper.com[10] and PriceGrabber[11].

---

[6]http://www.sls.lcs.mit.edu/
[7]http://www.scansoft.com/
[8]http://www.ibm.com/
[9]http://www.schwab.com/
[10]http://shopper.cnet.com/
[11]http://www.pricegrabber.com/

The Internet also has an influence on other technologies, such as the TiVo[12] TV appliance, which replaces VCRs and TV guides. There's even an application that lets you connect the Internet to your refrigerator, making it your personal shopping and cooking consultant.

These are a few examples of the ways in which technology can perform tasks for users instead of simply supporting them. Currently, there are few such applications in the typical office environment, but it's only a matter of time before that changes as well.

1.3 Trends in Computing

As you can see, we are about to complete the third wave. In desktop-based computing, we have full access to information and services through a Web browser. In mobile computing, not quite. Only when we reach the convergence of desktop and mobile computing will we be ready to move forward to the fourth wave.

In a study by Forrester Research[13], Carl D. Howe tries to identify the major issues with the third wave and why we need to move to the next level. While the Internet retains seeds of ongoing, sustained growth, Howe thinks that it needs to overcome three root problems:

1. The Internet is dumb. This is because static Web pages presenting news, sports, and weather hardly improve the same content presented on paper—nor do they take advantage of the powerful computing systems delivering them.

2. The Internet is boring. This is because the bulk of Internet use comes from fetching static Web pages. Today's Internet experience is more like reading in a dusty library than basking in the birth of a new medium.

3. The Internet is isolated. Today's Internet is so remote from the real world that the media calls it by a different name—cyberspace.

Although Howe might be exaggerating a bit here, he is not completely wrong. The big problem is that people think that the Web is the Internet and the Internet is the Web, making it difficult to understand the possibilities of the Internet beyond the Web.

As we move toward the fourth wave, we can see several trends (see Table 1.1) that are imminently affecting today's computing environment.

---

[12]http://www.tivo.com/
[13]The Forrester Report, May 2001, "The X Internet."

Trends in Computing

We are able to see a set of trends in computing that will eventually lead to the fourth wave of computing, although in some areas we have not yet even reached the third wave.

- **Increasing Bandwidth**—Internet traffic is growing exponentially and the telecommunications industry is introducing faster access technologies.

- **Reducing Information Overload**—People are not able to find what they were looking for, because there is too much information available.

- **Introducing Me-Centric Appliances**—The convergence of mobile telecommunications and computing devices creates a new set of intelligent me-centric devices.

- **Automating Processes**—Companies start to use Internet technologies for automating internal and external processes.

- **Using Personalization**—Services and information are presented in a personalized way to the users.

- **Modularization**—A modular Internet can be adjusted more easily to the needs of the individual person or organization

- **Web Services**—New services are about to be introduced on the Internet that are highly modular, personalized, automated, and available on all devices.

Table 1.1. Trends in Computing

1.3.1 Bandwidth Growth

During the Internet hype phase of the late 1990s, the telecommunications industry laid down an astonishing amount of fiber. Although the hype is gone, the Internet traffic is still growing exponentially and more users join the network every day. The bandwidth soon to be available on the Internet backbone, as well as to many offices and neighborhoods, is immense.

Nonetheless, bandwidth to many end users will remain limited by several technical factors. Many users will still connect via analog modem, or at best, ADSL over the old telephone company copper wire loop. Many other users will connect via low-bandwidth wireless networks, such as the mobile phone or wireless LAN which allows up to 22 megabyte per second (Mbps) currently. Most users can expect to see no more than 128 Kbps to 10 Mbps available at their desktop or palmtop. Although this seems good enough for most services today, it is clear that future applications will require much higher bandwidths.

Perhaps more importantly, the gap between the so-called low-bandwidth "edge" of the network and the high-bandwidth "backbone" of the network will increase dramatically as the backbone benefits from increased quality and availability of fiber, while the edge remains limited by the fundamentals of wireless and copper connections. Currently, only about ten percent of the available backbone bandwidth is used, with users still experiencing slow and lagging networks on their ends. This also means that if a big backbone provider goes bankrupt, for example, it will not affect Internet traffic at all, except for some hiccups in the first few hours after shutdown. The focus on bandwidth growth needs to be placed on the edge of the network. New algorithms like DivX[14], which makes it possible to reduce video sequences or complete movies to up to one hundredth of the original size, can help to overcome the bandwidth limitations by reducing the amount of data that needs to be transferred.

ATM networks, for example, not only increase the bandwidth of the backbone, but also introduce some important new features to the network, such as Quality of Service (QoS), allowing for the introduction of high-speed multimedia services. We expect that this trend will continue even as local connections improve past 1 Mbps in the next few years, since backbone bandwidths are improving much faster than local bandwidths. It is easier to replace a single connection between two cities than to replace thousands or millions of edge connections.[15]

1.3.2   Overcoming the Information Overflow

There appear to be two major factors affecting the ability of people to access information effectively: information literacy and application usability. Information literacy is the ability to effectively access and evaluate information for a given need. Application usability refers to the interactive environment that a software application or system provides to a user searching for information.

---

[14]http://www.divx.com/

[15]QoS is supported by IPv6 (Internet Protocol version 6), which makes it more likely that the Internet will be able to delivery QoS to the edge, eventually

Information literacy is the human aspect of information access. The purpose of information literacy is to raise the levels of awareness of the knowledge explosion and understanding how computers can help identify, access, and obtain data and documents needed for problem solving and decision making.

Being able to understand what is required to find information is an important element in the process of overcoming information overload. Some skills that contribute to information literacy are problem solving, decision making, critical thinking, information gathering, and interpretation. These skills are needed in addition to a basic competence and familiarity with computers. The application usability side of information access requires that computer-based information systems be designed for ease of use. Important interface concerns include selection methods (command languages versus menus) and representation methods (screen layout and graphic/text combinations).

We tend to think of machines as being good at processing information. The Internet started to become the most effective way to process information on a global scale. But in reality, Internet users are already overwhelmed by the sheer volume of available information, and the problem will get worse as the Internet grows and connections get faster. Search engines, shopbots, portals, collaborative filtering, and e-mail filtering are existing technologies that allow the user to reduce the torrent to a manageable stream, but these technologies are still quite limited.

Computers can only process information according to programmed procedures, and these necessarily operate on known data or inferable judgments. What machines aren't yet very good at is mimicking the human power of making complex decisions based on ambiguity and uncertainty. Such questions as "Is this relevant right now?", "Why?", and "What information is missing here?" are far too complex for machines. Learning and processing information in this way are, like any human function, grounded in physiological processes that cannot be easily replicated by a computer. It'll be a very long time before a computer can write *Romeo and Juliet*. But we can't parallel-process or multi-task the way computers can. And we get tired after a few hours and need to nap and watch television to get our minds off the information.

If we are to successfully handle information overload in the future, we have two options: One is to restrict production of "excessive" information. The other is to use software intelligently—meaning that we rely more on agents and search engines to distill information for us so that we may absorb it easier.

What we see today are general-purpose search engines that search everything. In the future, we will see more dedicated search engines that employ more specialized algorithms that will find particular types of information with a greater reliability. With the introduction of XML (see Chapter 6), each document will have a specified context, making it easier for the search engine to understand whether a certain piece of information is relevant.

Additionally, *agents* must be available as Web services that do a pre-selection of information based on the needs of the user. Armed with these two applications, the information overload problem will be less of a concern in the future.

1.3.3 Me-Centric Appliances

Me-centric appliances, of which there will be many in the future, are appliances we interact with that understand our intent and do what we want them to do. Such appliances will be one of the biggest areas of growth in the computer industry. Virtually every device will access Internet services to accomplish user tasks, even if users have no idea that such access is taking place. Moreover, new hardware products such as the Tablet PC and PDA/phone combinations are just starting to hit the market. Research indicates that by 2003 there will be over 1.25 billion mobile phone owners globally with Internet access, and that this number will increase exponentially in short order. This revolution in computer usage will be unleashed by founding computing architecture around knowledge of the user, giving the user the capability to delegate work to computers; thus, computing functionality will begin in the interface the user accesses to various devices, and then work will be tasked from this interface to various computers, applications, and intelligent agents distributed around the world on the Internet or its successors.

By 2006 the number of people who use data-enabled phones, PDAs, and other net-enabled devices is expected to exceed the worldwide Internet subscriber population. Much of this connectivity is at the expense of the PC, as more and more business users use wireless, mobile, and information appliances in their daily work. It is projected that in a few short years there will be three times as many of these devices worldwide as PCs. The result is that increasing numbers of people worldwide will first experience the Internet on a wireless device.

Typically, these devices today have unreliable, low-bandwidth, high-latency telephone or wireless network connections. A trend in mobile computing will be to make these connections more reliable and faster. This is not necessarily needed for phone calls, but through these better connections, these devices will be able to handle much more than pure voice traffic. Games, Web browsing, videos, and music, for example, will become accessible through these new devices, without having to set up additional antennas for these services.

The major reason why mobile devices are becoming very popular is the fact that many people don't want to miss the services and information they have on their desktop systems. They want to use them anywhere and anytime. Mobile computing also provides the enterprise with several compelling competitive advantages. It allows for faster, decentralized decision making and increases the responsiveness to customers. Through mobile computing, the sensitivity to market changes is increased and the time for staff to commute is lowered. As a direct result travel costs are reduced company-wide, and staff morale and productivity are increased. Probably the most obvious Internet service is e-mail. Through Web-based e-mail services, users can access their e-mail from any device, in any country, at any time.

Web terminals have become commonplace in public spaces, such as cafes, airports, and hotels. Eventually users will have full access to all of their files and applications from any terminal, as soon as the security and bandwidth problems have been solved and the technologies are standardized.

A new generation of mobile applications will be able to adapt themselves to the requirements of the user and include the context to reduce the amount of information the user has to enter. One clear trend in mobile computing is context-sensitive services. One simple example is a map service on the Internet. Today these services do not know where you are. In the future, they will receive your location as contextual information and will therefore be able to show you the right part of the map; the system knows what is of interest to you and therefore shows you the right restaurants, shops, and museums on the map and how to get there. Without the contextual information, the user is either overloaded with information or needs to specify the information manually each time. Map systems in cars (such as Hertz NeverLost[16]) today know already where you are, because they are connected to the GPS system.

The Internet infrastructure is changing to support these needs. One basic technology, IPv4 is being replaced by IPv6[17]. This means that every device on earth can have its own IP address. With IPv4, the number of devices with their own IP addresses was very limited. Another

---

[16] http://www.hertz.com/

[17] A detailed description of what this means can be found in Chapter 3 of the book *The E-Business (R)Evolution* by Daniel Amor, ISBN 013085123X, Prentice Hall.

important step is the introduction of QoS on the Internet. With this technology, it is possible to guarantee bandwidth or service availability, which can lead to the creation of service level agreements (SLA). This means, for example, that it becomes possible to view video and audio streams over the Internet in good and consistent quality. It also means that you can have a service-level agreement that you will be always connected. IPsec, also a new technology being introduced to the Internet, provides enhanced security features, making it more difficult to break into communication.

Parallel to the rise of the devices is the development of new infrastructure and standards that will make mobile and wireless computing a reality. Wireless LANs, Bluetooth, 802.11, and other technologies are rapidly evolving, facilitating connectivity and access. Telecommunication firms around the globe are rolling out third-generation networks that promise increased capacity for data and information delivery. But as a measure of market penetration, the rapid acceptance of applications is more important than the rapid growth of applications.

Though the hardware and network resources are being established, the market for products and services has barely been tapped. IBM estimates the overall market for mobile services alone should equal 30.5 billion dollar/euro by 2003. Jupiter[18] Media Metrix estimates that U.S. wireless Web users will increase to 96 million by 2005.

Mobile entertainment alone is expected to be a 1 billion dollar/euro business in Europe this year. By 2004, one-third of all Europeans (which sums up to more than 219 million consumers) will regularly use their mobile phones to access Internet services. The Nordic countries, including Finland, Norway, Sweden, and Denmark, have wireless penetration rates above 70 percent. The next five years will see dramatic wireless subscriber growth, with the worldwide penetration rate doubling from 10.6 percent today to 21 percent in 2006. This continued growth has been marked by the long-awaited surge by China into first place, with the country passing the U.S. in wireless subscribers during the third quarter of 2002.

The Internet appliances used in the future will take on a variety of forms including wristwatches[19], handhelds (much thinner and lighter than today's), and tablet devices. We will see a convergence of services into single devices (PDA, voice, and paging services on your handheld device, for example) and at the same time, a divergence toward single-use devices, such as earpiece/microphone units that communicate wire-

---

[18]http://www.jupiter.com/
[19]At Comdex 2002, Fossil showed a watch with Palm PDA and connectivity built in, for example

lessly with handheld devices. The limited screen size of the appliances will be overcome in many cases by "heads-up" displays embedded in eyeglasses that will become a technical fashion statement.

These devices will provide location-based, context-sensitive, just-in-time information and me-centric services. For example, as you drive to meet with a client, an alert could be routed automatically from your appointment calendar to your car's on-board computer about an impending merger involving the client.

1.3.4   Automation

Besides mobility, automation plays an important role in the future of computing. In the early days of the Internet, much of the emphasis was centered on processes initiated by people. For example, a person would visit a site, perform some searches, and then place an order.

While this model is acceptable for an individual, it falls short in cases where the purchase cycle tends to be repeated frequently, such as when a corporation purchases a variety of items from multiple sources. Requiring a person to manually perform a certain process can be time-consuming and error-prone. Automating such processes would certainly streamline a company's operations significantly.

Unfortunately, on the Web, the information returned from the transaction is a mix of presentation-related data (such as graphics and formatting instructions) and business data (such as product names, codes, and prices), and normally is not in a format that can be easily integrated into other systems. Consequently, someone needs to distinguish manually what is actually relevant in these interactions. Consider how expensive it is for a purchasing agent to re-enter information returned from a purchasing system into an accounting system. This seems rather antiquated, but many companies are still performing much of their processing manually because there are few, if any, standards for information that's being passed around. What is needed is a universal format or at least a way to separate business data from presentation data, which led to the invention of XML.

One hot area is B2E (business-to-employee) portals. Many organizations are increasingly using Internet protocols for their own needs for information distribution. All access to an intranet is managed by a single organization. Thus, new technologies can be deployed quickly, since little coordination is needed with outside organizations, and security (within the intranet) is of less concern.

In the first phase of a B2E portal project, employees get access to information, and then self-service features are introduced. In phase three, many tasks are automated to reduce the costs within the organization. While many companies have started to introduce internal information Web sites, the trend clearly moves towards self-service and automation.

1.3.5   Personalization

Unlike broadcast media, the Internet makes it possible to customize access for each user, as the users can provide some information about themselves. Web technologies allow customization at the client and the server. Many Web sites include their own site-specific customization features, but the customization is increasingly provided by third-party "proxy" sites. These proxy sites act as an intermediary between the service and the user. As a means to both reduce information overload and customize service access, proxy sites will become more and more important. In particular, as portable devices become more prevalent, highly specialized proxy sites will be provided to meet the special needs of mobile users. These sites can transform information and services in such a way that they are easily usable from any device.

The way your personal assistant will ultimately be implemented might best be thought of as a personalized intelligent proxy that aggregates knowledge about you and and your environment, and intermediates transactions with various agents to employ your resources appropriately.

1.3.6   Modularity

One of the goals of IT architecture, in the integration stage, is to create applications that can be easily extended to handle new interface devices. However, opening the IT applications is more than just putting a new interface to an old system. Practices that were acceptable in-house are no longer acceptable on the Web or a mobile device. A customer expects data to be consistent across all applications the company provides; he also expects fast access and no downtime, twenty-four hours a day.

The IT industry is not finding the integration stage easy, for three main reasons. The first is a huge legacy of existing applications that run businesses and are not easily changed. The second is that internal IT organization and methodologies are designed around the notion of funding, developing, testing, and deploying standalone applications, not integrated systems. Third, to serve integration well, there needs to be better cooperation between IT and business.

It's difficult today to find a single Web site that will solve multiple problems. For example, consider a consumer who wants to book an entire vacation online (flight, car, lodging, and local activities). The traveller or travel agent has to cobble together a package by visiting multiple sites and then ensure that all the relevant criteria, such as identification, dates, and locations are matched. Often, you end up giving the same information at multiple sites. Anyone who has ever planned a vacation has experienced the amount of work involved.

This clumsy user experience exists because it's currently too difficult for the site operators to break the sites into discrete sets of sub-processes that can be merged or integrated into an experience that's relevant to the consumer. The reason for this is the lack of standards that would make integration seamless. The focus of each site is narrow; typically the riding school is offering riding instruction, and the airline is offering flight services. A vacation could be composed of visiting a riding school in a certain location and using a certain transportation vehicle, e.g., a riding school in Pisa, Italy, with accommodation on a farm nearby. As far as the user is concerned, all of these events have to be scheduled and booked to accomplish his overall goal. Unfortunately, the site that offers riding instruction has no way of knowing that the consumer visiting the site is the same person who's staying at a local hotel on a particular date. Without that little detail, the riding site would have to ask for that information again. If you want to book your holidays individually and not in a package, it can become quite complicated to organize all the bits and pieces that are necessary to make it a nice vacation. And even Web sites of travel agents are not good enough to book complete holidays online.

You can see that most of the trends today are moving towards mobility and automation. These two features are key requirements for a me-centric computing world. Only if we can provide all services and information anywhere, at any time, through any device, can we build an automated me-centric world.

1.3.7 Mobility

Mobility is becoming a key concern for corporations worldwide. Executives are looking to extend the functionality and information accessible on the desktop to the PDAs, phones, and laptops they carry and use regularly. The need for this extended network is growing. But the key question remains—why undertake the effort? Why create connectivity at all times? What is the benefit to the corporate bottom line? Companies are turning to these systems to boost productivity, slash operating costs, improve competitive advantage, and cultivate customer loyalty.

In today's scenario for mobility, the majority of wireless services are delivered by a mobile network operator (large wireless carriers) to end-users via a mobile phone. These services are are predominantly voice-centric. In fact, the majority of mobile network operator revenue today is derived from voice. Because of this the mobile phone today is the primary device used to communicate wirelessly in a wide-area network, mobile network operators (who are provisioning service to the end-user via the mobile phone) tend to have a fairly strong relationship with the customer.

A connectivity that brings the power of the Internet provides for quicker access to information and transforms the work environment. Remaining competitive in today's global business environments means that organizations are constantly looking for ways to quickly and easily extend the reach of their most powerful applications, data, and services to users around the globe. Driven by the promise of increased efficiencies, businesses are looking to provide mobile workers, trading partners, clients, and customers access to corporate and commercial applications and content. FedEx[20] and UPS[21] have being doing this for some time and, in the process, revolutionizing the delivery business. There is virtually no transportation company without online tracing.

Similarly, the application of wireless technologies is clear for many industries. For example, to close a sale, a salesperson visiting a prospective customer might need to access an ERP system to view inventory details and establish availability in real-time. What are the sales possibilities? A utility company worker could move from job to job by information accessed through a handheld tablet instead of going back to the central office to grab the next clipboard and assignment. A businessman could manage his sales force automation programs through a wireless device. And in fleet management, supply chain solutions, CRM, and corporate information, wireless access can provide for substantial efficiencies. Some more detailed examples can be found in Chapter 2.

Applications will be smart and use multiple sources of data to minimize the time to relevant data.

Consider the following scenario: Richard, a salesperson, synchronizes his mobile device prior to leaving for work in the morning. A smart application uses the appointments on his calendar to proactively download driving instructions between meetings, linking calendar, address book, and third-party mapping services. Up-to-date account information from his company's CRM application is preloaded as well, linking calendar and CRM applications, ensuring that Richard can answer any questions that may arise. During the day, Richard's afternoon

---

[20]http://www.fedex.com/
[21]http://www.ups.com/

flight is delayed and his travel system sends his wireless device an alert. This alert includes a list of alternative flights that Richard can take to his destination, preventing him from having to search for this information later. That afternoon, as he boards his rescheduled flight, Richard checks his stock portfolio by using an application that downloads the prices every fifteen minutes during the trading day. These examples show how smart applications anticipate what a user will need and proactively bring the information onto the mobile device where a user can access it quickly without depending on wireless network availability or access speeds.

This need for information and access to applications is not confined to the business market. Wireless solutions providing entertainment, shopping, and travel services will be available to the consumer market. Instant messaging, games and other entertainment offerings are swiftly being embraced by the youth market and transforming the way people interact. In the education market, the wireless network is transforming the way students learn, providing the ability for a personalized curriculum and greater assistance for teachers and students.

While the "promise" these examples offer is compelling, the present realities are quite different. Current software and information products are not optimized (or ready at all) to deal with the limitations of the small form factor handheld device. Most offerings were developed for the PC and did not contemplate alternative access methods. Moreover, the current infrastructure is not sufficiently complete to transfer large amounts of data across wireless networks. These challenges remain key obstacles to the rapid adoption of wireless devices as tools of the trade.

In the new scenario for mobility, the business relationship with customers is likely to be spread across multiple categories of players (both new and existing) as they will compete and collaborate to drive new services to the end-user.

Mobile network operators face a new set of challenges including new competition with other types of mobile service providers (WLAN service providers, proprietary network service providers, mobile virtual network operators) and the additional complexity of deploying IP-based networks (GPRS/3G, content distribution, multi-access portals).

Enterprises see mobility as a way to not only make their own operations more efficient, but also to drive new services to their customers to increase loyalty and revenue. End-users will value those services that are highly personalized and relevant not to just the different environments (work, home, car, customer site) but also to their roles (mobile professional, consumer, parent, spouse, friend, etc.).

It's clear that mobility is a force to be considered as we move into the next wave of computing. Here's a final, simple example of how organizations are dealing with this today:

CityCab,[22] a taxi operator located in Singapore, is one of the largest taxi operators in the world with about 9,800 drivers and a fleet of 5,000 vehicles. Hewlett-Packard,[23] CityCab, and Ericsson[24] have jointly invested $5.5 million to transform the operations of CityCab and to revolutionize the customer experience. CityCab's mobile solution lets passengers surf the web, send e-mails, check stock prices, catch up on the latest news, and even print information such as distance traveled and total fare—all from the back of the cab. Additionally, taxi drivers are able to use handheld appliances to access mapping and routing info, accept e-payment options, or process bookings. They will also be able to use dispatch services that allow them to see where customer demand is concentrated at any given time and bypass the Customer Contact Centre. This increases the total number of passengers that CityCab can service during a day because the dispatch services now are linked directly to their devices.

1.3.8 Software as a Service

In light of the new wireless environment, software *delivered as a service* becomes a driving factor. To ensure that the functionality of an application on a wireless device is the same as its desktop PC equivalent, while also assuring that it can be mobile, software and information developers will need to optimize applications to reside on servers and modularize code to deliver just what is needed to provide users access to a consistent user experience. In a world dominated by wireless communications, this will be defined by server-resident applications accessible from any device at any time, presented in a format appropriate to the device itself.

However, the current capabilities of small devices cannot match the power of the desktop PC. In reality, most mobile devices fall short even in terms of what is needed to ensure that the wireless paradigm is effective. To ensure the same functionality of the application while also assuring that it can be mobile, software and information developers will need to optimize applications to reside on servers and modularize code to deliver just what is needed to provide users rapid computing and access to up-to-date information efficiently and effectively. A consistent

---

[22]http://www.citycab.com.sg/
[23]http://www.hp.com/
[24]http://www.ericsson.com/

user experience in a world dominated by wireless communications will be defined by server-resident applications accessible from any device at any time, presented in a format appropriate to the device itself.

We are already seeing independent software vendors (ISVs) that develop wireless servers, mobile middleware, and databases that serve as the backend for the mobile device access. New so-called Wireless Applications Service Providers (WASPs) are being founded to build, integrate, host, and manage the wireless components of mobile e-business systems.

ISVs will also need to deliver applications that can be used while mostly disconnected and occasionally using the wireless infrastructure to synchronize their activities. Models will vary based on the development requirements and consumer preferences. What is clear is that the rise in wireless devices will ultimately go hand in hand with software as a service, significantly driving its demand and development.

1.4 Conclusion

If you look back a few years, each of the trends mentioned in this chapter was supposed to become the next big thing after the introduction of the Internet. But it has become quite clear that not a single one of these trends will be able to top the success of the Internet. The future will be composed of many new technologies and paradigms that are reflected in these trends.

If you take all these trends and try to merge them to create a future, you will see that they are part of a bigger scenario, which will eventually become the basis for me-centric computing. Me-centric computing can only be successful if the appropriate architecture is in place, with higher bandwidth, new devices, and new software technologies.

In order to understand how these trends can work together in the future, the next chapter offers a set of scenarios that show how the future may look. You'll see how important it is to get these trends working together in service of a single unifying vision.

Chapter 2

CONTRASTING THE PRESENT
AND THE FUTURE

If we try to contrast the present and the future, it is like showing the radical contrast between two different images of the universe. Just imagine the universe before and after Copernicus (visit the web site shown in Figure 2.1 for more information). He was the first to suggest what has since become known as the Copernican theory; namely, that the sun is at the center of the solar system (which was considered the universe at that time), not Earth as everyone had thought up to then.[1] The paradigm shift occurred slowly because Copernicus wasn't immediately sure how to present this revolution in a way that everyone could understand, but eventually the sun became the focal point around which everything was centered. If we use this analogy for today's computing world, we realize see that at present everything is hardware-centric, while the future will be user-centric.

For many people, today's computing possibilities seem infinite, but due to the technologies and paradigms used today, there are limitations. Look, for example, at all the dimensions of the computing infrastructure and the layers that are used to implement and deliver a user experience. Traditionally, networked computing was built on the OSI seven-layer stack that had applications at the seventh layer, with everything else being about networks, connectivity, and communications. The user interface (one of the things at the top layer) was just part of the application, and the user was actually not part of the model at all. This required users of the system to know lots about the application and its user interface.

In contrast, we should define a model that starts with the user at the center, layers various user interface modalities around the user,

---

[1] Nicolaus Copernicus (1543), *De revolutionibus orbium coelestium*, Nuremberg.

Figure 2.1. Nicolaus Copernicus

and supports these with user models that understand the context and intent of the user. Then we need to deliver value to the user in a manner consistent with concerns for security, privacy, trust, preferences, and other policies. To do that, machines will need to understand how to perform everyday tasks and how to do the master's bidding.

People will be able to tap into this virtual world using any device and have the experience that everything is unified. Neither device differences nor location differences matter anymore. The underlying system remembers the user's activities and other aspects of state; the user can communicate with the system, people, and services whenever convenient and appropriate.

To make this system successful, the user interface experience must be appropriate. Traditional personal computers that are dominating digital communication today will become a minority of access devices in this new system. Computers must understand user intent, most easily achieved using natural modes of communication. In some cases, this will still be the keyboard; in many other cases, it will mean a broad adoption of input devices that utilize speech, text, handwriting, gestures, images, and so forth. Users will adopt input techniques that enable them to convey intent to their appliances most naturally.

This will require efforts to standardize the semantics of processes and how they can be achieved. Thus, starting with XML and Web standards, we will have to fill out the semantics of tasks, people, goals, resources, etc., so that devices from various manufacturers can work with services provided by various service providers to get work done. HP's e-speak concepts, and other research projects in process automation, sketched out much of this (see also Chapter 6).

UDDI and Web services, explained in Chapter 3, are putting down the foundations for service-centric computing, service discovery, and service invocation. Much of what users will notice or care about will be the interface experience; under the covers, everything will be rearranged to delegate work to agents.

What this means is the disposal of current programming concepts and paradigms to make way for new ideas. It's not enough to enhance existing applications; we need to rethink the services behind the applications and rewrite them for the new me-centric environment.

Me-Centric Computing Features

This table provides you with an overview on the key features of a me-centric scenario.

Feature	Description
Me-Centric Appliances	Devices that have knowledge about certain tasks and can do work on behalf of the users
Me-Centric Services	Services that handle information and service requests automatically and autonomously
Me-Centric Environments	Environments that can operate me-centric appliances and provide access to me-centric services

Table 2.1. Me-Centric Computing Features

To give you a better understanding of how the future will look, this chapter offers some example scenarios through which you will see the impact of the new thinking and its radical simplicity. You'll see in each scenario how one segment of life exists in the present, and how it will change in the future. Hopefully you'll glean some input for your own business ideas. For more detailed examples, see *Internet Future Strate-*

gies,[2] which not only provides a set of scenarios, but also an implementation plan for each of them and a sample ROI calculation.

To put the scenarios in context with me-centric computing, we are providing a table of key features here (see Table 2.1), with a short explanation of what these features mean. At the end of each scenario, you will find a summary of how these features have been implemented in that particular scenario. Later in the book, we will dig into more detail of these features and how they create a me-centric architecture.

Some of the scenarios have been developed by the HP Labs[3] and some ideas have been taken from *Internet Future Strategies*.

2.1   Mobile Sales Force

2.1.1   Introduction

Heather works as a salesperson for services in an IT company. Her portfolio includes selling catalog solutions, as well as designing custom services with the help of the client solution design group.

As a salesperson, Heather needs to access information ubiquitously to provide answers to client questions, retrieve order information, upsell and cross-sell, forecast performance and quotas, and explore opportunities and client contacts. As a designer of custom services, Heather needs to acquire data from the client, understand the client's needs, report these needs to the solution design group, and act as a link between client, sales, and solution design. In general, about 80 percent of a salesperson's time can be divided into four broad activities:

- **Preparation**–These tasks include preparing offers, making travel arrangements, planning for meetings, and reading through the client's history, if available.

- **Travel**—This time is spent on going back and forth to clients and meeting other employees internally, such as the client solution design group.

- **Client Time**—This is the time spent at the client's site, when the salesperson sits down with the client to understand the needs and design a solution for the client.

- **Administrative**—Most of the remaining time is spent estimating forecast performance, regular staff meetings, or completing expense reports.

---

[2]Daniel Amor (2001), *Internet Future Strategies*, New York: Prentice Hall.
[3]http://www.hpl.hp.com/

Mobile technology can help reduce the amount of preparation time needed, it can make the client time more productive, and it can speed up the administrative tasks. And in those cases where the salesperson is travelling by means other than driving himself or herself from one client site to another, a mobile solution can provide ways of performing administrative tasks or doing something else productive, such as e-mail or on-line training, during travel time.

Specifically me-centric and mobile wireless solutions will provide her the following advantages on the following topics: sales cycles, trips to the office, preparation time, up-selling and cross-selling, administrative tasks, sales efforts, social networking capabilities, and the delegation of simple tasks. If we look at these points a bit more in detail, you will immediately see the advantages. In the sales cycle, for example, you will find that response time to customer queries can be reduced significantly through the availability of information anytime and anywhere. The salesperson can reduce the number of trips and phone calls back to the office significantly as all information is available on site. The same applies to order entry, which can be done anytime and anywhere. Due to the availability of information, preparation time can be done while travelling and can be delegated to smart agents and intelligent services. Intelligent appliances will be able to provide the right information whenever required.

Up-selling and cross-selling also become easier, as smart agents can find the appropriate products and services that can be used in conjunction with whatever the client is prepared to buy anyway. These personalized proposals can be made while entering the order at the customer site, for example. Many administrative tasks, such as travel expense reports, can be done during travel time and can be automated easily, for example, through smart credit cards that will make sure that all travel-related items will be put into the expense report automatically.

In the following paragraphs, we describe two scenarios in which Heather uses three kinds of connections, today and in the future: managed networks, spontaneous networks, and the Internet. Managed networks are probably the best-known types of network and the most commonly used. These networks include telecommunication networks that allow one to retrieve information from a certain location, by phone or a direct modem connection. Spontaneous networks, on the other hand, allow the spontaneous connections between nearby devices and services. These networks are set up only for specific times and purposes. Wireless LAN and Bluetooth technologies, for example, enable these networks. Although not as reliable as managed networks, they provide a shortcut for exchanging information and services on a very local basis. The Internet allows one to access information on a world-wide basis. Information and services can be anywhere and can be retrieved easily through the Internet.

2.1.2 The Present

Heather is about to visit a customer. The mission preparation in the office uses the Internet, connected through a managed network. Instead of going back and forth to the office to receive updated information, Heather and Jim, the field engineer, can synchronize through a wireless connection with people and data in the office. In addition, the managed network guides Heather and Jim to the client site.

Heather's primary repository for information is her PDA. She uses it to synchronize data and to communicate wirelessly with scanners, cameras, microphones, and client devices. Before Heather leaves the office, she downloads all information required for this customer to her PDA: mission preparation, updated answers for client, updated client accounts, ongoing actions, sales opportunities, sales forecasts based on account management. During the travel, the PDAs are working in standalone mode until Heather and Jim reach the client site.

Once at the client site, Heather updates Jim while they take the time to establish communications between their appliances. This lets them transfer files and cross-reference devices. During the meeting with the client, they use to-do lists to help increase efficiency in achieving goals and keeping the discussions on track; they use their PDAs to transmit feedback and input for service specifications to Jim's back-end support as well as to Heather's sales office; they can also use their cell phones to make phone calls, if needed. These connections let them share information with people in the room as well as with the back-end office. This information can take various forms, such as pictures, plans, and voice annotations, enabling a more interactive description of the specifications. If needed, they could also have video conferences, scan documents, and share spreadsheets, just to mention a few possibilities. Before parting, Jim and Heather synchronize their data once more and send the information back to the Internet.

All of the connections and service discoveries made during this scenario are made manually, requiring set-up time and some management operations. The Internet does not provide these low-level services automatically today.

Managed networks offer privacy, trust, and high QoS in a known environment. This enables Heather and Jim's devices to exchange and access company confidential information inside the client's campus during this scenario. Sending trip reports out immediately following the meeting increases the efficiency and lowers the latency of the answers from the back office.

2.1.3 The Future

While Heather prepares for her customer visit, agents work to carry out certain tasks on her behalf. Specifically, they:

- Revisit the last trip report to verify that action items have been completed (specifically, the answers to client questions)

- Check order status

- Explore potential up-sell and cross-sell opportunities with the company

- Make automatic forecasts based on the client's order history and the goals of the salesperson

- Update all information just prior to the meeting

- Call the client to verify the visit date and location

- Summarize the results of these tasks and download them to Heather's PDA

As Heather and Jim reach the client's campus, their devices automatically discover the local services provided near the campus. They confirm the location of high-quality printing facilities so that Jim and Heather can create updated documents as input to the meeting. At the site, their appliances communicate, synchronize, and interact automatically, taking care of the low-level administrative details such as the day-to-day operations, updates on prices, checking the to-do lists, and so forth. This also enables them to establish a private communication during the meeting, letting them dynamically adapt their strategy based on the client's reactions. They can delegate tasks during the meeting, either to their back-end offices (if any) or to services working on their behalf. For example, they could look for background knowledge on the client's project, or gather evidence on how to reduce the risk on the project by analyzing similar previous contracts and experience. Finally, after the meeting, their agents can fulfill such administrative tasks as trip reports, order forms, and so forth. Heather and Jim can delegate further tasks instantly, resulting in faster answers for the client.

As you can see in this scenario, Heather, Jim, and the client have more time to focus on important issues; their meeting is more efficient because data is exchanged in the background without human intervention. This is a high competitive advantage to the salesperson, as it reduces cost and time while increasing efficiency. The latency of answers drops considerably, and the salesperson is in a good position to close the deal earlier.

To look at the big picture, this setup is delegated to the devices and infrastructure, providing an automatic service discovery and capability to delegate tasks. This provides a virtual office environment to Heather and Jim for all their meetings, right at the client's site. Instead of storing information on a certain device, such as a laptop computer or a personal agent (a successor to the PDAs), the virtual office will store all the information in a central location, making it possible to access the data from anywhere with any device. Data items are downloaded and cached in anticipation of what might otherwise be long latencies or periods of complete unavailability or low QoS.

2.1.4 Summary

Let's look at the key features of a me-centric future. From an appliance point of view, not much will change. Small, handheld devices will still be used, but with one big difference—they will be connected anytime and anywhere, either through local networks, managed networks, or the Internet. Today, many appliances can connect to only one of these at a time. In the future, it is expected that an intelligent appliance will be able to roam through different networks without losing the connection. Many companies are already providing such solutions. Hewlett-Packard,[4] for example, is offering its Open Roaming solution. Other companies such as Lucent[5] and Cisco[6] offer similar solutions, which solve security and mobility problems for mobile professionals whether they roam within the office using wireless LANs or outside using the varying wired and wireless public networks. Users will maintain the security standards and the IP address no matter where they are or what they do. This is essential to a me-centric environment.

So while the devices do not have to change dramatically, the services that run on these devices do. With agents, processes can be automated to help users resolve issues much faster. As you can see in Figure 2.2, a set of services exists around the core service of mobile sales force support. One of the key services is roaming. The core mobile sales force service contains knowledge about the required processes

---

[4]http://www.hp.com/
[5]http://www.lucent.com/
[6]http://www.cisco.com/

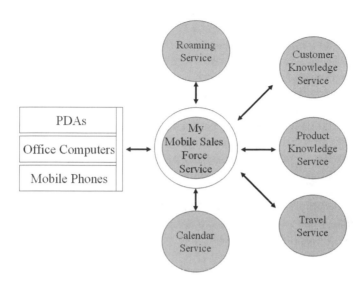

Figure 2.2. Mobile Sales Force Ecosystem

and maintains the connections to all other services. It provides the context on behalf of the salesperson that is required by agents and services to bring back the right information at the right time. By moving the context to this central location, the salesperson is not dependent on a specific device. The adjunct services are not dependent on a particular implementation of context, as the core service will provide translation mechanisms for different technologies.

Besides roaming, knowledge agents are providing an important service to find all relevant information about a customer and the desired products and services he would like to buy. A travel management service will help the sales force to optimize their trips to various clients and make sure that the sales agent's calendar is synchronized with all changes that may occur at the customer site. Therefore, a scheduling agent or service needs to be put in place that does all the timely coordination, based on the feedback from the travel management service and the customer. Additional services may be needed during negotiations, such as status order updates or answers to legal questions. Today these services exist as information pools that can be accessed when required. In the future, this information will be retrieved by agents that will provide contextually relevant information on time.

Through new sales knowledge services, it is possible to coordinate sales efforts towards a target customer group. This makes it possible for salespeople from different regions who work on similar clients to get insight on sales strategies of their colleagues, for example, and show how they can combine offers to create more sales. These collaborative services and agents can also create social networks with other salespeople and clients. These social networks make it possible to reuse existing marketing collateral, proposals, and service brochures more effectively. Asalesperson would only see relevant information for that particular kind of deal and it would also allow that simple and standardized tasks can be easily delegated to other employees or to smart agents.

As you can see, both infrastructure and business services must be introduced to make this me-centric scenario a reality. Building up such a scenario would probably be feasible, as the targeted audience of salespeople is enormous and the processes are standardized in many cases. A standardized service with configuration possibilities can help reduce the costs for sales activities drastically.

2.2   Real Estate Agent

2.2.1   Introduction

Henry, a real estate agent is creating a file to describe a house for sale. His goal is to record all information on the house, to present it in its most attractive form, to personalize this presentation for both identified and anonymous potential clients, and finally to diffuse this information in the most appropriate manner.

Collecting information on the house is the first order of business, including a plan of the house, pictures, noise levels in the house, garden, swimming pool, history, maintenance, and conformance to norms. The agent also needs to describe the facilities outside the house, neighborhood safety, risks linked to environment (such as hurricanes, earthquakes, floods), access to facilities (such as highways, train stations and airports), and facilities such as supermarkets and schools.

We develop two scenarios (short-term and long-term) in which our real estate agent uses three kinds of connections for accessing services and information required for the job.

2.2.2   The Present

To-do lists are prepared at the office, taking advantage of the Internet connection and the search engines to gather information on the home environment. Henry is in constant connection with the office using either a laptop, a PDA, or his cell phone. When he visits the home, all necessary information is recorded and a thumbnail image is sent to a Web site. Potential customers receive an SMS message describing the house. These messages can either be sent to a large base of customers or to a very targeted population, either automatically or handpicked by the real estate agent. More information about potential buyers can be downloaded on the fly while travelling. In addition, the real estate agent can place a key box on the door which sends information to the agency each time somebody visits the home, eliminating the need to go and check these key boxes twice a week as used to be done.

Today, preparation of to-do lists needs to be done at the office and downloaded to the personal agent. During the visit to the house, the personal agent is the primary repository for information and synchronization of data, wirelessly communicating among scanner, camera, and microphone. Communications are established automatically between appliances, and files can be transferred and referred across devices. To-do lists help increase efficiency in achieving goals. On the way to another appointment, the real estate agent needs to pass by a kiosk; the appliances connect to the services offered there and print a generic catalog of the house for sale.

When he reaches the house, the real estate agent connects to the local facilities and can query for information. All appliances can connect to the local network to communicate among themselves and connect to the Web. Therefore, all pictures and information about the home are directly posted on the Web site and are accessible by the clients. Brochures can also be printed out. If there is no network connection at the home, the real estate agent can take advantage of local coverage during his lunch break to synchronize with the office support system and send e-mail to the interested clients.

All tasks are triggered manually, and the end-user needs to verify the result of the action. The real estate agent triggers most operations, the managed architecture provides a reliable network, ensures a quality of service, and allows billing. But, compared to the future, where things do it for us, it is still a lengthy process that requires a lot of time today. Providing a more automated service would enable Henry to increase the quality of service by adding more details to the descriptions or spend more time talking to the prospective clients, for example, for which he does not have enough time today.

2.2.3 The Future

Our real estate agent is in constant connection with the office through his smart device. General preparation work for the house listing is generated automatically based on generic profiles like soccer mom, teenager, or specific profiles of existing clients existing in the office database or on recent statistics. This enables him to show the house to the right clients. The mission preparation is done by a support team. Once the preparation is finished, a precise mission statement, a to-do list, and a software agent are sent to Henry while he drives to the home and downloaded to his smart device.

A guidance system is used to organize visits according to road traffic, other appointments, and opportunities (such as good commission quota or probability of selling the house soon). Five minutes prior to the visit, Henry's personal agent calls the homeowners or clients to reconfirm. While the real estate agent travels to the house, he delegates his agent to conduct research on the neighborhood, safety records, schools, and so forth from police, county, and geographic records.

During the visit to the house, the personal agent actively helps Henry carry out the mission; in particular, appliances communicate and interact automatically with those in the home to collect data from them. The camera asks for pictures of the kitchen and gives a description of the important items to capture for all the clients. These pictures are automatically labeled and stored and are ready to be used. The catalogs are automatically composed and are print ready. Video recordings of parties and events casting a good image of the house can be requested uploaded to the house's web site. In addition, the size of each room can be precisely measured and transmitted to the personal agent, which updates the plan of the house and annotates each room's picture. All of this information can be immediately broadcast to potential clients, who can call Henry instantly for additional details.

Meanwhile, Henry follows his to-do list and focuses on taking pictures and collecting information on the house not available elsewhere, or gathering information requested specifically by clients.

The ultimate combination of appliances would enable users to go further and create a virtual home that future clients can navigate and discover at their pace. Interested parties can download the tour or software agents may deliver short lists of houses according to their specific choices. These virtual homes can be tailored to potential client tastes, providing a cozy house to a retiree or a wild party scene for students. Ultimately, a client can create avatars for his family, including the dog and goldfish, to see how these avatars would adapt in the new home, for instance how and when they use the swimming pool (the family, not the pets). We could also imagine the house twenty years down the road, estimating the maintenance costs and the evolution of the family.

All links between tasks are automatically made for the end-user. All the appliances collaborate in such a way that the user does not need to know where the information is stored, which software is used, or which connections are employed. The end-user is in control of the end results only; the process is completely invisible.

2.2.4   Summary

Let us look again at the key features of this scenario and how they have been implemented. The me-centric infrastructure is built on a high-availability, broadband network connection that links Henry with the office. The reason for a high-speed network is the number of large pictures that need to be transferred back and forth. Unless a new algorithm becomes available that can pack images much better than JPEG without losing quality, the size of the images will be probably around 1 MB. So either a WLAN network or Universal Mobile Telecommunications Service (UMTS) network will be required to make this system work. Roaming does not play an important role here. Speed is more important, and typically you can have either roaming or broadband access. The WLAN network would have a base station in every house that would transmit the information via cable or DSL, for example, back to the office. A UMTS network would require a base station near the house that would transmit the information via satellite to the Internet backbone and from there to the office.

The mobile device that will be used is a combination: mobile phone, PDA, and digital camera. We are seeing the first generation of these devices being introduced into the market today. Nokia[7], for example, introduced the Nokia 7650, with an integrated digital camera, which takes pictures that then can be sent via MMS (Multimedia Messaging Service) on a high-speed mobile connection. It also provides a photo album for storing pictures and an advanced user interface that runs downloadable personal applications via Java technology. To make it easier to use, it includes joystick navigation and a color display. Although the quality of the pictures is still very poor (the Nokia provides only 640x480 pixels), the bandwidth is not very high, and the PDA functionality is not very good yet, we can expect to see devices that will match our requirements soon.

One of the biggest challenges in this scenario is the services required to run the business. If you look at the ecosystem in Figure 2.3,

---

[7]http://www.nokia.com/

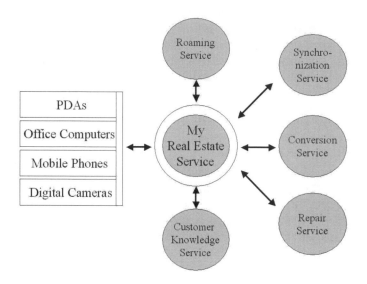

Figure 2.3. Real Estate Ecosystem

you can see that many of them do not exist in an optimal way. A synchronization tool is required to make sure that all data between the office and the device is up to date. While the images are quite large, the synchronization tool needs to check the bandwidth first and update the data only when enough bandwidth is available.

This means that if only little bandwidth is available, it should only synchronize small files, such as text files, and copy the descriptions of the images. If there is an urgent need for a certain image, it would be possible at least to search for it and download it immediately. The device should provide extensive descriptions to the pictures. The real estate agent should speak while taking the pictures and the device should save the spoken words and convert them into text. The device should also note where the pictures have been taken and use the construction plans of the house to create a virtual environment for prospective buyers.

An intelligent agent could be used to collect information about all repair work in the house. While Henry walks through the house and makes comments about repairs that need to be done in order to increase the sale price, the intelligent agent could start searching for the best offers from house repair companies, providing Henry with some time and cost estimates immediately. Another intelligent agent could collect all the information about the house and create an advertisement for the local newspaper and the local radio/TV stations automatically. Another intelligent agent could start to look through the customer database to find people who may be interested in the house and make appointments with them, if interested. Henry would receive a list of appointments before he even leaves the house.

Obviously, to have all of the services described in this scenario would be expensive and may not be profitable to implement. While most of the scenarios in this chapter are realistic and affordable, we wanted to show you some other ideas that may currently seem otherwise. However, if you look back in history, there have been many technologies and ideas that were considered unrealistic and expensive but have still become commodities today. One of the questions that needs to be answered is what economic model will cause a proliferation of so many diverse services that somehow come to be effectively aggregated into easy-to-use, coherent me-centric customer solutions.

2.3   Family Life

2.3.1   Introduction

Janice, married with three children, works for First Commonwealth Bank (FCB) handling commercial accounts. Her husband, Mike, is a painting contractor. Their oldest, Matt, has started junior college and still lives at home. Claudia is in high school. The youngest child, Sharon, is in middle school.

Janice's desk job comes with a wired phone that is part of the FCB's virtual private network (VPN). She keeps her cell phone on "vibrate" and in her purse during work; it's bad enough being interrupted by one phone when meeting with a client, much less two (one wired and one wireless).

It's a cold, clear winter day, and Janice realizes that she will have to stay an hour later than expected. She would rather not stop at the Bi-Lo or cook dinner. She decides to call Mike to see if he can handle dinner.

2.3.2   The Present

Janice calls Mike on his cell phone to ask if he can stop by the store and pick up barbecued chickens on his way home from work. But, as is often the case, Mike is on the phone. She gets his voicemail and leaves a message:

"Sweetie, could you pick up a couple of barbecued chickens on your way home? I'm going to be late. Let me know if you can't, and either I'll call Matt or pick them up myself. Thanks. Bye."

Half an hour later, she has not gotten a call back from Mike. She checks her cell phone: one unanswered call. She retrieves her voicemail and learns that Mike is actually working on the other side of town and won't be able to stop by the store. She calls Matt. Again, she gets voicemail:

"Matt, this is mom. On your way home from school, could you buy two barbecued chickens at the Bi-Lo? Thanks. If you can't, please give me a call at work right away. See you tonight. Bye."

To make sure that Matt gets the message, she sends him a quick text message asking him to check his voicemail and call her. Janice is finally ready to leave work. Still no call from Matt. "I wonder if he got the chickens?" She calls home: The line is busy. Claudia is no doubt chatting. She calls Matt again: voicemail. As soon as she walks out the door, her office phone rings: Matt leaves a message on his mother's voicemail:

"Mom, I got the chickens. I put them in the oven to keep warm. Bye."

The disadvantages of using the present system are pretty clear. It requires too much manual intervention and depends on humans being simultaneously available for synchronous communication requiring their nearly undivided attention.

2.3.3   The Future

It is 6:30 am. Mike and Janice finish their coffee and perform a ritual that's been going on for almost two years now: they synchronize their organizers. Mike is using the latest Nokia communicator; Janice has an HP iPaq. Lying on the kitchen table, the two devices exchange packets of infrared light.

That afternoon, Janice realizes that she will have to stay an hour later than expected. She would rather not stop at the Bi-Lo or cook dinner. She takes out her iPaq and sees that Mike is working on the other side of town. However, Matt finishes his last class at 5:30. She calls Matt, but gets his voicemail:

"Matt, this is mom. On your way home from school, could you buy two barbecued chickens at the Bi-Lo? Thanks. If you can't, please give me a call at work right away. See you tonight. Bye."

Janice picks up her iPaq and selects the shopping page. Touching the Bi-Lo link and then the deli link, she then drags two chicken icons into her "shopping basket." She then opens the basket and selects a 6 o'clock pick-up. As nobody is at home, automatic delivery would not work without a special storage.

Janice drags the shopping icon into the "message board" space and touches "annotate." After a couple rings, a recorded voice welcomes her to the ATW message board and asks her to speak her full name. "Janice Weaver" is all that it takes for her to authenticate herself and gain access to the message board. Janice says "family" and then when prompted, explains the situation: "Hello everyone. I have to work late tonight so I'd really appreciate it if someone could pick up two barbecued chickens at the Bi-Lo. I've reserved them for 6 o'clock. If you can pick them up, please give me a call. If I don't hear from you, I'll get them myself, but dinner will be even later. Your choice! Thanks. Bye."

Janice goes back to work while the message board attempts to contact and deliver the message to the family. Mike's cell phone is called, but the message board recognizes that the call has been re-directed to voicemail (caller ID has certainly improved over the last few years). After the greeting message goes silent, the message board plays Janice's message and hangs up.

In a similar manner, the home number is called. The fourth call attempt doesn't receive a busy signal, and Sharon answers. She hears her mom's recorded message. Putting down the phone, she calls upstairs to her sister Claudia: "Mom wants you to pick up some chickens. You should call her."

Matt's cell phone doesn't get called: He receives an SMS containing his mom's message, while he's in the middle of an exam. His personal agent refuses to pass on the message to Matt, as the message has only low priority. It will be delivered to him after the exam.

Claudia is the first to phone back, but she calls her mother's cell phone instead of the office number. Nobody picks up the phone. Therefore she decides to ask the message service agent for more information on the details. Fortunately, Janice linked her shopping agent to the message service agent to form a workflow, making it easy for Claudia to see the details of the order. Claudia confirms taking on the task to the message service which would know how to close the loop with Janice and also close the task out, keeping others from taking it on or being bothered with the message.

Janice is finally ready to leave work. Still no call from Matt, but an automatic message telling her that he will get back after the exam. She calls home: busy. Claudia is no doubt chatting. As soon as she walks out the door, her office phone rings: Claudia's agent reminds her to leave a message on her mother's voicemail in addition to the automatic notification of the message service agent:

"Mom, I got the chickens. I put them in the oven to keep warm. See you later. Bye."

2.3.4 Summary

If we look at the key features of the me-centric implementation in this scenario, we can see that the community is the most important feature. There is no need for high-tech devices or high-speed networks. Today's PDAs and mobile phones can be enhanced to make this scenario reality. The difficulty lies in coordinating the communication within the family, which is sometimes already difficult enough, even when everyone is in the same room.

The future scenario is an example of the use of a standardized template for tossing a task out to a small community of potential volunteers and a way for the task creator to be notified of successful delegation and a way for other volunteers to be freed from further communication about the task and prevented from unnecessarily taking on an already spoken for task redundantly.

In Europe, many children age six and up already have their own mobile phones. Parents give them phones to call home (for the younger ones, it is the only number they are able to dial; all other numbers are disabled). One advantage of having a mobile phone is that it is possible to locate the person easily. Although GSM[8] provides only rough location capabilities, newer phones have GPS built in, enabling exact positioning. This means that parents can check where their children are without having to call them. An agent could be introduced to make sure children stick to a routine path when walking home from school, for example. The agent could alert parents if their child starts moving in the wrong direction, or begins to move too fast as though they had entered a vehicle.

In our scenario, an intelligent agent could coordinate the locations and the supermarkets and check in advance if a certain market has the desired chicken in stock. Another agent could coordinate and synchronize the agendas of all family members. GPS could also be used to locate the person closest to the market for convenience.

In Figure 2.4, you can see the basic infrastructure requires a similar set up like a company, where each family member has certain privileges and rights in the system. A communication agent should track where each family member is and how that family member can be reached best. If Mike, for example, tells his mobile that he is in a meeting, this information could be relayed back to somebody who may be try-

---

[8]Global system for mobile communication

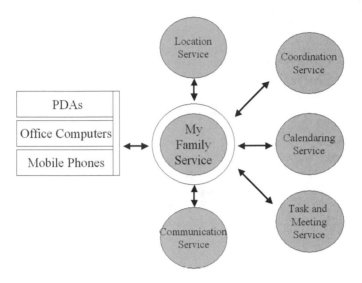

Figure 2.4. Family Life Ecosystem

ing to call him. Additionally, important information could be relayed to Mike in text form while he's in his meeting, so Janice could speak to the voicemail system and the agent could evaluate its importance. Today's voicemail systems allow the caller to specify the importance of the message, which is no good, as callers always think that their calls are of utmost importance. The agent acts on behalf of its user and not on behalf of the caller, which makes the agent trustworthy.

The ecosystem should also support task distribution among family members. In this case, Janice could send out the task to be completed to everyone in the family, and a task agent would coordinate the task with everyone's agenda and capabilities to find who would be ideally suited for the task. The task agent would also coordinate the family with the outside world, e.g., with friends and other relatives, and would connect to other agents that may be of interest to the family, such as shopping agents or intelligent vacation agents.

2.4   Work-Life Balance

2.4.1   Introduction

Chris is a working parent and is involved in two entertainment activities right now, one for work and one at home, which he needs to
coordinate in order to maintain a good work-life balance.

At work, Chris is in sales and has a need to keep in touch with his
customers and develop new ones. Chris sells a line of teen-oriented
clothing. A number of his customers are into a future-shock, cyber-
punk role-playing game, called "bunk," that connects them through
phone, pager, Web, and e-mail. Chris has chosen to play this extended
online game so that he can meet potential customers, interact with his
existing customers, keep tabs on the latest lingo and fads, and just to
have fun.

At home, Chris likes to relax in his media room and is very into
music, music videos, and photographs. He has a collection of old college
buddies who are into this too, but they are spread all over the world. He
and his friends like to get together to share music, talk about the bands,
concert dates, new videos, and so forth. He also likes to have access to
his music when he's in the car on the way to his next appointment or
just when he's ferrying his daughter to her horseback riding lessons.
Ozzy Osbourne is a great accompaniment to dressage.

2.4.2   The Present

In the near future, we have serious bandwidth issues for our wide area
wireless providers and very spotty coverage for 802.11. The appliances
Chris uses speak both. Chris likes to travel light, so he has a very light
headset he uses for both music and phone work, a palm-sized computer
that doubles as a phone dialer/communication hub, and a wristwatch
that shows simple paging info and doubles as a control panel for playing music, etc.

On his way to the mall to talk to his next client, Chris is notified
through his watch that a bunk player is nearby who has some info he
needs. He uses his PDA to IM and makes a stop at the Jamba Juice to
chat and trade bunk secrets, PDA to PDA. On his way to his customer,
he passes a print kiosk where he prints a small booklet about the next
bunk challenge and some info he needs.

His new-music-notifier service also sends him a page, based on his
music interests, showing that there is a new Ozzy track. He vows to
track that down later. At his customer's place of business, he finds out
what the needs are, beams over a catalog customized to his customer,

picks up some information about what's selling (the local store inventory has been told to allow him to get aggregate info on his products only), checks on the status of some open orders, and swaps bunk stories with the manager. Because his watch has swapped interests with the manager, he finds they are both Ozzy fans, and the manager tells him about a new single that is out. They share bunk IDs so they can help each other later in the week. A new custom catalog will be printed and shipped out that same day, and an online catalog will be uploaded that the customer can peruse.

On the way out of the mall, Chris stops at the music store to get a demo track of the Ozzy song, adding it to his playlist. He will listen to it now and then share it with his buds tonight when he gets to his media room. On the road again, Chris fires up his playlist on the car stereo that was synchronized with his home system overnight when the car was in the garage. The Ozzy single will be waiting for him at home. He can listen to it and share it with his friends later tonight.

2.4.3 The Future

In the farther future, we have better bandwidth for our wide area wireless providers and less spotty coverage for 802.11 WLAN technology. The appliances Chris uses can connect to both types of networks. Chris likes to travel light, so he has a very light headset he uses for both music and phone work, a palm-sized computer that doubles as a phone dialer/communication hub, and a wristwatch that shows simple paging info and doubles as a control panel for playing music.

The personal agent informs Chris about new music from Ozzy, which is automatically downloaded to his music repository and which will be charged only after he has listened to it twice. The first listening is free and and lets Chris decide if he likes the song enough to purchase it. The song is encrypted and cannot be copied so the record label does not suffer from pirate copies of the song. Once he decides that he likes it, he receives not only the audio file, but automatically also the video file with it. Depending on the device Chris is using, the quality of the video is recalculated on the spot or only the audio track is heard.

While driving to the customer site, Chris can already start talking to the customer about his needs, because his car has a built in camera and displays the incoming video stream on the windshield, so that Chris is not distracted from driving. At the customer site, the print-on-demand service has delivered the new catalogues, and Chris can use the time to have some discussions with the manager about the future.

2.4.4 Summary

If we analyze the me-centric implementation in this scenario, we see that mobility plays an important role, as Chris moves around and requires lots of bandwidth. The major issue is the design of the device that Chris will be using. The light headset, the wristwatch, and the PDA need to be connected wirelessly and need to be able to operate on their own, if the other components are not reachable. While the wireless connection can be achieved easily with today's technology, such as Bluetooth for local connection and WLAN for external connection, it can be difficult to create self-sufficient devices.

Each of the devices should be able to take over the functionality of the other. The headphone should be able to provide spoken page information, while the PDA should be able to play music, if required. Therefore, the devices themselves should not hold any information or services, but rely on the connection to a service provider that can provide the required information and services to each of the devices. The only job of the device is to convert the information to its output interface. An agent needs to configure the devices that Chris uses. The devices should work together automatically and respond to the service provider the configuration in which they work. In case a device is switched off, the service provider may need to reconfigure the service to make it useful for Chris. This means that when he uses his earphones, the music will be streamed to that device; if he is at home, the music will be played on his personal stereo. The device should have a fat cache to operate well with downloaded data and programs, and continuously when offline.

In Figure 2.5, you can see the networking infrastructure, which provides a seamless network to Chris and his music. Depending on the type of network, the quality of the music is automatically adjusted. On low-bandwidth networks, the quality is automatically dropped, and as soon as Chris connects to a higher bandwidth network, the quality is enhanced again. This requires seamless roaming just like in the first scenario.

Some bandwidth needs to be reserved to support the agents that help Chris with his work. Chris's car can be used for video-conferencing and can provide all the relevant information that Chris needs for his work. An agent collects the past orders of a certain dealer and compares the information with other dealers and their recent orders. The agent prepares a proposal for that dealer based on this information. Another agent would check the stock level at that dealer and restock the bestsellers automatically.

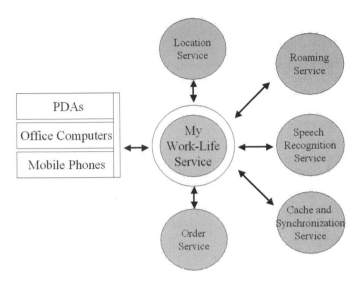

Figure 2.5. Work-Life Balance Ecosystem

2.5   Construction Site

2.5.1   Introduction

On a construction site, a new set of technologies is going to be introduced. Every worker will receive an online connection that allows him to communicate with the other workers and that monitors progress. This is done, for example, by monitoring the number of bricks that are already used for a wall. The computer in the back can verify that everything is going according to the project plan. It can also make projects, monitor when the next step is going to be complete, and order electricians just-in-time, as needed. A satellite will check the construction from space and make sure that it is built to its specifications. The architect can always have the full picture. He is able to see a 3D model of the construction on the screen, both the desired solution and then the actual solution, and make modifications on the fly. As every worker is connected, it is possible to make changes while building, because everyone will be able to receive the update immediately.

2.5.2 The Present

Although very ambitious, it would be possible to start with such a project today. First, a framework must be created that enables all parties involved to work together. A collaboration tool needs to be introduced that can be used by anyone on the construction site. As the workers won't be able to use a laptop while working, other devices are required to allow them to work in a group and exchange information electronically. Although very expensive, it is possible to build intelligent helmets for workers and display the content and the services on a small monitor that can be built into the worker's glasses. But it may not really be necessary for all workers. Information and services can be provided by mobile phone, for example, and it may not be required that the workers be online all the time. Therefore, it is necessary to think about the processes involved before setting up the infrastructure.

Although it may seem that a construction site is organized in a decentralized manner, there is a management of the whole site that makes sure that everything is done in the right order. Therefore, it would be important to support the management functionality of the site first. This would mean, for example, that materials are delivered at the right time, in the right amount. If the architect's drawings are the basis for all further planning, the software should be extended to support a project plan and procure the materials required for building.

The architect should just enter the drawings into a CAD program and provide a project plan based on the drawings. From this input, the system should be able to generate a list of items that are required to build the house. The materials list is sent to one or several marketplaces where companies can provide prices for the required building blocks of the house. In addition to the quantity, the delivery date can also be sent to the supplier. This reduces the space required on the construction site for storing materials. So far, it is not so difficult. It allows the architect to tell the sponsor of the project how much it would cost in total and if it is actually possible to build the house in time, as the architect now has a commitment from the suppliers to deliver the materials on time.

The service for the planning phase can be extended into the development phase on different levels. First, communication can be enhanced through mobile devices that can transmit voice and data. Simple instructions could be sent via voice, and more complex issues could be sent as data, making it possible to visualize a part of the house. While it may be impractical for many to have anything larger than a PDA, it actually may be sufficient to display on a small screen the parts of the house that the worker is actually working on.

Although security is not a major concern, it still needs to be taken into account. If a hacker could invade the construction network, he could create confusion and damage. Therefore, the wireless network needs to be protected. End-to-end security is a must again. The server, the transmission and the clients need to be part of the overall security model. Security is further enhanced by using devices that contain smart cards or require fingerprint verification, for example. This ensures that nobody can steal passwords without someone noticing it. If a hardware device gets lost, it can be excluded. Through this procedure, it is easier to secure the network, as only devices that are used by authorized persons are allowed on the network, and any device that is not owned by the construction company is automatically denied access.

The communication service could be enhanced by providing feedback from the workers about their status. Once they have finished their task, they could send a status update back to the server, which allows the construction management to track the progress. To make it easy for the workers, there should be a button labeled "I have finished this task" on the mobile device. By clicking on this button, and confirming the data that has been collected during the task, the worker sends the information back to the server. As each mobile device is attached to a certain worker and a certain worker has a certain task, this concept could work quite well and would not require the workers to have a deep understanding of the technology.

The planning service consists of components that exist today. CAD applications, project management tools, and marketplaces are common, but the integration is missing. This means that the main focus for the planning part of the service is integration of different software solutions that are not necessarily Internet-enabled. Most construction companies will have CAD applications and project management tools in place. In order to create this new service, it needs to be determined whether an extension of the current products makes sense or a replacement with newer software is required. Both will require some investment. Both applications require an Internet-enabled interface that allows them to share information with the marketplace and other services, such as communication services on-site. Introducing a messaging backbone and a central database for this service is not cheap, but still within the range that a company would like to pay for.

More expensive are the mobile devices and the infrastructure required to make them work in a collaborative environment. As we are talking about a system with special buttons to make use as easy as possible, special hardware needs to be introduced. Although it is an expanding market, companies will charge a premium for these devices in the beginning. Today it may not be feasible to introduce such a new communication infrastructure.

Although possible to implement today, only the planning phase would make business sense; introducing the collaboration part of the solution will be probably be too expensive on the hardware side, even though the software and the infrastructure can be set up at a low cost.

2.5.3 The Future

In the future the solution overview that was laid out in the preceding section can become reality more easily. The major reason is that mobile devices will become more common and prices will drop significantly. Not only will the prices for the hardware drop, the software components in the solution will become service offerings, reducing the need to buy a certain piece of software. It can be easily rented instead. Due to the new e-services infrastructure that will be in place, exchanging information between the services will become much easier and cheaper. First, there will be a connection to a security service that authenticates and authorizes the devices and workers who want to use the service.

Other than in a national security marketplace, it is not necessary that a governmental organization run the authentication service, but governmental organizations may want to enforce proper staffing on the construction site. Governments may actually require their service to be used on the site. Illegal workers will have a hard time and companies that try to save money through clandestine employment will have an even harder time with this type of authentication in place.

All construction-related data is stored in the construction management system, with contributions from the architect, the marketplace, and the workers on the construction site. Information can be pushed to the parties involved, but it is not stored there. This reduces the need for memory on the required devices. In the near future, it will also be easier to integrate new devices into such a network. Through wireless LAN technologies, any device can be made part of a network easily. Thus, creating new devices for a particular cause, such as providing feedback about the status of a workstream, is easy. Imagine a mason building a wall with a scoop. Instead of giving the mason a new device, it would be possible to enhance the scoop with wireless LAN access. The mason presses a button when he starts to build the wall and another button once he is finished. These simple functions can also be included in other tools the workers require anyway. Thus, the information technology is hidden away from them and does not require additional learning to improve the performance of their job.

To make the CAD application as effective as possible, it needs to be based on a client-server architecture. Just like all other applications, it should be provided as a service to the client in order to make it easy to exchange information with other services that are required for this meta-service.

In addition to the CAD application, a special visualization tool is required. It not only visualizes the current state, but also the complete plan and the delta between the two. It shows this not only from an architectural point of view, but also from a project management point of view. Ideally, the tool would also allow the user to create projections and reports for management. Very important also is the feature of visualizing information not only on high-resolution screens, but also on small displays of personal agents and cellular phones, which require different levels of detail.

The same applies to communication. The system should be able to transform messages from one format to another on the fly. Voice, text, e-mail, and fax, just to mention a few, need to be converted and stored in a single format, to make sure that everyone on the construction site is able to access the information in the way that best suits a particular moment. Unified messaging will be a key service for collaboration on the construction site. It will allow people to receive voice mails that are transformed automatically into e-mails and SMS that will be forwarded as fax, for example.

2.5.4   Summary

Let's look at the key features of a me-centric future in this scenario (see also Figure 2.6). While the workers do not require highly advanced technology to communicate with each other, the architect will require some highly sophisticated devices and services to support him in constructing the building. The worker communication is similar to the family from the scenario in Section 2.3.

The system needs to know the location of the workers and their status, i.e., what they are doing and what they should be doing according to the project plan. The device could be an enhanced mobile phone integrated into the helmet of the workers to make sure that they are not distracted from their work. The mobile phone needs to take lots of context into account, such as the location and the process, to send back to the central service provider.

In the construction site ecosystem, you can clearly see that tasks could be done more effectively with a little support from this central service, although the workers would probably not like it. While this advanced communication system would improve the performance of the

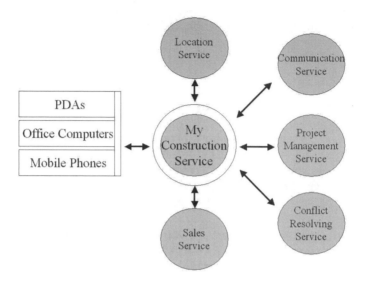

Figure 2.6. Construction Site Ecosystem

workers, only additional technology and services would help the architect to ensure the quality and the timing of the project. Satellites are able to shoot high-resolution images of any spot on Earth. Using these high-resolution images and the original construction plan can help the architect to verify that the plan is executed correctly. An agent would compare the plan with the images every day and would try to correct issues itself; only if this is not possible would it inform the architect about the issue. Another agent would compare the images with the project plan to see when which wall should have been built, for example. Again, the agent would try to resolve conflicts on its own where possible and would inform the architect only in cases where it cannot resolve the issue.

The agent would also provide a completion date, passing on the information to an intelligent sales agent that would send out the information about the building to some prospects. They would be able to wander through the 3D construction plans, which would be completed by the images of the satellite. The sales agent could be owned by the real estate agent from the scenario in Section 2.2.

Based on the progress of the construction, another agent could check with the project plan and start negotiation processes with suppliers for bricks or windows, for example. The bricks or windows would be delivered just-in-time to the construction site, reducing the need for storage and its associated costs.

2.6   Holiday Break-In

2.6.1   Introduction

Dan and his family leave for a long-needed holiday. They plan to spend two weeks at the Cannes Film Festival. On the third day of their trip, burglars break into their home and steal most of their valuables, including their computer system, home theater system, silverware, and several pieces of priceless jewelry.

During their raid, they also deliberately break several items in the home, including their cabinet of fine china and an antique curio holding Dan's wife's Lladro collection, the value of which the burglars do not realize. A neighbor notifies Dan at the hotel and the family cuts their trip short to return home and assess their losses.

2.6.2   The Present

Unfortunately, this scenario is all too common. Today, there are a few options to protect against such a scenario, but the biggest problem would be the assets in the home. Dan did what he could to prepare for such a scenario.

A year before this burglary took place, Dan's neighbor suggested that he videotape the contents of his home for insurance purposes. Dan takes this a step further and describes each item he photographs to the best of his ability, including his idea of each item's approximate value. Dan stores the videotape in a safe deposit box at his bank.

He also has a motion-sensor alarm system installed, which notifies a central alarm office when activated. The central office first telephones the home to determine whether the alarm was tripped accidentally or it's a real security breach. If they receive no answer within a few minutes, they then notify the police, who are dispatched to investigate.

In this case, the police are notified within ten minutes of the break-in and arrive at Dan's house within twenty minutes. By this time, the burglars are long gone and the damage is done. Dan files his insurance claim using the videotape he created for reference. The problem is that the tape is over a year old, and many of the stolen items are not recorded. To compensate for items he may not remember, Dan claims several items that were not stolen, and fudges the age and approximate value of many of the known items. The insurance company settles his claim without incident and he is satisfied with the reimbursement. However, a month later, he discovers that his insurance premium is increased by fifteen percent as a result of both his claim and the continuous problem of insurance fraud that plagues the industry.

2.6.3 The Future

As we have seen in this chapter, tomorrow's world will be much different. More things will have chips built into them that will enable them to communicate with other devices nearby, as well as with the Internet. These chips provide information such as the status of the object and its location.

Instead of Dan's videotape, which contains ad hoc and unreliable descriptions of his home's contents and their value, every item in his home - including furniture, cupboards, even walls and artwork, in addition to electronic devices - will register itself into an electronic catalog. The system will check each item's status and record the appropriate information, including exact descriptions of each item's age, condition, and value. Some items, such as the priceless jewelry, will be keyed in manually because they will not contain chips to identify themselves. But high-quality photographs will accompany all items, facilitating claim procedures and assessments.

After an online registration, all of this information will transfer over a WLAN into a database on the home server, which in turn is linked to the insurance company over the Internet, as well as a replacement service that will monitor the status of each item and process replacements should that status change.

Before Dan leaves for his vacation, he tells his alarm system to automatically notify the police if triggered. The system thus knows that Dan isn't home without him having to disclose this sensitive information to another human being. Once Dan activates the service, the objects with chips built in begin to monitor their own status and that of neighboring objects. An XML description is used to communicate the status of each object. Either at regular intervals or in real time, changes in the status are filtered through the database and reported to the replacement service, the insurance company, and to Dan.

When the break-in occurs, the police are dispatched immediately and arrive at the home within five minutes. Dan is automatically notified via his cell phone that a burglary has been reported and that the status of stolen and broken items has changed. The police aren't in time to prevent the burglary, but the thieves only manage to get away with Dan's stereo equipment and some jewelry, and in their scramble to get out of the house, they topple the curio housing the Lladro collection. As soon as the pieces shatter, the replacement service is notified and replacement pieces are processed immediately. They use an XML description to report the shipping status of each piece.

Within a half-hour, the police use a GPS system to track the chips in Dan's stereo equipment. A van is pulled over minutes later, the burglars are arrested, and the equipment is returned. Dan is reimbursed for the jewelry and the Lladro collection. He claims that his receiver was broken during the burglary, but what he doesn't know is that his son broke the receiver just before they left for their holiday. The database informs the insurance company that the receiver was in fact broken before the burglary took place, so he is not reimbursed accordingly. A month later, Dan discovers that his insurance premium has been lowered by two percent because of the efficiency of the system he has in place.

2.6.4 Summary

This implementation combines several of the me-centric features that we've seen already in this chapter, with several advantages to these features easily recognized in this scenario.

In the present situation, items in the home are too diverse to be treated by a single system such that we will see in the future. Although many household devices today have chips built in, they lack an Internet connection or even a local connection to exchange information. No system knows about the existence of any others, and there is no central system that knows about all the items in the home. To realize such a service, it would be necessary to create an online service where homeowners can register all the items they have in the house. There are several problems with this approach. First, there is no standard way to describe the objects. Either one builds a catalogue of all products that have been built and sold over the last hundred years, or one lets the homeowners describe their goods themselves. With the catalogue, one could be sure that every item is described in a very precise way, but the catalogue would be too big to be handled by the homeowners. Every category would contain thousands of different items, and often the owner does not know how to describe the item best.

The other option of free text does not really help either, because it makes it difficult to find a suitable replacement. Probably the best way would be to create generic categories (such as cabinet), define some attributes (such as size, material, and color), and add a free text field where additional information can be entered to make sure that the item is described as clearly as possible. This still means lots of work without immediate reward, and is still not always accurate.

To make it work, the system could focus only on consumer electronics and household devices. This means that the television set, the DVD player, the stereo, and the refrigerator would be registered at the service. These devices are easy to register because they have code names and numbers and are all standardized. Having their model names and numbers will not only make sure that a certain product is correctly described, but also the age and the approximate cost for the object. This makes it easier to find an equivalent replacement. It also helps insurance companies to evaluate the damage.

The number of objects to be entered into the system will be probably be pretty low—around ten—meaning that the effort is manageable and will ensure that many people will participate. However, the majority of household items would remain unprotected. Additionally, a change in each item's status would be impossible to monitor. We would still rely on unreliable user descriptions of broken or stolen items.

Using today's technologies it is possible to implement the basic idea of this scenario, but due to the complexity of it, we doubt that there is a business plan to support the effort. It would not be possible to implement the technology with reasonable costs. Too many unknowns are in the project to make it reality.

From an infrastructure point of view, the future scenario does not require much upgrade of today's networks. In-house communication can be based on WLAN, an agent will make sure that all affected parties are notified, and stolen items will be tracked via GPS.

To make this service work, it would be necessary for every object in the house to be scanned into the catalog in some way. It will be impracticable for the next few years to introduce chips to all objects, but putting a bar code on each object would work. In this case, broken items would be re-scanned for replacement purposes. Soon, though, we can expect to buy furniture and other items that include a small chip that can transmit the existence and state of each object back to a central service hub automatically.

In fact, each item in the home would have its own agent that would work on behalf of that item and make sure that everything is in order with it. The central service hub would know when to repair or replace the item. The service's ecosystem, shown in Figure 2.7, shows the required infrastructure services and the application services for the different parties involved.

Another advantage to this system is that insurance fraud would be virtually eliminated. Because items report their own status to a central system, insurance customers will no longer be able to make inflated or even false claims, thus keeping insurance premiums for all customers

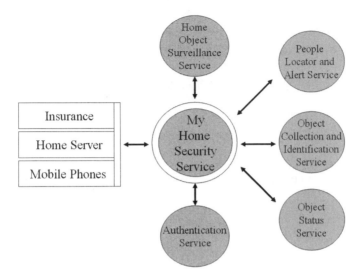

Figure 2.7. Home Security Ecosystem

at reasonable levels. Likewise, customers can rest easy knowing that accurate information is recorded for all of their valuables, so insurance companies cannot underestimate the value of any given item. Finally, stolen goods are easily tracked, not only ensuring their return to their rightful owners, but also increasing the likelihood that thieves will be caught red-handed.

2.7   Extended Manufacturing

2.7.1   Introduction

A manufacturer wants to automate its design process by moving it to the Internet. Instead of creating large-scale designs of its products on paper, it wants to use the Internet in order to reduce the complexity of the task and the number of errors in the designs. Internal designers work on the projects, but also some external companies and freelancers. Today, the designs are sent back and forth by courier. A tracer had to take the paper designs and put them into CAD applications in the end. The idea is to use the Internet as the collaboration platform for all parties involved in the design process.

2.7.2   The Present

In this case also, the technology is available today to move the whole design process to the Internet. To implement such a solution, several steps can be envisioned. It may be a pure communication medium, which allows files to be exchanged through a secure channel, or a full-blown collaboration services that enables people to work together on-line on a certain design.

If we look at the communication needs, a simple Web site that hosts a set of newsgroups and file exchange would basically do it. In basic technology, there are some challenges that need to be considered when implementing such a solution. As the competition would be very inter-ested in knowing which designs are in progress, the site must be well-secured. To achieve this, security needs to be enforced on the server, during transmission, and on the clients. Only with end-to-end security implemented properly is it possible to use the Internet as a communi-cation medium. This requires a set of tools for the server security, such as a firewall, a secure operating system, and a security procedure. This also requires application security. In many cases, hackers get onto a server by using design flaws within the application, so your applica-tions must stick to the same standards as your secure server. This means that you can make the server as secure as you want, but if your application does not stick to the same standards, the whole system will break at its weakest link.

You must also ensure that data cannot be intercepted during trans-mission. Today, 128-bit SSL encryption can be used to ensure that nobody can eavesdrop on the connection and steal, alter, or remove in-formation that is flowing between parties. To ensure the security on the client-side, data should only be accessible by password on an en-crypted filesystem, making it impossible to hack the client's computer and steal the information. In many cases, the client is the weakest link, as the operating systems are either not secure or not securely config-ured. Special applications for most client operating systems exist that can create data vaults, making it impossible for hackers to steal the data. They still can hack the system but are locked out of private com-pany information.

Security is further enhanced by introducing smart cards. This en-sures that nobody can steal passwords without someone noticing it. An additional card-reader and software needs to be installed on the client's computer as it is still not common to use smart cards in a Web environ-ment.

Once the security infrastructure has been set up, it is possible to use a communication portal Web site to exchange information and data. Information can be exchanged either through Web e-mail or newsgroups that are hosted on the system. The advantage of using secure Web e-mail is that no special e-mail client is required and no additional software needs to be installed by the client. Through Web e-mail and newsgroups, files could be also exchanged and stored on the server.

This simple application would be the first step towards an online collaboration tool. To make this tool happen, several other technologies need to be introduced. First, a design repository is required, which allows all designers involved to contribute. A project management tool and a revision control system are also required to support the collaborative private network. Through this set of tools, designers can share their work online and create project groups online. The revision control system ensures that people can check files in and out, thus making clear who is working on which part. The information about the file usage can flow back into the project management system, if files are grouped into projects and the work can be assigned to the files. Several technologies are available to handle this part of the collaboration.

At this stage, the collaboration process is online, but the actual work is still done offline. In order to move the work online as well, it is necessary to have some visualization tools and CAD applications online. The first part can be realized quite easily today, but online CAD tools are not yet available. Most CAD applications can export DXF files, which means that this should be the base format for all online activity, if designers come from different companies and use different technologies. By allowing only DXF on the server, the system is independent of the CAD system used. DXF can also be easily converted to X3D, which is a new format based on VRML (Virtual Reality Modeling Language) that has been available for several years now. X3D can be visualized in a Web browser, making it possible that work groups can view a certain part of the design and use the newsgroups or e-mail to exchange information about it. This could even be done in realtime via an online chat. Modifying the design online would require a CAD application running. Via VNC[9], for example, it would be possible to export the display of a client to the others, but this is not really a convenient or good way to work.

Building a basic communication portal is not very costly, since there is free software that could be used for this task. A Web server, Web e-mail server, and a newsgroups server are required. The costly part of the communication portal is the security infrastructure required. The costs are not fixed for the system, but depend on the number of people that are going to use the system. For every user, a digital certificate

---

[9]http://www.uk.research.att.com/vnc/

needs to be created. This requires a public key infrastructure to be built up. Every client computer that is going to use the service will require a data vault. Although the cost per user and client computer is decreasing with the larger number, it still means that a large investment needs to be made today.

The collaboration portal would cost significantly more. The project management software, the revision control system and the visualization tools can be quite expensive and the integration of these tools with the communication platform will create some additional costs. To save costs, an offline integration could be done that will exchange information between the different applications in a batch-mode. This means that the information would be updated every few hours only. Although the information would not be always up to date, it would reduce the integration costs significantly. Once the system proves to be successful, a tighter integration could be envisioned. Still, it will be expensive, as each application has it own set of interfaces and no common exchange format exists.

Designers would create a design, upload it to the server, and have an online discussion about it. Another designer could check it out, modify it, and upload it back to the server. The revision control system would track all changes, making sure that the pre-defined steps in the project plan are followed. In case of major changes in the design or failure to follow the project plan, the project manager would need to revisit the project plan and make adjustments to it.

To many unknowns are in the project to make it reality today, as it is highly complicated to build up such a solution using today's technologies. We doubt that there is a business plan to support the effort or implement the technology with reasonable costs.

2.7.3 The Future

The solution tomorrow will look very similar from an architectural point of view, but the integration will be much easier. Several companies are working on online services that allow the tight integration of the different modules and provide a common interface to the designers. Over time, the need for paper printouts of CAD designs becomes less relevant. More designers will be able to integrate their drawings and ideas into an overall project and can see immediately the effect of their designs in the overall context.

From a technical point of view, things become easier as the integration between the services is standardized. The core service will be connected to various other services. There will be a connection to a security service that authenticates and authorizes the person who wants to access the extended manufacturing portal. In the ideal future, this service is run by a governmental agency, offering all companies an identification service, which can be combined with a role model that is flexible and can be adapted for each business case. The current problem of proper user identification can thus be easily outsourced, and if run by the government, the element of trust would be very high. Alternatively this service could be run by banks, as their trust factor is also very high, but it would require people to register several times, depending on which bank a particular web service is using. Another model has the governmental agency holding the master database for identification, while the service is operated by the banks. The master database would be required to hold several types of data to provide different authentication mechanisms. Personal data, iris and retina scans, fingerprints, and a digital certificate need to be part of the digital identity of every single person.

Many companies try to set up their own trust centers, but they will not work efficiently if they are not trusted by the companies and people wanting to use the service. Microsoft and Sun are already trying to compete with rival technologies, but neither will win, as they are not considered to be a trusted third-party by the majority of people and because they are too technology-driven.

As the web services infrastructure provides an encrypted exchange of information, it is not necessary to implement something for this particular project. A data vault is not required on the client computers anymore, as the CAD editing service provides the possibility to edit the designs online. Therefore, a local copy of the data is not required, reducing the risk significantly. The CAD editing service is basically the client-server version of the standard CAD application that used to run on a single computer. This service could be hosted at an application service provider that also offers other applications online. This is probably the most complex part of the solution, as redesigning a CAD application to run in client-server mode will be expensive and difficult to achieve. Broadband Internet access and high-end computers will be required to make this service possible. High-speed access is required to download the application on demand and high-end computers to actually execute the application, as it most likely will be written in Java, which is not necessarily the fastest programming language. A part of the CAD application could be the visualization tool, but typically it should be another application, because it provides a different functionality. While the CAD application focuses on the editor, the visualization tool includes features to display the model in different views and qualities and provides a chat feature for online meetings.

E-mail, chat, and newsgroup services can be bought from a community provider and easily integrated. The flow of information between these services is limited, but a tight integration into the project management service and the visualization and CAD tool needs to be provided. The total solution will consist of a Web front-end that will allow designers to do all their work through a unified interface. A separate interface needs to be built for the project managers where they can create their project plans and provide updates to the designers. The project manager can also register designers and assign work packages to them.

Multiple access for the designers to the portal is nice to have, but not a requirement. Designers will require a computer to make changes in the designs. This is not possible through a mobile phone, for example, but in order to participate in discussion groups, alternative access devices should be supported.

2.7.4 Summary

Let's now look at the me-centric features of this implementation. A broadband networking infrastructure is required to support the needs of the designers in order to keep the data flow up. Security is an important issue in this scenario, as the designs could range from product designs for new cars to design plans for a space station. Everyone connected to this virtual community network requires a security clearance, and this applies to the devices that are connected.

In this scenario, no fancy devices or WLAN are required (although they do not harm the scenario). Traditional personal computers are mainly used for this kind of work, but the applications and services need to be made more intelligently. This means the community needs to employ agents to regulate the communication and the workflow and make it more efficient. These agents are especially important if the work is done in a distributed environment. They could ensure that the work is well coordinated.

If you look at the extended manufacturing ecosystem (see Figure 2.8), you can see the importance of the security aspect in this scenario. The security is important to make sure that nobody breaks in, but also to make sure that only people within a design team can add, modify, or delete the portions of the design they are responsible for. The data vault that contains all the information also needs special security features. Intelligent agents would be in place that act as security guards to protect the information. Another agent would be responsible for backup services and high availability of the solution. These agents would work autonomously and try to resolve all the issues related to

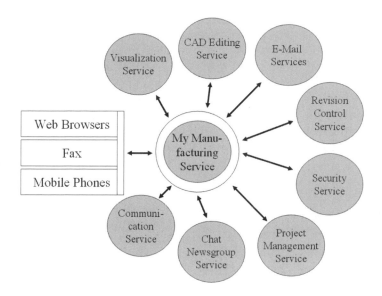

Figure 2.8. Extended Manufacturing Ecosystem

their tasks themselves. This would mean a huge advance in IT management. Today an administrator needs to monitor the whole IT environment; using these intelligent agents, an administrator is required only once in the beginning to set up the agents and tell them what to do.

The communication agents make sure that every party involved in the design knows about updates in the process and changes of decisions. They also ensure that people are working according to the project plan, making automatic static updates to the project plan, and informing other agents about the progress. It is important to note that there are two types of intelligent agents: one that is working on behalf of a person and one that is working on behalf of a process. The agents that work for people help to create the me-centric experience for the user, while the process agents help to get on with the predefined process.

2.8   Fleet Management

2.8.1   Introduction

A large corporation wants to track all its vehicles in use. It therefore sends out an RFP to fleet management companies to introduce a new service for automatic vehicle detection systems, in order to make sure that employees do not misuse the cars. Part of the new service requires a tight integration into a satellite navigation system, connection to all gas stations, and a fleet management system that is able to track the use of the cars.

In the past, employees used company cars for private excursions, and used the company gas card to refill their private cars. It was never clear which car was used by whom and for how long. The new system is designed to cut down on employee abuse. Additionally, in case of emergencies, accidents, and breakdowns, fleet management would be able to react quickly and efficiently.

2.8.2 The Present

If we look at the possibilities today, it becomes quite clear that the required technology is available. GPS, mobile Internet, and fleet management software packages can track the location and the use of the car. Due to the different technologies used for all these components, it is quite expensive to integrate them and make them work efficiently. The problem becomes apparent if you look at the number of vehicles that need to be tracked. If we talk about five or ten cars, it would be almost possible to track them manually, but fleet management service companies often have thousands of vehicles in operation and rented out to many different companies by a fleet management service provider.

In order to make this system work, the information would need to flow from the car via the satellite to the fleet management service provider, which in turn offers an extranet that allows the company to check the status of each car. Although not very common yet, telemetric data could also be sent with the location to make sure that the fleet management service provider is able to track repairs and mileage of the cars out in the field. This would require adding lots of technology to the cars, as very few support this type of integrated information exchange today.

To realize such a fleet management service, it would be necessary to create an online service where companies can register all cars they use. There are several problems with this approach. First, there is no standard way to describe vehicles. Every manufacturer uses a similar, but not identical way of providing a description of a car. Therefore, the company needs to create its own vocabulary to describe the vehicles in use. This vocabulary can be used to build a catalogue, where one could be sure that every item is described in a very precise way.

Such a system could be very expensive, even for a large corporation, which may outsource the whole operation to reduce the cost significantly. Once all cars are registered, employees can book vehicles based on a set of specifications provided by the company. This could range from car transportation between two offices to doing a roadshow with large trucks. The system would check which vehicles are available and their proximity to the desired location. It does not really help if a car in South Africa is available and you need one at the airport in Milan, Italy. The Web site could provide not only a set of vehicle specifications, but add a different view by providing use cases, meaning that an employee does not select the type of car, but the type of situation he or she is in, and the Web site will select the vehicle accordingly.

Once the employee has decided what he needs the vehicle for, the exact route can be specified by an online route planner. This would enable the employee to calculate gas costs and provide the duration of the travel. Today, the information can be stored on a PDA or printed out, for the convenience of the driver. If the vehicle has a built-in navigation system, the employee can re-enter the data and be guided by that system. Today, it is not possible to transfer the data between an online system and a car navigation system automatically.

The employee picks up the car and sets off on the journey. With GPS tracking enabled, the vehicle can be tracked. This way, fleet management could offer additional help if the driver hits a traffic jam or has a breakdown.

En route, drivers would be able to refill the fuel tank using a gas card, with the money being deducted automatically from the account of the company. In theory, this works very well, because it is limited to the car that the employee is using. In reality, this means that the drivers may use the card to buy fuel for something other than the company car. Although the cashier at the gas station should check the license plate, this is often not done thoroughly; hence, the high rate of fraud. It is difficult to overcome this problem today.

Once the vehicle has arrived at the destination, telemetric data could be sent back to the fleet management for statistical reasons. Imagine lots of employees travel from Milan to Florence every day for business reasons. You would like to know which time is the best to get there, how long it takes at a certain time of day, and how much it costs to get there. By collecting this telemetric data and creating the statistics, it would be possible to determine that it is not a good idea to leave Milan at nine o'clock in winter, because the motorway is often very foggy. In summer, it is okay to leave at nine, because most people are already at work and the motorway is free. Many other statistics can be created, to make the use as efficient as possible. Another example could be that ten people are driving from Milan to Florence in the morning, but all use their own cars. If you can find three people that leave at the same time and return at the same time, you could have them car pool, thus reducing costs heavily.

The complexity of this scenario makes it impossible to introduce such a solution today, although most components are available and could be interconnected.

2.8.3   The Future

The solution in the near future will look quite different. Several companies are working on introducing new technologies to make life easier for fleet management. New cars will all include an online connection either to the Internet or to a dedicated wireless connection to a server. The technology to do so is becoming cheaper every day.

All vehicles need to be equipped with mobile connectivity that connects them securely to a telemetrics service. This service collects data and provides the information to the fleet management service. The telemetrics service is responsible for maintaining the connection between the vehicles and the fleet management within the company. This includes operating the satellites and transforming the data that comes from the car. As companies often have cars from different manufacturers, and no standard has been set on how the information should be transmitted, the data is structured differently for every car type or manufacturer. The role of the telemetrics service is to convert the data from the car and present it in a unified way to the fleet management.

The gasoline payment service is an automated gas station that detects which car is filling up. This can be done via a camera that takes a picture of the number plate and compares it to the database of the fleet management service and makes sure that only the cars that are eligible can pay through the corporate gasoline card. More advanced systems will include a Bluetooth service that enables the gas station to communicate with the car, meaning that the car can tell what type of gas it requires and send the company credit card information electronically. The Fraunhofer Gesellschaft[10] in Germany is even a step ahead by providing robots that fill up the gas automatically. By combining these new technologies, vehicles could be served faster and more efficiently.

The central fleet management service consists of an employee Web front-end, which allows employees to perform the required transaction for booking a vehicle and for getting more information about the service. Employees can register for the service or can be automatically

---

[10]http://www.fhg.de

eligible for the service because of the role the employee has in the company. More importantly, the fleet management service provides many administrative functions for managing the fleet and providing information to the users. Tightly connected to the fleet management service is the route planning service that will not only help employees find their way easily, it is also the basis for statistics. The statistics service takes all the data, puts it into a data warehouse, and provides management statistics to the fleet management service.

The travel service provides the fleet management service with information about delays, traffic jams, important news, and other related information. This would mean a huge reduction in effort and lower the entry barrier significantly, if the fleet management service portal ensures that the information is securely stored and only authorized systems and people are allowed to see it.

Multiple access for the employees to the fleet management portal needs to be guaranteed. This means that employees can use the service via the Web, the phone, fax, or any other means of communication. The same is true for the information that comes from the fleet management system. Depending on where the employee is, the information should be sent as e-mail, SMS, voicemail, fax, or any other means of communication.

2.8.4 Summary

Let's take a look at the me-centric features of this scenario. Broadband access is not a requirement here. Although everything needs to be connected, the amount of data that is flowing back and forth is minimal compared to the other scenarios. Telematics data can be easily transmitted in XML files over low-bandwidth networks.

The biggest issue to solve is coordinating a large number of vehicles and their users (see also Figure 2.9). While the company does not need a car for each employee, it can reduce the number of vehicles drastically with good fleet management. Therefore, agents needs to collaborate and find out who should use which car when. Each employee who needs a car should also have an agent that makes car pool reservations on his or her behalf based on the schedule of the employee.

To make sure that employees use the cars only for the intended business travel, the route can be planned by the coordination agent, which allows the user to predict the time of the journey and when the next person can use the car. By using the GPS to track the car, it is also possible to see if the employee is taking the shortest route to the business meeting or if the employee is going some other routes to do some other things. This can also be used for filling up the car with gas.

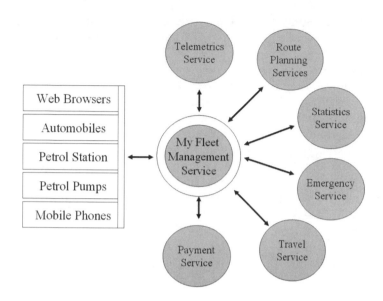

Figure 2.9. Fleet Management Ecosystem

The telemetrics system sends back information about gas usage and allows an intelligent agent to look out for gas stations in the vicinity. The prices are prenegotiated, and the driver can stop at the gas station and fill up the car. The driver does not have to pay personally. As soon as he leaves, the company pays for the amount of fuel that was bought. This ensures that only company cars are filled up.

2.9   Conclusion

As you can see quite clearly, these scenarios are built upon the trends we talked about in Chapter 1. If you look at these scenarios, you will find the kinds of interactions that "agents" would have to have and the kind of protocols that would be efficient or inefficient. You will find more detailed descriptions of agents throughout this book. These agents, their interactions, and their protocols are the basis for me-centric computing architecture—they make it possible to receive and perform delegated work.

   The ecosystem of me-centric appliances is glued together by infrastructure that provides enabling communications and servers/services, and to the extent the appliances are mobile, this is about wireless mobility. The key elements of this me-centric architecture are the smart infrastructure, the smart services, and the smart devices. These scenarios should help you to understand what the future can look like and help to validate the general proposition that there are countless arenas to be addressed, with many similarities but with a wealth of diverse functionalities, as appropriate to the domain.

From these examples, it has become quite clear that me-centric computing will be everywhere, changing the nature of every occupation. Me-centric computing consists of a set of capabilities/roles operating in an ecosystem glued together by pervasive computing and communications. In the next chapters, we will go into more detail how these futuristic scenarios can become reality soon.

Part II

Design Elements for Radical Simplicity

Chapter 3

HUMAN-COMPUTER
INTERACTION

3.1 Introduction

3.1.1 Definition

One of the biggest challenges in providing me-centric computing is the way that humans interact with computers. Interface design used to be machine-centered, so if something failed, it was the user's fault. Over time, people learned to complain about the design and blamed the designer. As a result, designers want to help the user. At this point, we have established a user-directed attitude, i.e., designing for the user. However, how to act on it is not entirely straightforward. Good intentions are not enough; the design and the design process must relate to the users somehow.

On one hand, it is important to accommodate the growing number of computer users whose professional schedules will not allow the elaborate training and experience that was once necessary to take advantage of computing. On the other hand, computers should become accessible to those who cannot afford these training courses. Increased attention to usability is also driven by competitive pressures for greater productivity, the need to reduce frustration, and to reduce overhead costs such as user training. As computing affects more aspects of our lives, the need for usable systems becomes even more important. There has been lots of effort going in this direction over the past fifty years, and it is known as "human-computer interaction" (HCI).

The ACM SIGCHI[1] defines HCI as follows: "Human-computer interaction is a discipline concerned with the design, evaluation, and im-

---

[1] Hewett, Baecker, Card, Carey, Gasen, Mantei, Perlman, Strong, and Verplank (1996). "ACM SIGCHI Curricula for Human-Computer Interaction".

plementation of interactive computing systems for human use and with the study of major phenomena surrounding them."

To simplify, HCI's aim is to optimize the performance of human and computer together as a system. Human-computer interaction studies both the mechanism side and the human side of computing devices. As its name implies, HCI consists of three parts: you the user, the computer itself, and the ways you work together. In Table 3.1, you can see the key elements of HCI.

Key Elements of HCI

If a system is designed well regarding its human-computer interfaces, it will include the following features:

- **Learnability**—It is easy to learn how to use the system, and the learned skills are retained well over time.

- **Throughput**—Tasks can be performed quickly (or only a few people are required to perform a task), and the user error rate is very low. Users and systems can recover from errors easily.

- **Flexibility**—The system is suitable for the expertise of the intended users and can be customized to suit different ways of working and/or different levels of expertise.

- **Attitude**—The users' subjective satisfaction with the system is high.

Table 3.1. Key Elements of HCI

HCI not only looks at interfaces for individuals, but also for groups of humans and organizations; therefore, interfaces for distributed systems, computer-aided communications between humans, or the nature of the work being cooperatively performed by means of the system are also part of the considerations.

Design in HCI is more complex than in many other fields of engineering. HCI is an interdisciplinary area. It is emerging as a specialty concern within several disciplines, each with different emphases:

- **computer science**—application design and engineering of human interfaces.

- **psychology**—application of theories of cognitive processes and empirical analysis of user behavior.

- **sociology and anthropology**—interactions between technology, work, and organization.

- **industrial design**—development of interactive products.

Furthermore, the developer's task of making a complex system appear simple and sensible to the user is in itself a very difficult task.

From a computer science perspective, other disciplines serve as supporting disciplines, much as physics serves as a supporting discipline for civil engineering, or as mechanical engineering serves as a supporting discipline for robotics. A lesson learned repeatedly by engineering disciplines is that design problems have a context, and that the overly narrow optimization of one part of a design can be rendered invalid by the broader context of the problem.

Because human-computer interaction studies a human and a machine in communication, it draws from supporting knowledge on both the machine and the human side. On the machine side, techniques in computer graphics, operating systems, programming languages, and development environments are relevant. On the human side, communication theory, graphic and industrial design disciplines, linguistics, social sciences, cognitive psychology, and human performance are relevant. And, of course, engineering and design methods are relevant.

3.1.2   Roots of HCI

As discussed above, HCI arose as a field from intertwined roots in computer graphics, operating systems, human factors, ergonomics, industrial engineering, cognitive psychology, and the systems part of computer science. The first human-computer interaction techniques were introduced in the early days of computing, when systems first started using graphics in combination. Since then, interfaces and graphics have improved a lot. Today, we have algorithms and hardware that allow the display and manipulation of ever more realistic-looking objects (e.g., detailed buildings or images of body parts). Many fields in computer science have a natural interest in HCI. Just look, for example, at computer graphics, which sees HCI as "interactive graphics," allowing the user to manipulate solid models in a CAD system.

The roots of today's HCI go back quite some time. Have a look at the ubiquitous graphical interface used by Microsoft Windows, which is based on the Macintosh, which is based on work at Xerox PARC, which in turn is based on early research at the Stanford Research Institute (SRI) and at MIT[2].

In the 1960s, several research topics related to HCI were first investigated, related to HCI, such as the "man-machine symbiosis" and the "augmentation of human intellect." These research areas led to a number of important building blocks for human-computer interaction. These building blocks are all included in modern operating systems: a windowing system, the mouse, bitmapped displays, personal computers, the desktop metaphor, and point-and-click editors. These early developments led to operating systems with advanced techniques for interfacing input/output devices, for tuning system response time to human interaction times, for multiprocessing, and for supporting windowing environments and animation.

Closely related to HCI is the science of "human factors," a discipline derived from the problems of designing equipment operable by humans during World War II. Many problems faced by those working on human factors had strong sensory-motor features (e.g., the design of flight displays and controls). The problem of humans operating computers was a natural extension of classic human factors, except that the new problems had substantial cognitive, communication, and interaction aspects.

Ergonomics is similar to human factors. As with human factors, the concerns of ergonomics tended to be at the sensory-motor level, but with an additional physiological flavor and an emphasis on stress. Human interaction with computers was also a natural topic for ergonomics, but again, a cognitive extension to the field was necessary, resulting in the current "cognitive ergonomics"[3] and "cognitive engineering."[4] Because of their roots, ergonomic studies of computers emphasize the relationship to the work setting and the effects of stress factors, such as the routinization of work, sitting posture, or the vision design of CRT displays.

In the early years of the 20th century, companies needed to raise productivity, which led to industrial engineering. Industrial engineering emphasized in the beginning improving manual methods of work, such as a two-handed method for laying bricks, instead of using only one. It also led to the design of specialized tools to increase productivity and reduce fatigue, such as brick pallets at waist height so bricklayers didn't have to bend over. Last, but not least, industrial design also led to the design of the social environment, such as the invention

---

[2]http://www.mit.edu/
[3]http://www.eace.info/
[4]http://lorien.ncl.ac.uk/ming/resources/cal/cogsci.htm

of the suggestion box. Interaction with computers is a natural topic for the scope of industrial engineering in the context of how the use of computers fit into the larger design of work methods.

At the end of the 19th century, cognitive psychology derived from attempts to study sensation experimentally. After World War II, cognitive psychology became an experimentally oriented discipline that is concerned with human information and performance. It has influences from linguistics, computer engineering, and communications engineering. Cognitive psychologists concentrate their research on the learning of systems, the transfer of that learning, the mental representation of systems by humans, and human performance on such systems.

Finally, the growth of discretionary computing and the mass personal computer and workstation computer markets have meant that sales of computers are more directly tied to the quality of their interfaces than in the past. The result has been the gradual evolution of a standardized interface architecture from hardware support of mice to shared window systems to "application management layers." Along with these changes, researchers and designers have begun to develop specification techniques for user interfaces and testing techniques for the practical production of interfaces.

3.1.3 Me-Centric Interactions

Human-computer interaction is, in the first instance, affected by the forces shaping the nature of future computing. Among these forces are the decreasing hardware costs leading to faster systems with more memory. At the same time, the hardware is being miniaturized and requires less power, leading to more mobility. Through new output technologies, such as new displays and voice communication, computational devices change their form. At the same time, information technology is spreading into the environment, leading to many technologically enhanced devices at home and at work (e.g., VCRs become TiVo-like devices, microwave ovens become food management devices, washing machines become clothes management devices). Through specialized hardware, new functions (such as rapid text search) can be implemented easily.

New developments in infrastructure allow new forms of network communication and distributed computing. Through lower prices, reduced complexity of applications, and new input techniques, computers are increasingly widespread among people who are outside of the computing profession. These new input techniques also allow improved access to computers by currently disadvantaged groups, such as young children and the physically/visually disabled.

In the future, computers and smart appliances will communicate through high-speed local networks, nationally over wide-area networks, and portably via infrared, ultrasonic, cellular, and other technologies. Data and computational services will be portably accessible from many if not most locations to which a user travels.

Some of these new systems will have large numbers of functions associated with them. Some others will have fewer functions than typical desktop computers. And there surely will be so many systems that most users, technical or non-technical, will not have time to learn them in the traditional way (e.g., through thick manuals).

These systems will handle images, voice, sounds, video, text, and formatted data. These will be exchangeable over communication links among users. The separate worlds of consumer electronics (e.g., stereo sets, VCRs, televisions) and computers will partially merge. Computer and print worlds will continue to cross-assimilate each other.

Computation will pass beyond desktop computers into every object for which uses can be found. The environment will be alive with little computations from computerized cooking appliances to lighting and plumbing fixtures to window blinds to automobile braking systems to greeting cards. To some extent, this development is already taking place. The difference in the future is the addition of networked communications that will allow many of these embedded computations to coordinate with each other and with the user. Human interfaces to these embedded devices will in many cases be very different from those appropriate to workstations.

Interfaces to allow groups of people to coordinate will be common (e.g., for meetings, for engineering projects, for authoring joint documents). These will have major impacts on the nature of organizations and on the division of labor. Models of the group design process will be embedded in systems and will cause increased rationalization of design.

Ordinary users will routinely tailor applications to their own use and will use this power to invent new applications based on their understanding of their own domains. Users will thus be increasingly important sources of new applications at the expense of generic systems programmers (with systems expertise but low domain expertise).

One consequence of the above developments is that computing systems will appear partially to dissolve into the environment and become much more intimately associated with their users' activities. One can make an analogy to the development of motion power. Once, strikingly visible, large, centralized water wheels were used to drive applications via belt drives; now electric motors are invisibly integrated into ap-

Possible Issues with Smart Appliances

Product developers often incorporate multiple functions into a device to provide flexibility and to serve a wider user community. However, extensive functional capability may well impose an unreasonable cognitive load on the user, unless considerable effort is devoted to the design of the user interface. The following are some problems that apply to many devices and can lead to errors:

- **Control Sequences**—Can be illogical or cumbersome

- **Language, Prompts, Symbols, or Codes**—May be unfamiliar or missing

- **Display Formats**—Inconsistencies may occur

- **User Expectations**—Conventions may contradict

- **Feedback**—Uncertain or no feedback after input

- **Functionality**—May be hidden from the user

- **Status Information**—May be missing

- **Complex mental calculations**—Requirements may be unclear

Table 3.2. Possible Issues with Smart Appliances

plications from VCRs to refrigerators. Of course, this will not always be trouble-free. In Table 3.2, you will find some of the most common issues.

Of course, personal computers in some form will continue to exist (although many might take the form of electronic notebooks), and there will still be the problem of designing interfaces so that users can operate them. But the rapid pace of development means that the preparation of students must not only address the present state of technology, but also provide the foundations for future possibilities.

3.1.4   Human Characteristics

It is important to understand something about human information-processing characteristics, how human action is structured, the nature of human communication, and human physical and physiological requirements. There are many aspects that need to be considered when a human processes information.

The first issue is how people use their memory. The difference between short-term and long-term memory needs to be understood and how it can be achieved that important messages are saved correctly. The motor skills of the target group are also important. Interfaces should be designed in a way such that the target groups can easily operate them; although this may seem trivial, it provides a serious stumbling block for children or elderly people, if they have to use an interface designed by young people for young people.

Perception, attention, and vigilance also play an important role when designing good interfaces. Only if these aspects are taken into account can you make sure that the user is able to perceive the interface in the correct way and stay with it. If it is designed badly, the user may decide to abandon the interface and not execute the necessary task.

One should also not forget to take problem-solving skills into account when designing an interface. Technical people may be able to understand "error: 30" because they know the specification of the system, but if the target group consists of less technical people, one should create meaningful error messages and help the user to solve problems actively. The same is true for learning and skill acquisition. Depending on the user group, help should be provided appropriately. Only if this is done correctly can motivation of the users be improved, making the interface and its associated services and appliances successful.

On a more cognitive level, it is important to make sure that symbol-system and engineering models are applied correctly. Every culture has a different symbol-system relationship that needs to be taken into account. If the wrong symbols are used in the interface, it can cause a delay or a break in the process of using the interface. Therefore, it is important to understand the users' mental models and how they act. Fortunately, humans are diverse, which makes life more interesting. From a designer's point of view, this can be a nightmare, as this diversity needs to be accommodated in the interface systems.

Important aspects are language, communication, and interaction. Language is the communication and interface medium and needs to be taken into account when designing the interfaces. Therefore, it is important to understand such aspects of language as syntax, semantics, and pragmatics. Besides that, the formal models of language and pragmatic phenomena of conversational interaction, such as turn-taking and repair, need to be taken into account.

Over the last forty years, specialized languages, such as graphical interaction, query, command, production systems, and editors have been established and need to be revised to make them applicable for the next generation of smart appliances.

3.2   Intelligent Input Interfaces

3.2.1   Introduction

With the miniaturization of devices, traditional point-and-click interfaces will no longer suffice. We will interact with devices the way we interact with each other—through speech, eye movement, gesture, and touch. To make these interfaces useful, they need to accommodate such sensory channels in parallel. Perceptual user interfaces will provide unobtrusive (for example, vision-based) sensing and mimic aspects of human communication, reacting to our identity, posture, gesture, gaze, and even mood and intent.

Humans can already process input on multiple channels much the way we'd hope computers could do. Brain activity and eye movement have been used successfully to enable paralyzed people to use computers. The Air Force uses gaze input as an alternative for fighter pilots to control their cockpits if temporarily paralyzed in high G-force dives.

Interaction methods hampered by intensive processing requirements and noisy signals will be overcome by high-speed Internet appliance processing capabilities. For example, researchers have struggled for years to remove environmental noise from speech signals. With advancements in wireless microphones and the new device capabilities, speech is more realistic. Speech alone will not be reliable as an input means, but combined with an alternative like gaze input, it will enable us to interact with the smaller interfaces. These multi-modal interfaces, capitalizing on multiple senses, will become the norm.

These new intelligent interfaces will make me-centric computing successful, because the devices can adapt to the needs of the user. The user needs to perceive the interfaces as invisible and the service as useful. Although many people do not realize it, using a PC means learning to interact in a totally new way. You have to learn how to use a mouse, a GUI, and cryptic key shortcuts, which interrupt the task you are trying to perform. New devices such as mobile phones or PDAs have no better interface; they often just use a subset of the user interface of a computer, making it even more difficult to interact, as the instructions on screen are even more cryptic. The best-known example for cryptic commands may be a car stereo's clock. In many cases, you have to remember a complex key combination to change the time. The same applies to VCRs, where many people still do not know how to record a program in advance or do anything other than simply play a tape. Partly the interface design is a problem, and partly it is a problem of loose integration into the television system.

In a me-centric computing world, manuals should become obsolete. Using these devices should be intuitive and natural. A secretary, concierge, or restaurant wait-person does not require a user manual to delegate tasks and have desires addressed. If you look at simple tools, such as a screwdriver or a hammer, nobody expects a hundred-page manual for these devices, and this means that me-centric devices need to become as simple to use as these. Inside the devices, complex algorithms may be in place, but for the person using the device, it should not matter.

3.2.2   Input Purposes

In order to decide which input technology is the most appropriate, it is important to understand what type of input is required from the user. Therefore, it is important to design the service first, and then the appropriate device. Many high-tech devices have failed because they were impractical, even though they may have been technically highly advanced.

One aspect of this paradigm change is that a specific device will be used for a specific task only. The personal computer was more like a Swiss army knife that could be used for many different tasks. It handled many different tasks, but was not perfect at any of them. With the introduction of smart devices, this changes dramatically. These devices will be able to do only one thing, but in a highly supportive and effective way.

There are many different types of input purposes and associated services. Just imagine a user who wants to order a pizza through his mobile device. All he needs to do is to select the pizza, and the rest, such as delivery address and next pizza service, should be handled by the device. A driver in a car needs to have continuous control over the car and therefore a totally different type of input device. On the other hand, a chemist trying to create a new formula will need to enter lots of parameters into his device.

For the pizza selection, a simple selection-ball could be used together with a small display allowing the user to scroll up and down and press the ball for the selected pizza.

A steering wheel has been used to control a car for the past hundred years, but more and more automobile manufacturers are looking into alternative control elements, such as joysticks or even automatic steering to make life easier and safer for the driver. The chemist, on the other hand, could work with traditional desktop PC to enter all the complex data, as this may still be the best solution. If he does not have his hands free due to some other tasks, a head-up display with voice recognition could work as well.

With input devices, six basic tasks can be achieved:

- **Positioning**—The user chooses a point for an object to be placed in an n-dimensional space.

- **Selection**—The user chooses from a set of items.

- **Orientation**—The user chooses a direction in a two or higher dimensional space. This is used to rotate a symbol on the screen or to control the operation of a robot arm.

- **Path**—The user rapidly performs a series of position and orient operations. The path may be realized as a curving line in a drawing program, such as the route on a map.

- **Quantification**—The user specifies a numeric value. It is a one-dimensional selection of integer or real values to set parameters, such as the page number of a document or the size of a drawing.

- **Text**—The user enters, moves, and edits text in a 2D space.

These pure input types can be combined to produce the impression of a wide variety of different types of "inputs." For example, in PTC's[5] CAD product, one generates solid shapes by applying a wide variety of transforms to chosen objects for a specific period of time or until a particular condition is satisfied. This gives you the impression that you are inputting transformations and control parameters for transforming processes. But, in fact, these are actually being provided by a combination of selection, positioning, orientation, path, and quantification inputs.

3.2.3   Input Technologies

To communicate with computers, different technologies have been established to enable the input of information and commands and the selection of data. The following gives an overview on the most commonly used technologies. The role of interfaces is to communicate the system

---

[5]http://www.ptc.com/

image to the user. They should teach users about the system and help users to develop skills and achieve their goals. Interfaces should map intent onto results and enable tasks to be performed. They should also provide direct access to system functionality.

Keyboard

Since punch-cards were abolished, keyboards have been the most popular input device for computing devices. Through the keyboard, it is possible to enter commands into a command line, as with a UNIX shell, or to navigate through menus, as with Windows using the Alt key. Many systems are keyboard-driven, such as the terminals at airports that are used for check-in. In other places, such as supermarkets, keyboards have been replaced with scanners, because it is faster and less error-prone to scan the prices instead of typing them.

Mice, Trackballs, and Pens

Mice became increasingly popular in the late 1980s. Operating systems such as Amiga OS, Atari OS, and Mac OS were the first that introduced this concept to a broad audience. Windows followed later, and today it is almost impossible to think of a computer without a mouse or similar device such as a trackball or a pen.

The most common mouse used today is opto-electronic. Its ball is steel for weight and rubber-coated for grip, and as it rotates, it drives two rollers, one each for x and y displacement. A third spring-loaded roller holds the ball in place against the other two.

The mouse can be used to point and click commands or select files, directories, services, or data. It can be used to select areas of an image, for example using rubber-band lines, and it can be used to drag and drop objects from one place to the other. A trackball provides the same features and similar paradigms to operate a system. Pen-based technologies can be used in the same way as a mouse or a trackball, but can provide additional functions, such as handwriting or gestures, which are difficult to achieve with a normal mouse.

Speech

Most people would feel more comfortable if they could communicate with their computing devices via speech. Actually, many do this already today. If something goes wrong, they start shouting at their PC, unfortunately with no response from the system. Speech recognition has been researched for many years. Voice recognition usually refers to systems that identify users by the characteristics of their voices.

Actually, a toy company had its first product decades before major research in the area was even considered. "Radio Rex" was a celluloid dog that responded to its name. Lacking the computational ability that powers recognition devices today, Radio Rex was a simple electromechanical device.

The dog was held within its house by an electromagnet. As current flowed through a circuit bridge, the magnet was energized. The bridge was sensitive to 500 cps of acoustic energy. The energy of the vowel sound of the word "Rex" caused the bridge to vibrate, breaking the electrical circuit, and allowing a spring to push Rex out of his house.

This toy was invented in the 1920s. If you look at speech recognition today, some may wonder if any advances have been made at all. Just imagine the computerized telephone hot desks, where you have to state your name and the purpose of your call, before you can get through to a human. In some cases you have to type numbers, but some systems use "highly advanced" speech recognition systems that still respond to 50 percent of all input with "I do not understand."

In the early 1990s, many thought that all problems with speech recognition were solved. The reason for such excitement was that the technical problems that had bottled up the technology in labs for decades were finally being addressed. The most basic issue had been associating specific vocalizations with specific phonemes. Phonemes are the basic units of speech. By recognizing phonemes instead of words, the complexity was largely reduced for these systems.

Making the associations required compiling huge databases of how the more than 40 English-language phonemes are spoken by those of different ages, genders, and linguistic cultures, and under different phone-line conditions. Developers then had to write programs that could find the degree of fit between a given user's vocalization and one of those samples.

It turned out, however, that speech recognition is only partly a technical problem in phonology. Recognition implies a conversation, and conversations make sense only in the context of relationships. When humans enter relationships, they immediately impose a structure of assumptions and expectations. Is the person smart? Knowledgeable? Nice? Lazy? Snobbish? That structure controls the interaction. If a comprehension problem comes up during a conversation with a smart person, we assume we are at fault and take on the responsibility of working it out. We do the same if we think our respondent is not too bright but basically nice. On the other hand, if we think the other party is lazy, doesn't care, or (worse) is trying to manipulate us, we behave very differently.

Those relationship issues are just as important when talking with machines as with people; even more so, since most users were and are uncertain about how to talk to software. To show you that speech recognition is not perfect yet, consider two examples: an automated call-center of a retailer and a navigation system in cars.

"Wood order blue kirk!" That's how a call center equipped with cheap speech-recognition technology might interpret a customer's request "I would like to order a blue skirt." That's because many systems can understand only precise, clear syntax that bears little resemblance to the way most people speak. Computers in cars that are used for navigation, for example, can also be controlled via voice in order to reduce the distraction for the driver.

Most speech recognition systems currently claim accuracies of 90 to 95 percent, but some say that such claims are averages, which hold true in a car at 30 mph but not at higher speeds. At 70 mph, for example, some engineers say that the accuracy figure dips to about 70 percent. Even if you have 90 percent accuracy, one out of every ten phone digits that you dictate is going to be wrong. A human ear can easily distinguish between these different audio sources, but most speech recognition systems have problems with it. Therefore, few applications have really been successful.

During the past few years, the underlying technology has continued to improve. Good speech recognition is perfectly capable of handling a complete sentence, such as "I want to take the TGV from Brussels to Paris a week from Saturday," but most users still want a highly structured interaction that prompts for each element of the transaction. In order to make me-centric computing successful, users will need to relax by having more experience with speech recognition applications, and conversations will get more ambitious and wide-ranging.

IBM Research[6] is planning to launch the Super Human Speech Recognition Project that aims to solve common speech-recognition problems and deliver systems capable of not just linguistic comprehension but contextual understanding.

The development of software that uses a language model to predict which words are most likely to follow other words is among the numerous approaches the company is taking. IBM Research is also using an acoustic model in which software predicts all the ways a particular word might sound given various pronunciations, cadences, or background interference.

The real challenge is building systems that can understand multifaceted conversations or respond to open-ended questions. To that end,

---

[6]http://www.research.ibm.com/

IBM is working on an approach called domain-specific interpretation. Systems designed for use in, say, a travel agency would be programmed to minimize the relevance of conversational elements not related to travel to generate the best response.

One of the first applications that IBM has produced in cooperation with Honda[7] is a telematics system for cars. These questions include information about the route and about nearby restaurants and sights to visit. The car will then respond in voice. This system, implemented in the Honda Accord, is planned to be launched in the United States. More "talk-to" applications are on the way. Nokia and Ericsson[8] have introduced this feature in their mobile phone. Instead of typing in a number, you can tell the mobile phone the number or a name from the address book.

We believe that we can see a major breakthrough in human-machine conversation. Extempo[9], for example, provides technology to build intelligent characters (Figure 3.1). The tools enable the character to get the gist of a conversation, have emotional reactions, and work towards its own purposes interactively with the human. It doesn't need perfect input. It can be coupled within various sensory inputs and outputs. Max the dog and Erin the bartender, two characters developed by Extempo, have both great tolerance for ambiguity and wicked senses of humor! So we are slowly getting there.

Speech recognition plays an important role in situations where it is impossible to use the hands for typing or for devices that are too small to have a keyboard attached. In our car navigation example, it is actually illegal in many countries to take your hands off the steering wheel and to not look at the road while driving. But there are many other situations where people do not have the chance to use their hands and are forced to communicate orally. Just imagine doctors in an emergency situation or workers on a construction site.

Speech recognition systems will need to understand people in many different languages and have good translations available for different languages. Language-specific expressions need to be matched in order to provide the right level of response.

Touchscreens

A touchscreen is an intuitive computer input device that works by simply touching the display screen—with a finger, stylus, or similar device—rather than typing on a keyboard or pointing with a mouse.

---

[7]http://www.honda.com/
[8]http://www.ericsson.com/
[9]http://www.extempo.com/

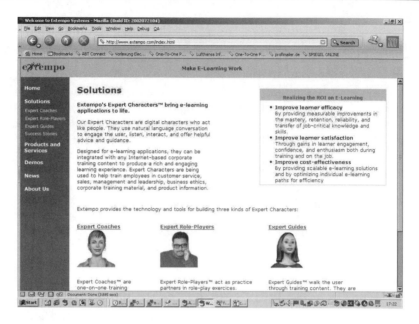

Figure 3.1. Extempo's Characters

Computers with touchscreens have a smaller footprint and therefore can be mounted in smaller spaces; they have fewer movable parts and can be sealed. Touchscreens may be built in or added on. Add-on touchscreens are external frames with a clear see-through touchscreen that mount onto the monitor bezel and have a controller built into their frame. Built-in touchscreens are internal, heavy-duty touchscreens mounted directly onto the CRT.

The user-friendly touchscreen is simple, intuitive, easy to learn, and is becoming the interface of choice for a wide variety of applications. Public information systems, such as information kiosks, tourism displays, and other electronic displays, are used by many people who have little or no computing experience. This makes information accessible to the widest possible audience.

Touchscreens are also commonly used in restaurant point of sale (POS) systems. The overall training time for new employees can be reduced. Work is done faster because employees can simply touch the screen to perform tasks, rather than entering complex key strokes or commands.

The touchscreen interface is also very useful in systems ranging from industrial process control to home automation. By integrating the input device with the display, valuable workspace can be saved. And with a graphical interface, operators can monitor and control complex operations in real time by simply touching the screen.

Self-service touchscreen terminals can be used to improve customer service at banks, busy shops, restaurants, and transportation hubs, for example. Customers can quickly place their own orders or check themselves in or out, saving them time and decreasing wait times for other customers.

Eye Movement

Eye tracking is a technique used to determine where a person is looking. The concepts underlying eye tracking are deceptively simple: track the movements of the user's eyes and note what the pupils are doing while the user is looking at a particular feature. In practice, however, these measures are difficult to achieve and require high-precision instruments as well as sophisticated data analysis and interpretation. Machines used to do this are called eye trackers.

Eye movements made during reading and identifying pictures provide useful information about the processes by which people understand visual input and integrate it with knowledge and memory. Until recently, most applications of eye tracking have been in psychological research for probing into subjects' perceptual or cognitive processes, for example when driving in traffic, reading text, solving problems, looking at pictures, scanning instrument panels, and performing complex tasks. Research into human visual search strategies has been based on tracking subjects' gaze during "target object" search tasks. Based on this research, the evaluation of computer displays has been modeled upon recordings of fixation patterns.

Commercial companies have found eye movement tracking to be of interest. It is used today for market research studies. It is actually used for Web site usability and new product designs. With eye movement tracking, it is possible to see how users react to visual input from these devices or Web sites. It can show if they are distracted or if they are able to understand the input efficiently.

Military research developed head-up displays (displays integrated in the windshields of aircraft, so that instrumental data is displayed "on top of" the surrounding flight scene) combined with eye tracking for guiding the missile system, thus freeing the pilot's hands for other tasks. This naturally required on-line processing of the tracking data, and this processing was not aimed at probing the pilot's perceptual or cognitive processes, but rather letting the pilot use the eyes as an extra manipulation channel. Later, the on-line processing of eye-gaze tracking data was extended to user-interfaces for non-military purposes. It is used, for example, in Formula 1 racing, where it enables the projection of messages into the driver's direct field of vision.

Besides this passive usage of eye movement tracking, it will become an integral part of me-centric applications. Eye movement can be used in various applications in a me-centric world. One is, of course, the passive tracking of the eye movements in order to test if the user is looking in the right direction. Another purpose is to assess the user's state of mind. Is the user angry or happy? Does he or she have trouble with the lighting? Is the user insecure? This input can help make the device easier to use without having the user state that there are problems. The device would be able to adapt, by adjusting the lighting, for example or adding information to guide the user.

Eye movement also has some medical use for disabled persons who are partially or completely paralyzed. In some cases, these people cannot even speak and can only move their eyes. Through eye trackers, these people are able to communicate with other people or use the Internet. Although it is a very slow communication, it means a lot to these people who would otherwise be completely cut off. And the group of disabled people is not small. In the United States, 22 percent of the population 16 years or older is affected, and more than 50 percent of Americans over the age of 65 report a disability. This is more than 54 million Americans and more than 750 million people worldwide, who could be easily helped, if low-cost devices were available to support their needs. Anyone can be affected by disability at any time.

The success of the computer mouse as a pointing device combined with direct manipulation interfaces comes from the fact that it is based on human abilities. Man has developed the skill of grabbing and moving objects with his hands and working on them. There are some problems with eye-gaze control in comparison to the mouse, however. There is no analogy to the mouse-button — you cannot "close your eye around an object" to pick it up, as you can with a mouse. It is not possible to "let go" of the eyes as you can with a mouse when you do not wish to manipulate anything in the display. The human eye-gaze pattern is not calm and controlled like the movement of the mouse. The eyes dart rapidly from spot to spot, and keeping your eyes fixed on a specific point is unnatural and can also perhaps be a strain. And it can be difficult to point at a blank area of the screen, because the eye normally is attracted to information-carrying features.

Although there are still some problems with the correct interpretation of the eye movement, it will become part of the me-centric devices to assist users in what they are trying to do.

Scanners and Digital Cameras

Scanners and digital cameras have become the input devices of choice for images and pictures. While images were drawn or pixeled on the computer screen in the early days of computing, most images we see on the computer today are direct representations of how we see the world. While scanners have been common for over a decade now, digital cameras have become so affordable nowadays that many people have at least one.

Figure 3.2. Picture taken by Digital Camera

While few people use their more advance features, scanners and digital cameras have lots of input parameters that can be tweaked to modify the resulting images. The scanner, for example, enables you to scan only certain colors or regions of a given image. The camera enables you to focus on certain aspects of the image. Figure 3.2 shows a digital photo of a tropical flower taken in Malaysia.

While photography has been a hobby for many people for over a century now, there are many who complain that they can't take quality pictures or that their images always look funny. Many would ascribe these failures to shooting technique or digital technology. But most models of digital cameras are designed to obtain adequate image quality with a relatively simple operation. The problem is that today's digital cameras do not provide agents that take pictures on behalf of the user; the digital camera just replaces the chemical film with a memory card. The images still need to be taken by the human, and the quality of the photo depends on how good the user is.

Gesture

Adam Kendon explained the difference between gestures and speech quite well: "Gesture has properties different from speech. In particular, it employs space as well as time in the creation of expressive forms, whereas speech can use only time. Therefore, the way information may be preserved in speech, as compared to gesture, tends to be very different."[10]

Gesture recognition is human interaction with a computer in which human gestures, usually hand or body motions, are recognized by the computer. Recognizing gestures as input might make computers more accessible for the physically impaired and make interaction more natural for young children. It could also provide a more expressive and nuanced communication with a computer.

In 1964, the first trainable gesture recognizer was developed. A prototype motion processor developed by Toshiba[11] allows a computer to recognize hand motions and to display them in realtime on the computer's display. Proposed applications include word processing using input with hand sign language, games and other entertainment, and educational approaches in which hand motion could result in multimedia effects.

Toshiba's motion processor works by emitting an infrared transmission light near the hand area and "reading" the light reflected back from the hand. Reflections from areas beyond the hand don't occur because the light is quickly dissipated over distance. The reflected light allows the computer to continuously build a 3D motion image of the hand, which can be displayed or not.

Research in gesture recognition can be divided into four areas: hand gesture, body gesture, mouse-based gestures, and sign-language recognition. The gesture recognition is done through various types of sensors.

There are many applications for sensor-based gesture recognition. Navigation commands come to mind, where the user can gesture toward a desired direction. Applications in medicine and industry include precise remote control of surgical robots, or of robots and other

---

[10]http://www.univie.ac.at/Wissenschaftstheorie/srb/srb/gesture.html
[11]http://www.toshiba.com/

machinery in outer space and other locations too dangerous for humans to access. Applications can even be enabled to enhance communications for people who are both deaf and mute—inter-communication between themselves and communication with hearing persons.

Imagine a 3D application where a user can move and rotate objects simply by moving and rotating his or her hand. The user can get more than six degrees of freedom simultaneously (X-, Y-, Z-rotation, X-, Y-, Z-translation, and additional degrees from the hand-form, e.g., how far the thumb is spread from the hand). The user gets the impression of an easy and intuitive interface, because she or he can change tools or give commands by showing another hand gesture. For example, moving and rotating is enabled when the hand is open, selecting is enabled when the index finger is shown, zooming when both the index finger and the thumb are shown. Many dialog states can be saved in this way.

The technology also has the potential to change the way users interact with computers by eliminating input devices such as joysticks, mice, and keyboards, and allowing the unencumbered body to give signals to the computer through gestures such as finger pointing.

Unlike touch-sensitive interfaces interfaces, gesture recognition does not require the user to wear any special equipment or attach any devices to the body. The gestures of the body are read by a camera instead of by sensors attached to a device such as a data glove. The device, for example, needs to decode facial expressions as displayed in Figure 3.3.

Haptics is the science of applying tactile sensation to human interaction with computers. A haptic device is one that involves physical contact between the computer and the user, usually through an input/output device, such as a joystick or data glove, that senses the body's movements. By using haptic devices, the user not only can feed information to the computer but also can receive information from the computer in the form of a felt sensation on some part of the body. This is referred to as a haptic interface. For example, in a virtual reality environment, a user can pick up a virtual tennis ball using a data glove. The computer senses the movement and moves the virtual ball on the display. However, because of the nature of a haptic interface, the user will feel the tennis ball in his hand through tactile sensations that the computer sends through the data glove, mimicking the feel of the tennis ball in the user's hand.

Mouse-based gestures have become of interest lately. They allow users to send commands to the system without needing to click through a navigation or select from a list. Depending on the context, a certain mouse movement will execute a command. This reduces the number of

Figure 3.3. Example Gestures

steps to get to the goal. One piece of software that uses this technology is the Opera[12] browser. For example, holding the secondary mouse button down while sliding the mouse downward will open a new window. Pen-based gestures that fall into the same category as mouse-based gestures are widely used on PDAs, for example. A gesture-based text editor using proof reading symbols was already developed at CMU[13] by Michael Coleman in 1969. Gesture recognition has been used in commercial CAD systems since the 1970s and came to universal notice with the Apple Newton in 1992.

Gestures are already widely used in touch-panel displays where fingers are used and on PDAs both for picking with a pen and for "writing" with Graffiti on the Palm. It is our belief that pointing and activating with fingers pointed in the air are likely to be very common. Wireless handheld mice are already used today to control presentations by speakers in audience presentations.

It is important to note that gestures may be specific to a certain culture. This means that it is important to understand who is actually making the gesture and in which cultural context. Otherwise, it may

---

[12]http://www.opera.com/

[13]http://www.cmu.edu/

lead to miscommunications that are not unknown in human communications today. Gestures are important, as they are part of non-verbal communication that is important to humans. Non-verbal communication is more than gestures; it includes processes without the use of language proper, e.g., body movements and smells; but also such extra-linguistic features of speech as intonation, speed, and pause. Non-verbal communication is expressive and manifest, as opposed to being about something outside the communicator, and tends to provide the context of verbal communication and has the power to disambiguate (but also to invalidate) the content of linguistic expressions.

Multimodal

Most computing interfaces still use only pointing and typing. But some systems like intelligent voice recognition (IVR) use a combination of speech and typing (e.g., for mobile banking), others use pointing and speech, but very few use gestures in combination with other interfacing modes. Few systems pay any attention to what we do with our bodies (e.g., position, pose, orientation, and gaze). So there is room for improvement.

In many cases, when people speak about multimodal systems, they speak about systems that can use only one modality at a time. In some cases, the different modalities are used to adapt to hardware configurations (e.g., using a PC-based Web browser or a mobile phone). In some cases, the user is simply given a choice, such as speech or typing.

In some cases, a multimodal system accepts input from the user through different modes at the same time or nearly simultaneously. This could be, for example, the two-handed input, which combines actions of the two hands to trigger a specific task. The most obvious trigger for multimodal interfaces are speech and hand gestures, because this mimics the behavior of transmitting tasks between humans.

Much research on multimodal input has been done, but little is really being used so far. It is expected that future devices and systems will become multimodal to make it easier for people to use. The device will adapt to the needs of the user and not the other way round.

3.2.4 Input Issues

Although many input techniques have been in operation for decades, there are still some issues that need to be taken into consideration when building human-computer interfaces. While the keyboard provides very exact input, its main issue is that it requires a lot of keystrokes to get things done. Using a command line interpreter to enter commands, for example, is a very effective tool for experienced users who can type very fast. Mice, joysticks, and trackballs are very good at selecting and clicking commands that appear on screen. The only issue with these input devices is exact positioning. If you miss the command on screen (e.g., because the ball inside the mouse is dirty and does not allow exact positioning) and you click on something else instead, you may be doing the exact opposite of what you wanted. Critical commands should be reconfirmed before they are executed.

Speech input unfortunately does not work perfectly yet and can lead to errors in communication. Just imagine that you wanted to go to Paris and your car navigation responded with "I don't understand." But what did the computer not understand? Was it the pronunciation? The usage? The logical thread? Humans react to this message the same way they would in a conversation, with resentment and irritation. They raise their voices and sound out words as if they are speaking to a child. Their voices become stressed. They change their pitch and may even swear. As a result, the program is even more confused. Even worse is a car navigation system that tries to guess, if it does not understand well. This creates even more confusion.

The crux of the problem is that vehicles, unlike desktop PCs, are subjected to a wide variety of noises that can confuse software-based speech recognizers. The systems have to worry about more than just the noise generated by the vehicle. There are many different sources of noise. The road, wind, defroster, fan, radio, windshield wipers, and backseat occupants are just a few.

Me-centric devices will have similar problems as car navigation systems. They will be used in all sorts of environments, such as at the airport, in hotels, at the swimming pool, on the road, on the plane, or anywhere else. With the introduction of me-centric devices, it is important to give the user as much help as possible, which might mean building another database (this time of the most common errors). Even more important is to support the user who gave an unclear instruction by proposing specific solutions to the user's perceived problem. For example, the computer could ask, "Do you want Paris or Brussels?" This does more than locate the problem as a pronunciation issue; it reassures the user that the program is intelligent enough to understand the situation and is willing to help the speaker solve it, which in turn makes users more disposed to working with the program.

Touchscreens are good for simple commands but not suitable for complex input, as it would take too long to key them into a touchscreen. Therefore, one should make sure that the application or service that runs on a touchscreen does not require huge amounts of input.

An important issue when designing interfaces based on eye-gaze control is exactly how to use the gaze direction. The point of regard in a display can be used as it is, for positioning an invisible mouse pointer perhaps, and using this to select from some sort of menu-based system. But it can also be processed further, using the knowledge of the connection between eye-gaze and interest.

One of the biggest challenges with scanners and digital cameras is the correct use of colors. While this seems trivial, it requires quite some technology to make a given image appear on every computer screen in exactly the same way. It becomes even more difficult if you want to print out an image. It's common for an image to look great on the screen, but not so great on the paper.

When designing gesture-controlled interfaces, it is important to understand that gestures are culture-dependent. Therefore, the target group of a given service or application needs to be analyzed quite well as to cultural background, and it needs to be made clear that other gestures that may be used will not interfere with the system.

For multimodal input, it is important to find ways to coordinate the input. It is also important to find out if input from different modes is contradictory; for example, you say "no" and nod your head. In most countries, nodding means "yes," but there are some countries where nodding means "no." In cases where the modes are contradictory, the system should verify the input by reconfirming what it understood.

3.3 Intelligent Output Interfaces

3.3.1 Introduction

Passing on information to the computational device is one part of the equation, but to be of use, the device also needs to be able to respond to the users. Output, in most cases, means output of visual data. Devices for "dynamic" visualization include the traditional cathode ray tube (CRT), liquid crystal display (LCD), and specialized devices like a pilot's head-up display. Printers are also very important devices for visual output, but they are substantially different from screens in that their output is static—it won't change over time except for the yellowing of paper.

In order to increase bandwidth for information reaching the user, it is important to use more channels in addition to visual output. One commonly used supplement for visual information is sound, but its true potential is often not recognized. Audible feedback can make interaction substantially more comfortable for the user, providing unambiguous information about the system state and success or failure of inter-action (e.g., a button press), without putting still more load onto the visual channel.

For the same purpose, tactile feedback or even smell might do very well, with keys and mice "reacting" to input.

3.3.2   Output Purposes

If we look at the output purposes, there are as many as for the in-put. Output can be used, for example, to give the user the percep-tion of the current situation in a certain process. The output device could propose a set of choices (e.g., "what to do next?"), display the state of the system (e.g., "searching for new information...") or show the results of the information processing (e.g., "you need to turn left"). It could also be used to summarize information (e.g., "It will be warm and sunny in France"), provide detailed information (e.g., "It will rain in Paris, but not in Nice"), illustrate processes (e.g., "Enter your name and birthdate to receive your horoscope") or visualize information for easier understanding (e.g., show a picture instead of text). Probably most important, the system should provide feedback to every action a user performs; otherwise, it becomes difficult for the user to know if and when things are going wrong—for example, when input is missing or incorrect, or the requested task cannot be executed because of ex-ternal factors, such as low battery or wrong context, or that it cannot accept input at the moment, as it is still performing another task.

3.3.3   Output Techniques

Display

Probably the most commonly used output for computing devices is a vi-sual display. Visual displays range in format, size, and color depth from large-screen displays and projectors to LCDs, mobile phones, goggles, and elevator displays. These displays can show information in various formats and media, such as scrolling texts, windows, animation, sprites (animated element), or fish-eye displays, just to name a few.

One purpose of displays is to visualize information, that is to give the user understanding of some complex phenomena. Visualizing infor-mation can either mean that a computer produces the data and gives a representation of it, or that it visualizes external data, such as statis-tics. Visualization requires mapping between the data and the repre-sentation. Through this mapping, the user can control the representa-tion.

To understand representation, consider how a word processor can show different views of the text (outline view, layout view, etc.), while a spreadsheet application can offer alternative views of the data it contains.

Sounds

Sounds have become a very important output device over the past few years. Sound, in the form of synthesized sounds, such as speech, music, and natural sound, are used to convey information to the user. Sound is not restricted to alert messages, but can be used to read e-mail messages, explain data sheets, or recite the user's appointments.

Sound is especially useful when the user has limited visual scanning possibilities. This can happen, for example, in a car. Sound can also be to used to complement the visual interface. It can be used when attention is required on the screen, in alarm situations, or data sonification.

The sound synthesis technology has made some huge progress over the last few years, which makes it possible to use it for the arrangements of digital recordings, creating sentences, phrases, or word segments. Sound can either be created by the concatenation of prerecorded phrases or by synthesis-by-rule (text or phonemes to speech).

Mice, Trackball and Joysticks

For the interaction process (i.e., the control of the cursor and the haptic output), mice, trackballs, and joysticks have additional technology built in that gives feedback about the movements by the user. Force feedback joysticks are probably best known as they are very commonly used with computer games. They are also used with aircraft simulators, for example, to give the crew the exact experience of the airplane.

Printers

Printers have been used long before display, sound, mice, and multimedia output were fashionable. The printed paper provides the users not only with the result of the computation, for example, but also with a haptic object that they can move and use. Although the paperless office was envisioned a few years ago, quite the opposite happened, as people print more than ever before. The main reason is that they can see the results without having to switch on a computer again (which takes time to boot up, etc.).

The printer can display text and images in any combination making it ideal for complex information, as reading on a paper is less tiring than reading on a computer screen. Because most printers are color nowadays, it is possible to print photos in high quality, for example. The only issue we can see with printers is the fact that so far they have been a one-way output street. Changes made on a piece of paper can be re-imported into the computer only with much difficulty (via scanning, for example).

Multimodal

Multimodal output representations are composed of unimodal modalities. A comprehensive set of unimodal modalities covering the media of graphics, acoustics, and haptics are systematically generated at descending levels of abstraction until the result is a practical "designer's toolbox" of unimodal modalities. Multimodal interfaces are more natural, so they are more engaging.

The best-known multimodal output is graphics and sound together. This is often referred to as multimedia. Multimedia is technology driven and is about particular media channels that are available, such as text, graphics, animation, and video. Although different in media, they share the same modality.

So far, much research has been conducted on multimedia, and we see many different applications in place. Unfortunately, not much research has been done on multimodal output outside of multimedia.

The basic idea behind multimodal output interfaces is to take advantage of natural human communication skills. As mentioned before for the input devices, this means that human behavior is almost always multimodal and that having systems behave like this makes it easier for humans to use them. As with the input, the output can be either simultaneous or not. This means that the modalities are fused (used as one), used in sequence, or used independently.

The current interfaces fall far short of what the human can do, adding extra complexity to the human-computer interaction. With multimodal systems, much higher bandwidth is possible, as different modalities excel at different tasks and different modalities may fit better to different user groups and timings. Through multimodal interfaces, where multiple modes are used to output the same information, errors and awkward behavior can be reduced dramatically.

Multimodal output leverages the human senses and perceptual system, because humans can perceive and correlate multiple things at once by focusing on a certain subject. Appliances need to find a way to filter information correlated to a certain subject otherwise they won't be able to process the information in a timely manner, as they would need to analyse every piece of information available.

3.3.4   Output Issues

Although output devices have existed since the beginning of computing, they still are not perfect. If we look at display technologies, we can find several issues related to the screen layout, such as focus, clutter, and visual logic, which make it difficult for the user to follow the instructions or get the information presented on screen. Another issue known from the Web is that different screens have various resolutions and color depths. Many applications cannot adjust themselves to these variables, making it hard to display the information in a useful way on screen.

Another issue that has appeared on the Web widely is the problem of interpreting information through application logic. Without digging into browser wars too deeply, we just want to mention that the display of Web pages in Internet Explorer and Netscape, for example, can vary a lot, to the extent that some elements are not visible in one browser or the other. In the me-centric world, in which we will have many different displays and display technologies, it is of utmost importance to provide the information in a device-independent format that adheres to some standard like XML to ensure the correct display of information.

With sounds, we have similar problems as with the sound input devices. But now the problem is with the human ear and not necessarily with the device. In noisy environments, you may have trouble understanding what the device is telling you, or you may misinterpret the information you are hearing. Therefore, it is very important that you reconfirm the instructions in critical situations before applying them. On the other hand, devices should be aware of their surroundings and adjust themselves automatically to make sure that the user is able to understand what the device is saying.

Haptic output by joysticks, mice, and trackballs is good for the experienced, but can provide problems for the novice, meaning that new users may not know how to react to haptic output, as they are not used to this kind of feedback from electronic devices. Once they understand that haptic output works the same as for other devices, they should be able to use it quite well.

Printing has always had some issues with the paper throughput that seems to get slowly better (e.g., paper jams). Today, technology in printing is so good that you can even print high-quality output on low-price printers (which are slower and more costly to run, typically). Timing may be a problem with printouts, as a printer may be shared by several persons through the network. If you need to print something urgently and someone else is printing 5,000 pages of a document, you will have to wait until the other person finishes.

Multimodal output provides a combination of display and sound output, which normally makes it easier for the user to understand, as it is more like the real world. One problem of multimodal output can be the wrong combination of display and sound, which may confuse the user. This could be because of lags in output or because the output was not properly coordinated. Apart from these issues, all the issues that may arise from display or sound output can be a problem in multimodal output as well.

3.3.5   Dialogue Techniques

To make interfaces successful, it is necessary to implement dialogue techniques properly. The basic software architecture and techniques for interacting with humans can be specified as follows. First, it is important to specify the dialogue interaction techniques that should be implemented for a specific interface. This includes techniques like alphanumeric techniques, form filling, menu selection, icons and direct manipulation, generic functions, and natural language. Also important for a good human-computer dialogue is navigation and orientation in dialogues and the associated error management.

There are problems associated with this type of dialogue. Humans expect a real-time response, as they would from speaking to other people; therefore, it is important for an interface to give immediate feedback, even if it is only acknowledging that the input was accepted by the system. In automated systems such as agents, it is important to give feedback from time to time to make sure that the user understands why there is no result yet from the system.

Also important is the dialogue genre selection, which describes the conceptual uses to which the technical means are put. Such concepts arise in any media discipline (e.g., film, graphic design, etc.). For your interfaces, you can use interaction metaphors such as the tool metaphor, which is used quite commonly today, or the agent metaphor, which will hopefully replace many tools today. Besides the interaction metaphor, it is also possible to think about a content metaphor with elements, such as a desktop metaphor or paper document metaphor, that make it easier for the user to understand the meaning of an object. This also includes workspace models and transition management techniques.

3.4 Context Awareness

3.4.1 Introduction

One radical change in computing is the introduction of *context aware-ness*. One popular definition of context is "that which surrounds and gives meaning to something else."[14] A context describes a situation and the environment a device or user is in.

Computing until now tried to avoid context as much as possible. Most of today's software acts exactly the same, regardless of when and where you use it or who you are, whether you are new to it or have used it in the past, whether you are a beginner or an expert, whether you are using it alone or with friends. But what you may want the computer to do could be different under all those circumstances. This comes from the desire for abstraction by software companies. They want to sell one piece of software to as many people as possible without any change.

Henry Lieberman and Ted Selker (both MIT[15]) have written a very good introduction on this revolutionary introduction of context[16].

Computers, so far, have been considered as black boxes. You have some input, the computer does something with it, and you receive some output. The nice thing about context-free computing is the high level of abstraction. If you look at mathematical functions, you can clearly see why. They derive their power from the fact that they ignore the context and work in all possible contexts. The fewer exceptions a function has, the better it is. This paradigm also works for grammars. Context-free grammars are much simpler than context-sensitive grammars and therefore are preferred to describe languages.

Selker and Lieberman believe that software has become too abstract and that there is a need for context sensitivity where it is appropriate. The divide-and-conquer model assumes that if you divide something into two, they are independent of each other. This strategy created a lot of independent modules that can be operated on their own, but it neglects the fact that there is sometimes the need to understand how each piece fits in its context.

There are several reasons why context is important. First and fore-most, explicit input from the user is expensive. It slows down the inter-action, interrupts the user's train of thought and raises the possibility of mistakes. The user may be uncertain about what input to provide,

---

[14]http://wombat.doc.ic.ac.uk/foldoc/foldoc.cgi?query=context

[15]http://www.media.mit.edu/

[16]Out of Context: Computer Systems That Adapt To, and Learn From, Context, http://lieber.www.media.mit.edu/people/lieber/Teaching/Context/Out-of-Context-Paper/-Out-of-Context.html

and may not be able to provide it all at once. Everybody is familiar with the hassle of continually re-filling out forms on the Web. If the system can get the information it needs from context, why ask for it again?

Devices that sense the environment and use speech recognition or visual recognition may act on input they sense that may or may not be explicitly indicated by the user. Therefore, in many user interface situations, the goal is to minimize input explicitly required from the user.

The same applies to explicit output. It is not always desirable to have it for each computational process, because it requires the user's attention. Hiroshi Ishii, for example, and others have worked on so-called "ambient interfaces" where the output is a subtle change in barely-noticeable environmental factors such as lights and sounds, the goal being to establish a background awareness rather than force the user's attention to the system's output.

Another issue with context-free computing is that it assumes that the input-output loop is sequential. But this is no longer true of modern user interfaces, where several inputs and outputs can happen at the same time.

Each context provides a relevant set of features with a range of values that is determined (implicitly or explicitly) by the context. By relating information processing and communication to aspects of the situations in which such processing occurs, results can be obtained much more quickly.

Context is a powerful and longstanding concept in human-computer interaction. Interaction with computation is by explicit acts of communication (e.g., pointing to a menu item), and the context is implicit (e.g., default settings). Context can be used to interpret explicit acts, making communication much more efficient. Thus, by carefully embedding computing into the context of our lived activities, it can serve us with minimal effort on our part. Communication not only can be effortless, but also can naturally fit in with our ongoing activities. Pushing this further, the actions we take are not even felt to be attempts at communication; rather, we just engage in normal.

Graphical user interfaces in operating systems adapt menus to such contexts as dialogue status and user preferences. Mobile phones have context-sensitive buttons to reduce the number of buttons required and even more advanced car stereos use context-sensitive menus to enable the car owners not only to listen to the radio, but also to change the time and date without having to remember a complex process.

Context is also a key component of mobile computing. While many people thought that mobile computing would only be about location awareness, it has become quite clear that this is only one aspect of context that can be used by mobile computing devices. These new devices (such as PDAs, mobile phones, and wearable computers) relate their services to the surrounding situation of usage.

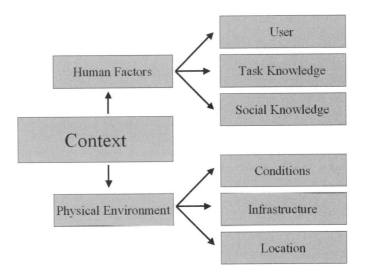

Figure 3.4. Context Types

A primary concern of context awareness is awareness of the physical environment surrounding a user and his device (see Figure 3.4). This has already been implemented in several products that provide location awareness, for instance based on global positioning, or the use of beacons. As mentioned before, location is only one aspect of the physical environment, and it is often used as an approximation of a more complex context. Beyond location, awareness of the physical conditions in a given environment is also important. This is based on the assumption that the more a mobile device knows about its usage context, the better it can support its user. With advances in sensor technology, awareness of physical conditions is now embedded in mobile devices at low cost.

Research in the area of context can be divided into two main categories: human factors and physical environment. Human factors can include information on the user, such as emotional state, knowledge of habits, or biophysiological conditions. It can also include information about the social environment of the user, which typically includes the co-location of others, group dynamics, and social interaction. Besides information about the user and the social environment, context about the user's tasks are covered by the category of human factors. This includes information about the type of activity (e.g., spontaneous or planned), a description of the task itself and the goal of the task.

All computing systems have some dependency on prior history or *state*. The complexity of systems, or power of systems, is related to how many distinct prior conditions they distinguish, and these distinctions show up in how they react to future events. So when a machine has state, it has also a sense of history and a variety of behaviors in the future that appropriately vary in response to its history. When people have this kind of memory, we refer to it as knowledge. So knowledge is what machines acquire through their interactions with people that enable them to behave more appropriately in the future. When we use this knowledge to predispose our systems to interpret new inputs or to respond appropriately, we are "contextualizing" our interpretations and response. So the long history of computing, going back to the first efforts to think about a hierarchy of machines that had more and more state and could use it more and more powerfully, is actually the forerunner of our modern-day appreciation of context.

Besides human factors, the physical environment plays an important role in context-aware computing. Probably best known is location awareness, which includes the absolute position of a person, relative position, and co-location. Besides location, the device can receive contextual information about the infrastructure, such as surrounding resources for computation, communication, task performance, and physical conditions, which include noise, light, and pressure.

The notion of context is much more widely appreciated today. Context is key to dispersing and enmeshing computation into our lives. Context refers to the physical and social situation in which computational devices are embedded. One goal of context-aware computing is to acquire and utilize information about the context of a device to provide services that are appropriate to the particular people, place, time, events, etc. For example, a cell phone will always vibrate and never beep at a concert if the system knows the location of the cell phone and the concert schedule. However, this is more than simply a question of gathering more and more contextual information about complex situations. More information is not necessarily more helpful. Further, gathering information about our activities intrudes on our privacy. Context information is useful only when it can be usefully interpreted, and it must be treated with sensitivity.

3.4.2 Human Factors

Human factors play an important role in context, which has been neglected so far, because it is very difficult to get reliable information into intelligent appliances, especially because human beings are not always logical. The appliances need to understand who the users are, the tasks that need to be done in that moment, and the social context in order to "behave" correctly.

User

As we talk about a me-centric or human-centric computing world, it is probably the most important task to accommodate users with different skills, knowledge, age, gender, disabilities, disabling conditions (mobility, sunlight, noise), literacy, culture, or income, just to name a few variables.

Since skill levels with computing vary greatly, it is necessary to adapt the application to the knowledge and skills of the user. This means that applications need to segment the user base. NASA[17], for example, provides a children's section on its space mission pages. Similar segmenting strategies can be employed to accommodate users with poor reading skills or users who require other natural languages.

A more difficult problem comes in trying to accommodate users with a wide range of incomes, cultures, or religions. The appliances and services need to make sure that the information offered is not offensive to the user, and they need to understand what the typical process in a particular country may be to support the users instead of confusing them. The most simple example could be a Web site that allows you to order goods and requires you to select a U.S. state, even though you may be living abroad.

Another set of issues deals with the wide range of disabilities or differential capabilities of users. Blind users will be more active users of information and communications services if they can receive documents by speech synthesis or in Braille, and provide input by voice or their customized interfaces.

Physically disabled users are more likely to use services if they can connect their customized interfaces to standard graphical user interfaces, even though they may work at a much slower pace. Cognitively impaired users with mild learning disabilities, dyslexia, poor memory, and other special needs could also be accommodated with modest changes to improve layouts, control vocabulary, and limit short-term memory demands.

---

[17]http://www.nasa.gov/

Expert and frequent users also have special needs. Enabling customization that speeds high-volume users, using "macros" (series of operations) to automate repeated operations, and including special-purpose devices could benefit many.

Therefore, appropriate services and appliances for a broader range of users need to be developed, tested, and refined. Corporate knowledge workers are the primary target audience for many contemporary software projects, so the interface and information needs of the unemployed, homemakers, disabled, or migrant workers usually get less attention.

Task Knowledge

In order to have smart devices help you more efficiently, two aspects of task knowledge need to be considered. First, the device needs a description of the tasks it can fulfill on behalf of its owner, and it needs to recognize when it should initiate such a task. In order to have a good description, a task analysis needs to take place.

The smart device needs to learn how to solve problems and get tasks done right. It needs to know the sequence of the work within a specific task and the related workflows and process specifications. This technical information can either be stored in the device itself or requested from a server on demand. Below the process layer, the smart device also needs to have some IT-specific how-to knowledge to get access, set privileges, change permissions, and delegate tasks and responsibilities.

The device needs to understand the normal and best ways to do things. It needs to learn how to allocate resources or get more resources available to do work. It needs to be able to choose among alternative sources or methods, based on up-front costs and opportunity costs. Only then can it avoid unnecessary additional costs or create unnecessary work. But first and foremost, the devices need to learn that perfection is not always the best solution and that a quick fix may help much more than a lengthy process that may resolve the issue, but may be too late or too expensive.

Social Knowledge

Social knowledge is about getting along with people. It means doing things in a courteous and appropriately informal way, comporting oneself when one is an agent working on behalf of a principal, and appreciating the efforts of people.

This is a huge challenge to computing today, as social knowledge can vary not only from country to country, but from family to family. Especially in diverse environments, like Paris, Berlin, or London, where many cultures live side by side, some people are integrated into the local culture and some are not. How should agents react if they need to communicate with a German butcher, Lebanese hairdresser, and Chinese bankers for a single service? Although technology and business are driving towards globalization, it is still the people who run the technology and the business and make the difference.

Implementing rules of conduct will be important, as they will help the appliances and services to interpret input from humans better. It also helps to reduce the amount of information that is required from a person, as it takes facial expressions and gestures into account and is able to interpret them in the correct way.

3.4.3 Physical Environment

Intelligent appliances can already gauge the physical environment fairly easily. Mankind has spent quite a lot of effort to measure physical conditions such as the weather and convert it into digital information. The challenge is to get information about local conditions through small sensors that do not affect the size or the longevity of the device. Lots of time and effort has also been spent on getting to know which other technical resources are available. In order to get the most out of an intelligent appliance, it needs to know which other services and devices are available to support a certain process.

Although this has been researched for decades, we are only slowly moving towards a semiautomatic discovery service, and it will be some time before we see automatic service and device discovery in every device. Last, but not least, location plays an important role. Through GPS and similar services, it is possible to detect the exact location of every single device or person on earth. This information can be used to provide specific information and services related to that location.

Conditions

Physical conditions, which can include noise, light, and pressure, can be used in many applications to reduce the amount of data that needs to be entered into a context-sensitive appliance. Imagine a personal MP3 player that adjusts the volume depending on the surrounding noise. This could also be used for a communication system embedded in helmets that are worn by construction workers.

Many cars already switch on the lights automatically if it gets dark, such as in the evening or when the car enters a tunnel. The weather conditions could also be used to force the driver to slow down in curves, where difficult conditions are expected. Rain could start the windshield wipers. Pressure can be of importance to applications in planes or submarines to indicate the altitude at which the vehicle operates. This could trigger some operations to be conducted automatically. It can be also used as an indicator for changing weather, which could force planes to reroute, for example, or move appointments back half an hour for business people driving in a car.

Infrastructure

The physical infrastructure around a certain device is also of importance. It includes the surrounding resources for computation, communication, and task performance. This area of research is very well developed. Sun, IBM, and Apple have been working on this issue for a while, and Apple[18] released its "Rendezvous" technology in July 2002, which allows a user to connect a certain device with all surrounding devices with no configuration required at all. This means that a user can walk into an office location and have the laptop/PDA/mobile phone automatically recognize all available resources that could be used. This would include printers and scanners from a hardware point of view, but also software services, such as configurations (e.g., proxies) or applications (e.g., databases) that help users to do their work.

   This so-called "Zero Configuration Networking"[19] has become a working group in IETF[20], which has established standards on which Rendezvous is based, for example. By knowing which devices are available, the device used can provide different services to the user. Steve Cheshire of Apple has an example of how Zero Configuration Networking can help in everyday life. Imagine having two TiVo Personal Video Recorders, one in the living room and one in the bedroom. Now what is the problem? At night the user turns on the bedroom television to watch a recorded episode of Seinfeld before he goes to sleep, but he can't because it is recorded on the other TiVo. Imagine if any TiVo in your house could automatically discover and play content recorded on any other TiVo in your house, or even exchange recordings with other TiVos in the neighborhood.

   Speaking more generally about Zero Configuration Networking, it means that we can easily move data and services among intelligent devices, if required.

---

[18]http://www.apple.com/
[19]http://www.zeroconf.org/
[20]http://www.ietf.org/

Location

A user's location is an important service customization criterion. It is an important service customization parameter for mobile me-centric services, for example. The most common forms of representing location information are physical and geographical. In particular, absolute physical location is the form of choice for most positioning devices such as GPS receivers. However, it is not easy for humans to express and comprehend a latitude-longitude pair.

Even with an accurate absolute physical location of a passenger travelling on a public transport bus, a service may not be able to conclusively determine the bus's route number. As a result, the service cannot offer richer services like estimating the time of arrival at the passenger's destination. In Figure 3.5, you can see the service of Info-Split[21]. They can track down a user based on the network connection he is using without involving GPS. You can see that Danny Amor is currently in Stuttgart, Germany, for example.

The city of Palo Alto will be recognized by those interested in technology as an important city in the San Francisco Bay area. However, a person who has never heard of that city won't know where it is. City and other common location descriptions such as zip codes and postal addresses convey physical location as well as certain implicit semantics. Such geographical location representations are useful for services requiring explicit user input, as they are easier for people to remember and communicate. However, this representation format can be ambiguous, difficult to sense with devices and too coarse for many applications. Geographic location representation carries more semantic information than physical, but there is still not enough information in either representation to determine the nature or purpose of a place.

To address these issues, HP Labs has defined an orthogonal form of location that they call semantic location. Semantic locations are globally uniform and unambiguous (URIs are by definition unique), and links to them can carry as much semantic information as required. They are represented by URLs, and are linked and accessed using standard Web infrastructure. This is a highly scalable approach as there is no central control point. Depending on the application, the place, and the desired accuracy, one of the many URL sensing technologies can be selected. Even at a single place, a heterogeneous set of technologies can be deployed.

Visiting a semantic location does not imply physical presence at the associated place. This impedes the ability of mobile e-services to con-

---

[21]http://www.infosplit.com/

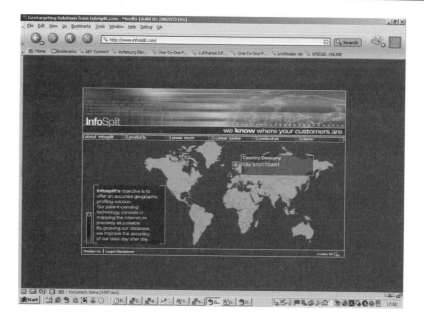

Figure 3.5. Location-Based Services

clusively track the physical movements of nomadic users, without restricting their ability to provide localized service.

3.4.4   Building Context-Aware Applications

Context-aware applications can be built by following a series of steps described in this subsection. First, it is important to identify the contexts that really matter. In many cases, there is no context at all that matters, so the first step is to analyze the usage of the artifact that should become smarter. You should try to find out if the artifact is used in changing situations, if the expectation of the user varies with the situation, and if the interaction pattern is different in various situations. Only if these questions can be answered positively should one consider this context to be of use for the application.

For all the situations that matter, you have to identify the conditions of the informational, physical, and social environment. Real-world situations that should be treated the same are grouped into one context. These situations typically identify a number of variables that discriminate the context. This can include information about time interval, number of messages, temperature, value, number of people in the vicinity, relationship with people nearby, for example.

Once the relevant contexts have been identified, it is necessary to find the appropriate sensors for these context artifacts. When selecting a sensor, the accuracy and the cost for providing the information should be taken into account. The resulting selection of sensors should be done such that the sensors cover all variables with sufficient accuracy at minimal cost.

Now that the context artifacts and the relevant sensors have been selected, you should build and assess a prototype. Here it is especially interesting to experiment with the positions of the sensors on the device. Then the sensing device is used in the situations that should be detected, and data is recorded to be analyzed later.

After the prototype has been tested and analyzed successfully, you have to determine recognition and abstraction technologies. Most sensors will provide too much information, so it is important to identify a set of cues that reduces the amount of data but not the knowledge about the situation. Based on the cues selected as above and applied to the data recorded, an algorithm is selected that recognizes the contexts with maximal certainty and is also suitable for the usage of the artifact.

Now that the cues have been identified, the integration of cue processing and the context abstraction needs to take place. In this step, the sensing technology and processing methods are integrated in a prototypical artifact in which the reaction of the artifact is immediate. A design decision can be that the processing is done in the back-end, transparent to the user of the artifact. Using the prototypical artifact, the recognition performance and reliability is assessed in the real-world situations identified. If recognition problems or ambiguities are identified, the algorithms or cues have to be optimized or the sensor selection may even need to be rethought. Once this works out and is accepted by the target group, you can go ahead and build applications on top of the artifacts that use the context knowledge.

3.4.5 Context Summary

As you can see from this section, context is a powerful and longstanding concept in human-computer interaction, which in turn is a key feature of me-centric computing. Context helps to reduce the amount of data that a user needs to enter. It makes it possible to concentrate on the real task and enables intelligent appliances to act autonomously on behalf of the user, based on the current context, no matter if it is a process step or the temperature outside of the appliance that will trigger the action.

3.5   Conclusion

Me-centric computing will only work if we have a positive experience in working with machines. To achieve a positive human-machine interface, it is necessary to specify the roles clearly. In me-centric computing we are talking about reassigning tasks to machines that initially belonged to humans. To make this possible, these machines have to be far more user-friendly than they are now, if they are to be an intrinsic part of human culture. This is fundamentally a problem of design and interpretation. Two systems that are capable of performing the same tasks often require totally different training because of this. A Windows user is not able to use UNIX without some extra lessons, although the basic tasks are the same.

The new breed of computers needs to simulate human cognition through a series of algorithms that interpret "natural" human communication as well as respond in a likewise "human" fashion that is understandable to the user. Only then will me-centric computing be interesting to the majority of people, because they can use these intelligent appliances without any technical training, with only process knowledge.

The work of defining patterns for human-computer interaction is far from complete. A first step has been taken whereby an initial set of patterns has been defined and validated to the extent that the patterns identified seem to be consistent with subject perceptions of valid patterns. But lots of effort still needs to be put into research to create human-computer interfaces that are really technology-independent and require only the process knowledge.

Resolving the open issues in HCI will enable universal access to resources on the Internet, i.e., information, communication, and transactions. It will allow more variety in technology, as it will support a broad range of appliances and services. It will grow the user base, allowing for more diversity by accommodating users with different circumstances. And it will help to bridge the gap between what users know and what they need to know. Closely related to HCI is the field of good design, which we will talk about in the next section.

Chapter 4

DESIGNING TO MAKE
YOU SMILE

4.1 Introduction

4.1.1 Successful Designs

New inventions are emerging all the time, but only a few become good enough to be used by the public. The inventions and the business opportunities related to them are immense, but whether they are seized or not depends on whether products are conceived and designed to deliver on the potential. Anyone who has tried unsuccessfully to program a VCR or understand all the functions of a mobile phone has experienced the problem of technology that was designed without considering the user.

Manufacturers are constantly designing feature-rich products to appeal to the widest market possible. This is fine, of course, but problems arise when they don't stop to consider the end-user during the design process. Consider an alarm clock/radio. Its primary function is to activate the buzzer or radio mechanism at the set time. Simple enough, but as more and more features are added to the device, even the most basic task of setting the alarm turns cumbersome. The instructions might look something like this:

Your clock comes equipped with two alarm times, Alarm1 and Alarm2, each containing five different Wake functions that can be combined within one alarm time or both. You may awaken to the buzzer, the radio, the CD, or the personal message mode for Alarm1 and choose a different mode for Alarm2. Or you may choose the same mode for both Alarm1 and Alarm2. You may also choose to use the Gentle Awake feature, which begins at a designated low volume and gradually increases in volume until the designated maximum volume level is reached, easing you into a wakeful state. Again, you may use the Gentle Awake feature for either Alarm1 or Alarm2, or both. To activate the CD mode for Alarm1, press the Alarm1 button twice, then press the Alarm1 and Mode buttons simultaneously. To set the time for Alarm1,...

You get the idea. Without the manual in hand (and even sometimes *with* the manual in hand), just setting the alarm is enough to give you a headache. This is a classic example of poor design. If you cannot operate the device without simply looking at it, or at least reviewing a short list of recognizable steps, it is not designed with the user in mind. Instead, it was designed with the functionality in mind.

A successful design, on the other hand, is one that most any user can look at and almost immediately understand. It's intuitive because either the user can associate the interface with something familiar, such as the start/stop/play buttons on a VCR, or because the visual design of the thing clearly dictates its operation.

One striking example is the Segway Human Transporter[1], named from the word "segue" (or moving seamlessly from one mode to another), which is a vehicle that is electrically powered and produces no emissions.

The device is a gadget from award-winning inventor Dean Kamen, who also developed the first insulin pump, a briefcase-sized dialysis machine, and a wheelchair that can climb stairs. The Segway scooter, shown in Figure 4.1, builds on "dynamic balancing" technologies Kamen used to create his wheelchair.

Before its official presentation in December 2001, it was one of the most hyped technologies and was known as Ginger. Segway is a self-balancing, motorized scooter that costs less than 5 cents a day to operate. The machine could replace private cars in crowded city centers and could also prove useful on factory floors. The two-wheeled device uses a complex array of gyroscopes and computers to mimic the human body's sense of balance. People lean forward to move forward, lean back to reverse course, and turn by twisting the handle. The device looks like an old-fashioned push lawn mower, with the handle sticking up in the air and a platform to stand on where the cutting blades would be. Falling over is impossible, and the scooter can handle ice, snow, and stairs with ease. At first sight, it seems like a product that everyone would like to have, but the Segway still has a long road ahead.

Though the product's potential is clear to the inventor and his team, he confronts a lack of imagination and understanding from the world at large, particularly from regulators. Most people think that Kamen's

---
[1]http://www.segway.com/

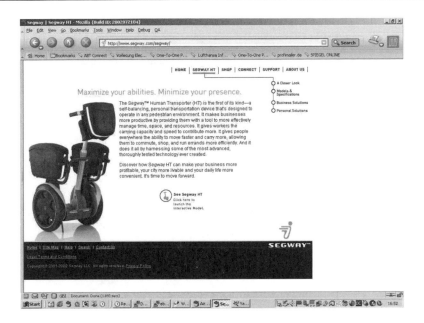

Figure 4.1. Segway Human Transporter

invention is a new form of scooter, instead of understanding the new level of mobility it provides to people. But as soon as people start to use it, they change their mind; it is intuitive and easy-to-use.

For at least ten years after Henry Ford started building cars, people called them horseless carriages. It wasn't obvious to call it a car. They used to call the radio "the wireless." Innovation is much more about changing people, their perceptions, and attitudes and their willingness to accept change than it is about physics and engineering.

Kamen wanted to make an innovation "that has the footprint of a human, that can walk around in a crowd like a human, that can bump into somebody without hurting him." But the world sees a vehicle, and therefore believes it needs to be regulated. In the United States, some states have defined the Segway as a consumer device that is only allowed on pavements; in other states it is considered a vehicle and only allowed on roads. But as Steve Jobs put it, cities need to be built around Segway to make it successful.

So what should R&D managers, marketing managers, and designers be doing to create successful products? They should be looking at places where people could off-load work onto machines, where people complain about and struggle with products and interfaces that seem to defy understanding or just aren't worth the effort to learn, and convert these "problems" into me-centric solutions.

To create me-centric solutions, it is necessary to introduce a new design methodology. This means that the interface becomes the application, which requires a outside-in type of design. The human-centered task-analysis needs to be extended with results from human factors research. This methodology needs to revolve around the ability to have your intent understood and implemented (through delegation) rather than merely populating your environment with more tools or buttons to automate what you already do. Airplane cockpit design, for example, is about making it easier for pilots to get the information they need and reduce the amount of work they need to perform to do their tasks. To become me-centric, cockpit design should include services such as the delegation of route planning, collision avoidance, etc., which are made possible over time by increasing levels of potential automation.

This means that the revolution in design starts from the idea that machines are genies that can do our bidding, but we have to first conjure them up and put them together so they can do it. This design, which we call "Radical Simplicity," goes beyond the hardware form of boxes and reach up into the me-centric ability to tell a bot what to do. By using this methodology, it is easier to hit sweet spots in the market and open up leadership opportunities.

The construction of intelligent appliances with human interfaces is both a matter of design and engineering. These topics are concerned with the methodology and practice of interface design. Other aspects of the development process include the relationship of interface development to the engineering (both software and hardware) of the rest of the system.

4.1.2   Consequences of Bad User Interfaces

On the other hand, bad user interfaces have many consequences, of which a financial failure may be the smallest problem. If a user interface is badly designed, it means that the users need more time for performing their tasks. This can not only cause financial problems, because the tasks get more expensive, but also increase the frustration level of the users over time, because they need so long to perform a task.

As a direct result, users are more likely to commit more errors. To perform more complex and longer tasks, the users also need more time to learn how to use the appliance and need to remember more steps in the process. This means that they will probably concentrate only on core part of the task and will not bother to learn to use the full functionality of the interface, much like our alarm clock example earlier in this chapter.

Good interface design is important for any kind of software and hardware. But it is of utmost importance in systems with high costs of failure (e.g., nuclear power plants), systems with high demands on operators (e.g., rescue coordination centers, combat aircraft, call centers), and mission-critical systems (e.g., space mission control).

Evaluating Human Factors for User Interface

Human factors are a key element in successful user interfaces. The following measures reflect the quality of the device employed by users in accomplishing their tasks:

- **Speed of Performance**—How long does it take to carry out the task?

- **Error Rate**—How many and what kinds of errors do people make in carrying out the tasks?

- **Success Rate**—How many tasks were successfully completed?

- **Time to Learn**—How long does it take for users to learn what actions are required to achieve the tasks?

- **Retention over Time**—How well do users maintain their knowledge and skills over given periods of time?

- **Subjective Satisfaction**—How much did users like using various aspects of the system?

Table 4.1. Evaluating Human Factors for User Interface

To make sure that your human interface does not fail, it is important to measure the human factors of every interface (see Table 4.1). Performance speed is one of these factors. A specific implementation of a task should not only measure its performance relative to the users, but also relative to other implementations of the same task to make sure it is at least faster than the average implementation for the average user.

Two more important factors are the interface's error and success rates. It is important to know what kinds of errors are committed when operating the device, as well as what tasks are completed successfully. The error rate can be used to drive efforts to make the system reliable, while the success rate indicates how well your design accomplishes its principal objective. This is closely related to the time required to learn an interface; shorter time obviously indicates a more successful design.

Another important factor is retention over time. If a user gets training for a user interface and does not use it for a year, how likely is it that he still knows how to use it?

Last but not least, subjective satisfaction should be measured and monitored to better understand which aspects of the system the users embraced and which they didn't.

Example of Bad Interface

On December, 20, 1995, American Airlines Flight 965, a Boeing 757, crashed near Cali, Colombia[2]. It hit mountainous terrain while attempting to perform an escape maneuver, about ten miles east of where it was supposed to be on the instrument arrival path to Cali Runway 19. Approaching from the north, the crew had been expecting to use Runway 1, the same asphalt but the opposite direction, which would require flying past the airport and turning back, the usual procedure. They were offered, and accepted, a "straight-in" arrival and approach to Runway 19, giving them less time and therefore requiring an expedited descent.

The crew were not familiar with the clearance they were given, became confused, and spent time trying to program the Flight Management System (FMS) to fly the clearance they thought they had been given. A confusion over two navigation beacons in the area with the same identifier and frequency led to the aircraft turning left away from the arrival path, a departure not noticed by the crew for 90 seconds. When they noticed, they chose to fly "inbound heading," that is, parallel to their cleared path. However, they had not arrested the descent and were in mountainous terrain. Continued descent took them into a mountain, and the Ground Proximity Warning System (GPWS) sounded. The escape maneuver was executed imprecisely, which led to the impact.

The aircraft should never have been so far off course or so low. The accident has been of great interest to aviation human factors experts. It was the first fatal accident to a B757 in 13 years of service. The first probable cause of this accident was the flight crew's failure to ad-

---

[2]Thorsten Gerdsmeier, Peter Ladkin, and Karsten Loer (1997), *Analysing the Cali Accident With a WB-Graph.*

equately plan and execute the approach to Runway 19 and their inadequate use of automation. The second failure of the flight crew was to continue the approach into Cali, despite numerous cues alerting them of the inadvisability of continuing the approach. Third, the flight crew lacked situational awareness regarding vertical navigation, proximity to terrain, and the relative location of critical radio aids. Last but not least, the flight crew was not able to revert to basic radio navigation at the time when the FMS-assisted navigation became confusing and demanded an excessive workload in a critical phase of the flight.

Contributing to the cause of the accident were the flight crew's ongoing efforts to expedite their approach and landing in order to avoid potential delays. Also contributing to the crash was the fact that the crew was trying to execute the GPWS escape maneuver while the speedbrakes remained deployed. Another big problem was the fact that the FMS logic dropped all intermediate fixes from the displays in the event of execution of a direct routing, and the FMS-generated navigational information used a different naming convention from that published in navigational charts.

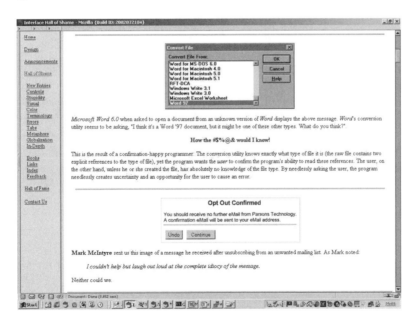

Figure 4.2. Bad User Interface

As you can clearly see, the pilots were unable to comprehend and master the situation because they were overloaded with information, and the systems that should support them increased the information overload instead of resolving it. While it is clear that human error was the cause of the accident, you can also see that the technology that was supposed to help the pilots did not work in the way it should work. In emergency situations, the technology should reduce the information output to show only the relevant information, making it easier for the pilots to focus on what needs to be done. Technology should also provide guidelines and processes on how to resolve the situation, and in the worst case, be able to resolve the issues itself. The cockpit should work like an autonomous agent, even though this may be psychologically not a good idea to mention to the passengers (that's also the reason why many trains still have drivers, although it is often not required).

Besides this rather complex scenario, many people have problems using "simple" computer programs. Have a look at Figure 4.2 to see some examples of bad interfaces on PCs.

4.1.3 Example Systems

Classic designs serve as extended examples of human interface design. These can be classified into four different groups: command-oriented, graphics-oriented, frame-based, and user-defined combinatorics.

Command-oriented designs include, for example, OS/360 JCL, is based on a batch-oriented command style and provides a baseline for seeing later improvements. MS-DOS is also still known as probably the most-used command-style interface. UNIX shells today still provide only a command-oriented environment, which make them hard for beginners to learn, but they are very powerful and very effective.

Graphics-oriented interfaces include Apple Macintosh's graphical user interface, which provides similar interface over many applications, and Star Office, an office productivity suite that offers a consistent look and feel over a set of applications.

Frame-based systems are not so well known to most people. Zog was the first commercial frame-based system available that provided a user-tailorable, rapid-response system, with a large number of frames. HyperCard was the first mass market frame-oriented system that provided a graphically-oriented frame-based system with a user programming language. Knowledge is split into chunks called frames. These frames are supposed to capture the essence of concepts or stereotypical situations, for example being in a living room or going out for dinner, by clustering all relevant information for these situations together. This includes information about how to use the frame, information about expectations (which may turn out to be wrong), information about what to do if expectations are not confirmed, and so on.

Last but not least, there are interfaces with user-defined combinatorics. UNIX operating systems, for example, have a strong combinatoric architecture, providing a logical infrastructure paired with weak human interface. While being highly structured and very powerful, it is difficult to learn how to use a Unix system, as it does not help you master your tasks, you need to learn a lot of cryptic commands, instead. Closely connected is the text editor Emacs, which is language-oriented and provides a large combinatoric command set. Another example is Nintendo's Super Mario Brothers, which even grade school children can learn without a manual.

4.2   Systems Development Methods

4.2.1   Introduction

A systems development method (SDM) is a work discipline chosen by product developers as a way to ensure successful results. Typically, an SDM specifies a series of stages that include information gathering, designing, developing, testing, delivering, maintaining, and enhancing a system or product.

Before SDMs came into being, developing new systems or products required using the experience and intuition of management and technical personnel. Still, development often took place in a rather chaotic and haphazard manner. With no existing models to use, and no similar practices taking place in other industries, systems developers had to guess when creating systems. Development often occurred in a vacuum, in a world without any predetermined rules or methods. The early systems that were developed reflected this lack of governance. Many were poorly conceived, crudely designed, and subsequently prone to almost constant maintenance and repair.

Fortunately, this time period did not last very long. Because systems developers tend to be somewhat organized in their practices, the early pioneers realized that creating effective and efficient systems required developing and consistently applying useful rules and procedures. The complexity of modern systems and computer products long ago made the need clear for some kind of orderly development process to enable complex solutions.

Frequently, several models are combined into some sort of hybrid process. Record-keeping is important regardless of the type of SDM chosen or devised for any application, and is usually done in parallel with the development process. The choice of method is typically done under time and/or resource constraints.

In this section, we'll take a look at some of the most commonly used development models to see which aspects of them work and which do not, with specific regard to how SDMs can be applied to develop human-centric solutions.

4.2.2 Waterfall Model

The waterfall model, also referred to as the systems development life cycle model (SDLC), is one of the oldest SDMs and is still probably the most commonly used. It provides a linear sequence of steps that progress from start to finish, with distinct goals for each phase of development. Imagine a waterfall. Once the water has flowed over the edge of the cliff, it cannot turn back. It is the same with waterfall development. Once a phase of development is completed, the development proceeds to the next phase and there is no turning back.

The advantage of waterfall development is that it allows for departmentalization and managerial control. A schedule can be set with deadlines for each stage of development, and a product can proceed through the development process like a car in a carwash, and theoretically, be delivered on time. Development moves from concept, through design, implementation, testing, installation, and troubleshooting, and ends up at operation and maintenance. Each phase of development proceeds in strict order, without any overlaps or iterations.

Typically, the following steps are used in the waterfall model.

- First, the existing system is evaluated and deficiencies are identified. New system requirements are defined, using the deficiencies in the existing system to propose improvements.

- Next, the new system is designed. The design provides the complete architecture, including hardware, software, and infrastructure.

- Once the design is ready, development can start. The new components and programs must be obtained and installed. Users of the system must be trained in its use, and all aspects of performance must be tested. If necessary, adjustments are made at this stage.

- After the test, the system is put into use. This can be done in various ways. The new system can be phased in, according to application or location, and the old system gradually replaced. In some cases, it may be more cost effective to shut down the old system and implement the new system all at once.

- After a certain period of time, the new system should be exhaustively evaluated. Maintenance must be kept up rigorously at all times. Users of the system should be kept up to date concerning the latest modifications and procedures.

The disadvantage of waterfall development is that it does not allow for much reflection or revision (it would be like climbing the waterfall to change something). It does not allow sufficiently for error discovery and redesign. Once a development stage has been completed, it is very difficult to go back and change something that was not well thought out in the previous stage.

Perhaps the greatest deficiency of the waterfall approach for designing me-centric devices is the assumption that one can conceive a successful user interface at the outset, without experimentation and iteration. That assumption generally proves incorrect. As a result, waterfall design practices work well only for familiar, well-trodden paths.

4.2.3 Participatory Design

Participatory design is a technique in which representative users provide continual feedback to designers as they develop preliminary prototypes in low-fidelity media (e.g., pencil and paper). It can be seen as a democratic approach to design, which encourages participation in the design process by a wide variety of stakeholders, such as designers, developers, management, users, customers, salespeople, and distributors. It enables technical and non-technical project members to participate equally.

This method gives users an opportunity to interact and make suggestions for the product before those suggestions are codified into a program. Often these interactions lead to practical improvements based on user suggestions. Such improvements can result in a product that better fits the need underlying the user's suggestion, as opposed to merely following the suggestion itself. The approach stresses making users not simply the subjects of user testing, but actually empowering them to be a part of the design and decision-making process. Studies have shown that systems designed using mental modeling techniques are better, it's advisable to use a feedback loop such as participatory design before implementing user suggestions in a final product. This proactive user input can both result in better designs and help shorten product development and testing cycles.

At Bellcore[3], for example, software engineers and prospective users play games in the labs. These games are tools to help the developers,

---

[3]http://www.bellcore.com/

with variables specific to a product, to help design the product. These game methodologies included PANDA (Participatory Analysis, Design, and Assessment), CARD (Collaborative Analysis of Requirements and Design), and PICTIVE (Plastic Interface for Collaborative Technology Initiative through Video Exploration).

Although the focus and precise rules of these games vary, they have the following common properties: engineers and end-users working together on a design, using low-tech tools like different colors of index cards, sticky notes, and felt pens; an initial focus on user tasks quite apart from GUI design; and resultant software specs that demonstrably shorten GUI development and testing cycles.

A complete participatory design exercise always includes the following top-level outcomes:

- **Task flows**—Task flows describe what the users want to accomplish with the proposed tool. These flows do not refer to underlying system architecture or data representations but describe the real-world steps the user must go through in any environment.

- **Task object design**—Task object design describes the attributes and actions for each task object and regroups them, eliminating redundancies as they appear, into a hierarchy of parent and child objects.

- **GUI object design**—GUI object definition translates their task objects into screens, lists, and controls and their representation.

This paper prototype, consisting of sketches, block diagrams of screens, and textual descriptions of the behavior, is handed over to the development team. This input is used to improve the design.

4.2.4 Exploratory Model

The exploratory model consists of planning and trying different designs until one of them seems to be the right one to develop. This model works best in situations where few, or none, of the system or product requirements are known in detail ahead of time. This model is largely based on educated guesswork.

There are several steps in the exploratory model.

- First of all, a starting point is determined for the work. All the information available is gathered together in an attempt to get an idea of what the new system will be expected to do, and how it can be done.

- Once that has been done, a rudimentary first-generation system is put together, based on the information gathered and the ideas formulated in the first step.

- It is then tested to see how it performs, what it can and cannot do, and what might be done to improve it.

- Based on the feedback, a second-generation system is developed from the first one, based on the improvements proposed in the previous step.

- It is tested, like the first. Its performance is again evaluated, and possible improvements are determined. This process is repeated as many times as necessary to obtain user satisfaction, or until it is decided that the project is unworkable.

This model resembles a prototyping approach, but it begins more nebulous and is less formal. It is not particularly cost effective and can result in less-than-optimal systems, so it should be used only when no viable alternative seems to exist. It could be used, for example, in situations, where a company is trying to extend their business into a new focus area, with little or no knowledge in that area.

4.2.5 Rapid Application Development

Rapid Application Development (RAD) refers to a development life cycle designed to give much faster development and higher quality systems than the traditional life cycle. It is designed to take advantage of powerful development software like computer-aided software engineering (CASE) tools, prototyping tools, and code generators. The key objectives of RAD are: high speed, high quality, and low cost. These goals are achieved by gathering requirements using workshops or focus groups, by prototyping, and by engaging in early, reiterative user testing of designs, through the reuse of software components, a rigidly paced schedule that defers design improvements to the next product version, and less formality in reviews and other team communication.

RAD is a people-centered and incremental development approach. Active user involvement, as well as collaboration and cooperation between all stakeholders, are imperative. Testing is integrated throughout the development life cycle so that the system is tested and reviewed by both developers and users incrementally.

RAD is a methodology for compressing the analysis, design, build, and test phases into a series of short, iterative development cycles. This has a number of distinct advantages over the traditional sequential development model. RAD projects are typically staffed with small integrated teams comprised of developers, end-users, and IT technical resources. Small teams, combined with short, iterative development cycles, optimize speed, unity of vision and purpose, effective informal communication, and simple project management.

Historically, RAD systems have tended to emphasize reducing development time, sometimes at the expense of generating efficient executable code. Nowadays, though, many RAD systems produce extremely fast code. Conversely, many traditional programming environments now come with a number of visual tools to aid development. Therefore, the line between RAD systems and other development environments has become blurred.

4.2.6   Shared Meanings Design Framework

Shared Meanings Design Framework (SMDF)[4] is a novel HCI-centered methodology that was initially conceived to support the development of human-centered systems. The approach offers support for developers, as it is focused on the semantics (i.e., meanings) of an interface, both the intended and unintended meanings it transmits. This approach is derived from an explicit semiotic paradigm and is still under development.

SMDF seeks to support the development of systems that are semiotically and logically valid, which engender trust and security, are not overly complex in terms of surface features, and are culturally neutral. SMDF provides a set of tools and technologies to help developers build human-centered systems. Therefore, it provides tools for cross-cultural design allowing for globalization and localization activities. To share the design with others, the Shared Meanings Markup Language (SMML) is being developed, and a Semiotic Textual Analysis (STA) tool is available for languages such as XML, XHTML, WML, and XSL.

Human-centered design is much more like designing for mass media than building a stakeholder-led application. Mass media has only an idea of the intended audience and the corresponding message. Semiotics has been successfully utilized to help make sense of such media.

4.2.7   Solution-Based Modeling

Solution Based Modeling (SBM) is a software development process by Neal Goldstein and Jeff Alger.[5] Their book, a bit overtaken by Ra-

---

[4]http://www.smdf.org/
[5]Neal Goldstein and Jeff Alger (1992), *Developing Object-Oriented Software for the Macintosh*, New York: Addison Wesley

tional Unified Processes (RUP)[6], etc., had more of an outside-in design approach than RUP, more like Smalltalk than like Java. In fact, Smalltalk had one really key motivating concept: the *simulation* is the application.

SBM has its origins in the Macintosh software development community. It is based on the idea that any software development project is a process of constructing *models*. The models consist of elements, relationships among those elements, and frames. Elements include natural world and program objects, categories, and classes. The relationship between a pair of elements can be structural (e.g., membership, instance, container, whole-part), behavioral (e.g., collaboration, creation, destruction), or calibration (e.g., implement, replace, same as).

Their idea was to model the world and to let the user interact with and control it. The simple principle behind this dictates that we observe how users interact with the model, how they work to solve problems, and then we design in such a way that lets them work that way. That orientation towards creating an application was very much an early landmark on the path toward me-centric systems, since the user gets to interact with an interface that is (virtually) a direct control of entities that themselves interact in realistically physical and natural ways. Humans control the entities through the application's model-view-controller (MVC) paradigm.

4.2.8 Conclusion

As you can see it is possible to use any of the above approaches, but as mentioned some have more and some have fewer advantages when creating human-centered solutions. Important in any case is to keep the user in the loop to make sure that the system you are designing and implementing will be of use. Building without involving the target user group will make it at least twice as hard to be successful.

The key is the user and not the system. It used to be the other way round, and as a result, we now have personal computers with highly complex applications that require lots of training. Instead of training millions of users, the applications and devices should be trained to adapt.

Although financial success is not the primary motivation for many inventions, it helps to keep an eye on finances. This not only means that the company that will produce the device will make money, but it also means that the device and its associated services are financially accessible by the customers.

---

[6]http://www.rational.com/products/rup/

Therefore, one should not forget to set business goals. Invest in research about the target market, intended customers, and primary competition. It always helps to see what the competition is doing, learn from their mistakes, and make sure that your project is competitive. Once you know who your audience will be, you should investigate in more detail the cognitive, social, and physical aspects to understand how they can best be supported. Find out about their expectations, motivations, and technical abilities, and try to generalize usage behavior relative to a certain context.

Then the associated processes should be reviewed and the expectations actively managed. The design should include all experiences and interactions of the user with the device and/or service. Therefore, the SDMs that integrate the customers are best, as they allow the designer to verify whether every way in which the person sees and touches the product or service has been considered and designed into the solution. This enables continuous evaluation of the design, and in some SDMs the evaluation is done only after implementation. The evaluation should continue when the product has been launched into the market, as customer feedback throughout the life of the product can be used to enhance it over time.

A good evaluation of the product takes into account productivity, figures of merit (e.g., time, errors, learnability, design for guessing, and preference), usability testing techniques, and linking testing to specifications.

There are many tactics and tools for implementation. You need to take into account the relationships among design, evaluation, and implementation when creating a new solution. Make sure that the device and the application are independent, which allows for maximum reusability, but tie the interface as much as possible to the device to get the most from the device. Prototyping as proposed by some SDMs can also help to reduce the amount of rework when reviewing the product in a later development stage. Typical prototyping techniques include storyboarding, video, and rapid prototype implementations. These prototypes can be easily implemented through toolkits, such as MacApp, PowerPoint, and HyperCard. But prototypes can also be done on paper, with interactive sketches that show the key functionality. Usability testing gives people tasks to accomplish with prototypes and heuristic evaluations help experts make assessments based on guidelines. This catches major problems before costly development and focuses design priorities on people using the product, not the people designing it.

In the future, human software developers will act as consultants to users, who with little computer training will be able to develop their own programs. Such a system will contain the specification subsystem (which could use voice input, for example), the generation and optimization subsystem, and the runtime and lifetime management subsystem. The architecture of such a system would be a combination of current CASE technology and expert systems. This would make it easier for users to participate in the development of complex systems, as they could provide smaller parts of the overall system themselves.

While possible, this prospect is less compelling than the idea that users, or product designers will be able to put together appliances from a set of reusable building blocks that can be linked to known services, it provides the semantic linkages between the user interface and the functionality. Lots of tools and end-user applications today have a similar kind of GUI for building a customized application (e.g. with VisualBasic or simCity)

4.3   Psychological Design Aspects

4.3.1   Introduction

While having the technical parts in place is important for human-centered design, it is equally important to have all the non-technical building blocks in place as well. Social sciences such as psychology and semiotics play an important role in building successful me-centric systems. It would be possible to write a separate book on the influence of social sciences on good design, so we provide you with a short introduction on these topics only. When starting a design, you should take these topics into account and involve some people with a deep understanding of them to make your design more powerful.

4.3.2   Gestalt Laws

Gestalt psychology began as a reaction to behaviorism and introspectionism. Gestalt's argument with behaviorism was the focus on systematic collection and analysis of data from the bottom up; investigating the elements individually without an appreciation for their importance as a whole that was greater than the sum of their parts. This concept of an integrated whole is described by the German word Gestalt, for which there is no English equivalent. Gestalt psychologists apply this concept to relationships between people, citing the group dynamic of a common enterprise where each individual puts forth his gifts to create something more meaningful than each member could individually.

An early influence on Gestalt psychology was the philosopher Immanuel Kant. He argued that we do not perceive the world as it is;

we impose cause-and-effect relationships on it, and therefore our perceptions are influenced by our experiences. Later, this understanding emerged in Max Wertheimer's explanation of a phenomenon known as apparent motion.

Max Wertheimer, considered to be Gestalt psychology's founder, was born in Prague in 1880 and studied at the University of Frankfurt. There, he became aware of a form of apparent motion known as the phi phenomenon. The phi phenomenon is experienced when an observer notices that two lights within close proximity to each other and flashing alternately appear to be one light moving to and from both locations. The observer perceives movement, even though none has occurred. This "apparent motion" is thought to occur because we perceive experiences in a way that calls for the simplest explanation, even though it may differ from reality. This is known as the Gestalt Law of Minimum Principle: "We do not perceive what is actually in the external world so much as we tend to organize our experience so that it is as simple as possible...simplicity is a principle that guides our perception and may even override the effects of previous experience."[7] Explaining apparent motion in this way marked the beginning of Gestalt psychology as a separate school of thought.

When designing smart appliances, we need to take into account Gestalt; otherwise, the devices can become unusable. There are five elements of Gestalt: proximity, similarity, closure, continuity, and symmetry. When placing objects close to each other, they tend to be seen as a group. Objects with the same shape or color are seen as belonging together. If parts of an object are missing, the missing parts are filled in to complete it, so that it appears as a whole. At the same time, lines tend to be seen as continuous, even if they are interrupted. If regions are bound by symmetrical borders, they tend to be perceived as coherent figures. As you can see, these five elements should be the basis for every user interface. If Gestalt is not applied, users will have difficulty figuring out which elements in the interface belong together. If done well, the interface can be simplified and reduced by leaving out parts of objects, as the users can complete the objects in their minds and use the interface as if the objects were complete. Symmetrical boundaries can also help to simplify the interface.

Kurt Koffka extended the basic Gestalt elements in his work. Among the many important concepts he introduced, we mention two here. The first is the concept of geographical versus behavioral environment. People behave in the ways they do based on how they per-

---

[7]John G. Benjafield (1996). *The Developmental Point of View. A History of Psychology, p. 173*. Needham Heights, MA: Simon & Schuster Company.

ceive the environment (behavioral) instead of how the environment actually is (geographical). The practical application of this would be understanding someone's behavior within the context of their environment instead of our own. The second one is the concept of distal stimuli versus proximal stimuli. Distal stimuli describes things as they exist in the geographical environment; proximal stimuli are the effects that distal stimuli have on sensory perception.

The Gestalt grouping laws represent repetition or redundancy in the visual world, which provide an opportunity for information compression. The laws can be applied both to the device itself and to the user interface. This means not only that the designers need to be aware of Gestalt, but also that the devices should behave according to Gestalt theory.

4.3.3 Mental Models

Smart devices and services should be designed in such a way that users can quickly acquire a good functional model of the system that is in accordance with their task model. An important goal of user-centered design is to understand the users and how they interact with the systems that they use. Using both syntactic knowledge (knowledge of procedures, such as pressing the "delete" key to erase a character) and semantic knowledge (knowledge of a domain, such as a theory) gained by experience with a system, users build a mental model of how that system operates.

Mental models are representations of the function and/or structure of objects in peoples' minds. They are analogical representations, or a combination of analogical and propositional representations, and can be dynamically constructed when required. There are two main types of mental models. The functional models are good for everyday use; the structural models are good for breakdown situations but are difficult to acquire from usage experience only.

For example, having been a student at a university for a while, one can establish a "mental model" of attending a university. That is, he goes to classes, talks to his classmates about how to accomplish the homework, knows how to interact with his professors, etc. Suppose now a virtual university is being offered to students for online courses, and a Web site is to be constructed for the virtual university. This Web site should understand and respect the "mental models" of targeted students in order to avoid confusion for the student trying to find his way around the virtual university.

In computer-based systems, a user's model of how to perform a task is directly influenced by how she perceives the data being presented by the computer. For example, let's say that in order to successfully accomplish a task, a particular switch must be open. The controller must not only know that the switch is to be open, but also be able to interpret the current state of the switch as displayed on the computer's screen (perhaps displayed graphically as a circuit diagram or simply as a "yes/no" field). Also, she must know how to tell the computer to send the command to open that switch (perhaps via a typed command or by clicking on a button).

The task flows more smoothly when the data displayed and the method of interaction match the user's expectations of how the system will operate, that is, her mental models. Thus, it is important that the designer incorporate the user's model of the task into the design of the computer's interface so that there is no disconnect between what the operator thinks she sees and does, and what the computer actually is presenting and executing. This problem is compounded by the fact that, to a certain degree, all users possess somewhat different mental models. This is often the reason why computing systems are not successful, because they do not match the majority of users and their mental models.

To implement mental models successfully, it is important to concentrate on small-effect operations where possible, since operations that do many things in one step are more difficult to model, understand, and use correctly. For modeling the state of objects, choose models that can be drawn and/or visualized easily. When designing a me-centric service, you should evaluate models and specifications, both for novices and experts. There are possible "intermediate" levels of abstraction between a raw representation and the abstraction in the requirements specification. These intermediate levels can provide more abstract views of the representation for use by implementers and maintainers. Recognize and document these where appropriate.

4.3.4 Cognitive Models

In contrast with mental models, a cognitive model is the attempt to represent conscious and subconscious mental processes and outcomes. Cognitive modeling is emerging as an effective means to construct predictive engineering models of people interacting with computer systems. A cognitive model is a theory-based, graphical representation of inferred relationships between hypothesized components of human thought. These overt models of the mind may be qualitative or quantitative, specific or general, and they are typically embedded in graphical models of human performance. Most cognitive models encompass the basic constructs of human information processing, such as sensory processing, perception, short- and long-term memory, and analytic processes such as problem solving and decision making.

Different models vary in their level of detail and sometimes in the theory that underlies their depiction of the flow of information and control within the model. Cognitive models aid analysts in getting beyond the behavioral aspects of human activities to their underlying goals, objectives, and thought processes. Cognitive modeling also documents operational decision points, information requirements, and the analytic processes followed in making decisions on the basis of available information, incomplete and uncertain though that information may be. Cognitive task analysis provides critical input to user-interface design and evaluation. Such models serve as frameworks for investigating and documenting the role of human information processing in operational settings.

In a specific operational environment, early and continuing cognitive modeling and cognitive task analysis can help to identify analysts' information requirements and can support the design of automated job aids. When a job or position is being defined or redefined, it is worth the effort to document cognitive tasks and information requirements as a basis for the user interfaces, position manuals, and training programs. When a change is contemplated for a computer system, design of user interfaces and operational procedures that are based on a thorough cognitive task analysis are likely to yield a more usable and operationally suitable product than will result from a design that gives low priority to human information-processing issues. A design's support for cognitive capabilities and compensation for cognitive limitations should be evaluated throughout the project's life cycle.

One of the most important assumptions of cognitive models is the fact that human performance is predictable. Human performance refers to the patterns of actions that people carry out to accomplish a task according to some standard. Tasks might include using Amazon[8] to find all the books about Shakespeare, or driving your car to the Virgin Megastore[9] in London's Oxford Street. Actions would include gaining access to the Internet or starting your car. The related standards to these actions would include speed and accuracy, for example.

Through cognitive models, these aspects of human performance can be predicted. These models are basically computer programs that behave in the way that humans behave and allow one to make accurate comparative and absolute predictions of how people will interact with a computer to do a piece of work. Given a few assumptions, for ex-

---

[8]http://www.amazon.com/
[9]http://www.virgin.com/megastore/

ample, we can predict how long a person would take to find all of the books mentioned in the example above or how long it takes to drive to the shop. A cognitive model might include just the discrete observable steps involved in the task, but it can also account for the processing in the various components in the human brain.

The brain includes four major components that need to be taken into account for cognitive models: perception, cognition, memory, and action. A person uses all four components when interacting with a computing device. More detailed cognitive modeling, such as that in the service of advancing cognitive psychology, is typically done using a cognitive architecture, a computational framework for building cognitive models that simulates and constrains fundamental aspects of human performance.

Cognitive architectures represent the hardware of human performance, the characterize the invariants that constrain it, and provide a framework for building predictive models. Methodologies for applying cognitive architectures to predict aspects of human performance are still evolving.

4.3.5   Semiotics

Until now, interface design has been mainly dominated by computer scientists and psychologists. Unfortunately, the problem is that computer science so far does not provide concepts for supporting human thought, whereas psychology so far lacks concepts for externalizing and materializing computational structures that accord with mental operations. There is, therefore, a need for a science that complements both sciences to make design more human-centered.

Semiotics is the study of signs and sign functions in all conceivable aspects of message exchange, and it concerns the conveyance and development of meaning through all sign vehicles. It can be seen as a framework for the comprehension of the world. Interest in the nature of signs began with Aristotle.

In the 4th and 5th centuries A.D., St. Augustine formulated the first general theory of semiotics. In *On Dialectics*, he defined the sign as "something which is itself sensed and which indicates to the mind something beyond the sign itself. To speak is to give a sign by means of an articulate utterance." The term semiotics appeared first in 1690 in John Locke's *"Essay Concerning Human Understanding."*

One of the basic assumptions of semiotics is that humans cannot "not communicate." We always communicate even when we are not consciously sending a message. Semiotics underscores that everything in the world communicates (from mountains to humans). Semiosis is a pervasive phenomenon, but there is a difference between the mountain's act of producing signs and the human act of communicating. In a simple semiosis, the sender isn't well defined (mountains aren't conscious addressers), while in the communication process, the sender has a central role.

Semiotics provides an abstract language covering a diversity of special sign-usages (language, pictures, movies, theater, etc.). In this capacity, semiotics is helpful for bringing insights from older media to the task of interface design, and for defining the special characteristics of the computer medium.

The core of semiotics is the sign that integrates a physical side (the signifier) and a psychic side (the signified). Therefore, semiotics can talk about representations (the algorithms and data structures as signifiers) as well as the user's interpretation of these representations (user interpretations and domain concepts as the signified), but it does so with a particular focus, namely the sign.

In human-computer interaction, the computer is the object of what is represented. The operating system, on the other hand, is the representamen. Think of the desktop metaphor as an example. A specific use is one possible interpretation, such as word processing. In such an interpretation much is left out, but this is intended. For a typist, the computer is not the computer with its many functions and components, but a typewriter with more possibilities.

The same computer can offer an interpretation as a database management tool or as a multimedia console based on the specific application a user is concerned with. By the same token, the object can be an application: PhotoShop (the metaphor of the darkroom carried over to the digital realm), database, or text processing, for example. In such a case, the representamen is the "representation" of the language one must command in order to achieve the desired performance. The interpretation is the performance actually achieved.

Semiotics can analyze only those parts of the computational processes that influence interpretation and only those parts of the interpretation that are influenced by the computation. Although semiotics cannot replace computer science or psychology, it provides lots of additional knowledge about humans that is required in creating good designs. Experts in semiotics need to acquire a solid understanding of the technical possibilities and limitations of computer systems in order to become creative in this domain.

4.4   The Interface Is the Application

4.4.1   Design Approaches

Interface design has different approaches, which we will summarize here shortly. Some of the more interesting approaches will be discussed in more detail later in this section. To make a design successful, it is necessary to get the graphic design basics right. This means that the design language, the typography, use of colors, spatial organization, and temporal sequencing need to be defined and selected according to the task that needs to be implemented. In an increasingly globalized world, the challenges for design in overcoming cultural, social, and political barriers are immense.

To make design successful, it needs to be done with the human in mind. This human-centered approach to design applies not just to products or graphics, but includes the design of entire systems of things that people use and expect to function in a certain way—software interfaces, public transit systems, museum exhibits, work environments. It goes beyond the physical human factors (ergonomics) traditionally studied by designers, and considers the cognitive, social, cultural, and emotional factors that comprise users' needs.

Human-centered design is a product development process that involves people during all phases of development and is led by a multidisciplinary, collaborative team working toward a common goal: the creation of a useful, usable, and engaging user experience. The process focuses on the physical, cognitive, and social abilities of humans to facilitate understanding and ease of use in interactions between people and their environments.

To make design successful, it is not good enough to work with a specialist in one single area anymore. Working in interdisciplinary teams is a must, as many products often contain different types of technologies and processes, so design teams must include people who know the technologies and business processes in detail. It is often also very helpful to adapt ethnographic methods from the social sciences, such as direct, video, and still-camera observation, which allows for gathering information about users of the new design. Besides observation, social sciences often use contextual inquiry, interviews, focus groups, and market audits and reviews to find out if a certain design attracts the user group.

The contextual inquiry studies the context of work tasks in combination with the direct observation, making sure that the design fits into the overall picture and improves the performance of everything. Interviews are used to supplement contextual inquiry. Interviews are typically fast and informal and provide quick feedback. Focus groups in design are similar to marketing focus groups but with the intention of finding out how people do things. Market audits and reviews can help to identify larger trends and patterns and tend to be quantitative and homogeneous. All these techniques help to make design better even before starting.

Human Factors in Design

There are four basic human factors that should influence the design of everything:

- **Physical**—How do people physically interact with things?

- **Cognitive**—How do people process and interpret information?

- **Social**—How do people behave in groups?

- **Cultural**—How do culturally based assumptions and preferences affect people's behaviors?

Table 4.2. Human Factors in Design

These guidelines help to solve complex problems by designing holistic systems of products and services that accommodate the user right from the beginning. This also means that it is necessary to advance the role of a designer from that of an implementor, who is carrying out someone else's orders, to that of a key business strategist capable of designing products and services that create entirely new markets.

There are four basic human factors that influence design: physical, cognitive, social, and cultural factors (see Table 4.2). These factors show the designer how people physically interact with things, how they process and interpret information, how they behave in groups, and how culturally based assumptions and preferences affect people's behaviors. Many designers do not take these factors into account and fail. But design in a me-centric world needs to adhere to these principles in order to be successful.

4.4.2   Task-Centered Design

Task-centered design is an approach where the design process is structured around specific tasks that the user wants to accomplish with the system being developed. These tasks are chosen early in the design effort, and then used to raise issues about the design, to aid in making design decisions, and to evaluate the design as it is developed.

This design approach combines a description of both people and their tasks to identify patterns of use so that appropriate content structures and relationships can be created. These relationships can then be put into context, relevance, and coherence. Context creates relationships to things people already understand, relevance shows how close the structure is to what people expect, and coherence makes sure all parts of the experience hang together as a whole. Task-centered design helps to create a taxonomy, rather than a hierarchy, because a hierarchy implies no overlap in the things we want and do.

This approach requires that designers find out which users will use the system and what they are going to do with it. As most systems are complex, it is important to choose some representative tasks first that will make sure that the whole design process is well defined. Once these tasks have been defined, one should try to find existing interfaces, learn from them, improve them, or create totally new interfaces, if the current ones available are bad. Once the interface design has been developed, a prototype should be built and tested by the user group. This prototype building should be iterated a few times, based on the feedback of the users, before it goes into production. One important thing to remember is that after the go-live date, the system needs to be monitored and changed, again based on the users' feedback.

But designers ought not be limited in their thinking to tasks that people do now. For example, a one-click purchase of books on Amazon.com[10] was a milestone, a revolution, and could be seen as a really inventive new task to achieve a human purpose not previously approachable in that way.

4.4.3   Human-Centered Task Analysis

Task analysis can be defined as the study of what a person is required to do, in terms of actions and/or cognitive processes, to achieve a task objective. The idea is that task analysis provides some structure for the description of tasks or activities, which then makes it easier to describe how activities fit together, and to explore what the implications of this may be for the design of products. But beyond simply "doing

---

[10]http://www.amazon.com/

what's needed," a successful system has to merge smoothly into the user's existing world and work. This can be particularly useful when considering the design of interfaces of products and how users interact with them. The following is a very simple introduction to some of the concepts of task analysis, and is illustrated by a design example.

- It is a discrete, step-by-step analysis of how people do things.

- It identifies the goals of the target group—what they are trying to achieve.

- It tries to identify typical patterns of use, sense of purpose, and sequence, and identifies problem areas.

Task analysis can be applied to studying how users use existing products, and such an analysis will assist in the process of understanding the difficulties they face in using existing products and improvements that might be needed. Task analysis techniques can also be used in a predictive fashion to represent how users may operate products that are being developed. Such representations can act as a vehicle for communication between developers and others involved in the development process, e.g., end-users or their representatives.

Task analysis techniques can also assist in the development of training manuals for products, as the structure that is implicit within the design of an interface is more easily revealed when represented in such a way. Task analysis techniques can also be used in the development of evaluation plans, as an understanding of what activities are the most important to the user or have critical consequences for their safety helps place priorities on any evaluation studies planned. Information on how often different activities need to be performed is also particularly useful for these purposes.

When doing an analysis, it is important to make sure that information is in the order that the user is likely to receive it. The design should make it easy to correct data that's often entered incorrectly, and the required hardware should fit in the space that users have available and look like it belongs there. These and a multitude of other interface considerations are often lost in traditional requirements analysis, but they can be uncovered when the designer takes time to look into the details of tasks that users actually perform.

Two processes are usually followed when a task analysis is conducted. The first is some analysis of sequence or dependency between different activities. Thus, it is important to understand a particular activity in the wider context. For example, a person using a communication aid may want to communicate hunger, but first needs to draw the attention of the person with whom she wants to communicate. After she has communicated hunger, there is a need for her to be fed.

The second process is one of representing how activities or tasks fit together. This is a process of representing how large tasks can be decomposed into smaller components, and the logical relationship between these. A common technique used is called hierarchical decomposition, which means breaking larger activities into smaller activities until a sufficient level of detail is reached. A good way of achieving such decomposition is to repeatedly ask "how" questions to break activities into smaller units.

Effective human-centered task analysis requires close personal contact between members of the design team and the people who will actually be using the system. Both ends of this link can be difficult to achieve. Understanding of the users themselves is also important. Knowing the users' backgrounds will help the designer to know what features the system should provide. Less quantifiable differences in users, such as their confidence, their interest in learning new systems, or their commitment to the design's success can affect decisions such as how much feedback to provide or when to use keyboard commands instead of on-screen menus, for example.

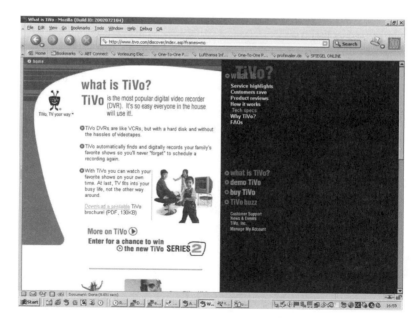

Figure 4.3. The TiVo System

Task analysis can be illustrated by going through the interface of TiVo[11] (see Figure 4.3), which though narrow and simple, addresses the design of a product and interface to record television programs (thereby taking on the task of capturing the ones you want). It makes it easy for you to specify which types (by show title, time, or subject), and which episodes (next, all). It dials out on a modem and through the Internet to determine the schedule, and then it traps the signals coming in on cable or antenna to its disk for you. You delegate the work of recording the show to the device, by selecting it from the menu, as you would select a nice steak in a restaurant and delegate the cooking of it. This is a me-centric appliance.

After establishing a good understanding of the users and their tasks, a more traditional design process might abstract away from these facts and produce a general specification of the system and its user interface. Then you should try to find existing interfaces that work for users and build ideas from those interfaces into your systems as much as practically possible. The rough description of the design should be put on paper, which forces you to think about things. But it shouldn't be programmed into a computer (yet), because the effort of programming, even with the simplest prototyping systems, commits the designer to too many decisions too early in the process.

After thinking through the paper description of the design, it's time to build something more concrete that can be shown to users and that can act as a more detailed description for further work. In the early stages of a simple design, this concrete product might be as simple as a series of paper sketches showing the interface while a user steps through one of the representative tasks. A surprising amount of information can be gleaned by showing the paper mock-up to a few users. The mock-up may even reveal hidden misunderstandings among members of the design team.

No matter how much analysis has been done in designing an interface, experience has shown that there will be problems that appear only when the design is tested with users. The testing should be done with people whose background knowledge and expectations approximate those of the system's real users. The users should be asked to perform one or more of the representative tasks that the system has been designed to support.

The testing with users will always show some problems with the design. That's the purpose of testing: not to prove the interface, but to improve it. The designer needs to look at the test results, balance the costs of correction against the severity of each problem, and then revise

---

[11]http://www.tivo.com/

the interface and test it again. Severe problems may even require a re-examination of the tasks and users.

4.5 Globalization

4.5.1 Introduction

While there is much debate about the positive and negative effects of globalization, it is quite clear that globalization is happening and has become part of everyday life. Many companies have failed in the past, because they did not keep the global market in mind when developing new products. Many companies find that over 60 percent of their revenues come from the international marketplace. More significant still is the year-to-year growth rate of the international sector. Many countries still have a huge potential.

To be successful in the global economy, it is important to provide products that have the look and feel of local products. Only about 25 percent of the world population understands English, and only a fraction of these people are native speakers and part of the Anglo-American culture. Again, smart appliances and online services need to adapt to the needs of the user and not the other way around.

The value of localizing solutions and their user interfaces for the international market is no longer in question. Localization can lead to greater potential for the introduction of products, both in terms of penetration of new emerging markets and by allowing you to reach more users in existing areas. It helps you maintain customer satisfaction in the face of increasing demands and expectations from international customers. It is often essential to meet legal requirements. And, last but not least, it helps you maintain a competitive advantage over other product vendors.

In typical product development, localization is treated as an afterthought. The base product is designed and developed with a focus on the home market, and the localization group or vendor is engaged somewhere towards the end of that cycle. The problem here is that you are likely to be introducing obstacles to effective localization as you develop. This typically has adverse impacts on your international offering.

If you do not consider localization from the beginning, it takes much longer to develop a product that meets the local requirements. For every month the foreign version of your product is delayed, you can be losing very large amounts of potential revenue, as well as losing ground to your competitors. Delay is bad, but in many cases it means that a certain product cannot be introduced into a market at all, as it may not be possible to localize the product for certain areas because decisions based on a home market focus during the development phase are too costly to re-engineer. For example, changing the code base of your product so that it supports the thousands of characters needed for Chinese, Japanese, or Korean can be a daunting proposition if the need only surfaces while you are desperately trying to fend off the competition by last-minute localization.

4.5.2 Internationalization

It is essential to understand the needs and requirements of the international marketplace as early as possible in your development cycle, and then to build the capability to support these into your design and development processes (see Table 4.3). As discussed above, a customer-focused design for products and services is essential. Including international customers in the reviews is a must. This will allow for easier internationalization of the product, which means that the design and development of the product allow for reduced time to market, reduced cost and higher customer satisfaction when the need arises to introduce the product to a particular market. Internationalization is, therefore, the process of creating a base design that can be readily adapted for use in various international markets. It does not mean that you can use it automatically everywhere, since some additional work such as translation is required, but the cost is much lower and the process is repeatable for every country, making a worldwide roll-out less risky.

To ensure the success of a product in other locales, it is necessary to check the relevance of the solution to the work practises and processes of the particular locale. Many computing solutions, for example, use text fragments that are composed dynamically for a given situation. If you would translate these text fragments and use the same rules in another language, you would create a very funny but unusable solution. Therefore, it is important to ensure linguistic appropriateness and translatability. The spoken words or written text need to be checked in context. With respect to written text, it is important to enable the application to use different character sets and encoding, and allow for multiple text directions. Besides these rather technical issues, there are two additional areas that need special attention: cultural and organizational issues. Different working habits and methodologies can have a major impact on the success of a product, if they are not taken into account, because they will determine whether the new smart appliance will be considered useful or not. Other cultural issues, such as locale-specific data format conventions and measurement systems,

Internationalization Issues

To make a product successful, you need to consider the following features:

- **Appropriateness**—The relevance of the solution to the work practices and processes of the international user.

- **Linguistic Issues**—Including text fragmentation and re-use, linguistic appropriateness and translatability, and message expansion.

- **Foreign Text Issues**—Including character sets and encoding, glyph complexity, character rendering, and text direction.

- **Cultural Issues**—Including differing work habits and methodologies, locale-specific data format conventions and measurement systems, and cultural bias.

- **Process and Organizational Issues**—Including ways of creating text or graphics and additions to the product delivery process.

Table 4.3. Internationalization Issues

must be taken care of in modern systems. The process and organizational issues also need attention.

Internationalization is simply a "quality" way of working, aimed at reducing non-conformance costs by addressing issues before they occur. However, internationalization does not mean one will need no change for any marketplace. Nor does it mean adding every bell and whistle you could possibly need for any market during the development phase. What internationalization does mean is developing your product in a modular, extendable, and accessible way, so that when the need to localize for a particular market arises, the localization can be done as easily and cheaply as possible.

4.5.3 Localization

Localization is making different versions of the same product for different international markets. The tangible factors of localization are straightforward and publicly observable elements. They include date, calendars, weekends, time, telephone number and address formats, character sets, collating order sequence, reading and writing direction, punctuation, translation, units of measures, and currency. The intangible factors deal with the elements that depend on culture.

Product localization is not just translation. Localization is the process of re-packaging and re-engineering a product and software application and their associated on-line help, "readme" file, documentation, printed manuals, packaging, and marketing collateral materials for a specific target language different from the market for which the product was originally developed, and ensuring that the functionality, usability, and screen content is acceptable in the local culture. The ability to effectively localize solutions for efficient release depends on the integration of project management, engineering, and linguistic and cultural review.

An example of misinterpretation is the use of the "trash can" icon in the Macintosh user interface. Thais, for example, might not recognize the American trash can, because, in Thailand the trash can is actually a wicker basket. Some visuals are recognizable in another culture, but they convey a totally different meaning. A black cat is considered bad luck in the United States but good luck in the United Kingdom.

Typical problems also involve symbols and gestures. Let's say a product includes a graphic of a cartoon character waving at the user. This is not considered a friendly gesture in Greece or Nigeria, for example. In those nations, the palm-forward wave is a nasty gesture indeed, as is the thumbs-up signal in Iran—not to mention the thumb-and-index-finger "okay" sign, which is most definitely not OK in Brazil.

Cultures perceive things differently. The influence of childhood, upbringing, education, and social aspects affect the way we interact with the environment. Members of each particular culture share similar attitudes and behaviors, as well as think and act similarly in certain situations. Cultures may be defined by country boundaries, language, or cultural conventions such as race or ethnic groups.

To make a system usable in a certain culture, experts of the target culture need to be involved in the design process. They will need to actively participate in the decisions on what sort of elements will go into the interface design. User interface designers work collaboratively with this group.

4.5.4 International Design

International design can start with two premises, as we have learned. Either you design an all-inclusive product that is shipped everywhere but with different defaults, or you create a modular product, which allows for localization of modules as required before shipping to specific locales.

The procedure for international design could be based on the following. First, you should identify all target locales and gather information about them. Within these locales, you should determine the target audiences. Then start an international impact assessment. This assessment should determine which features will function identically across international boundaries, which of the features are generally okay, but have to be implemented differently in target locales, and which features have to be discarded or completely re-engineered to make them work in a specific locale.

A good internationalized interface should use localized feedback. The United States, for example, has very low visual literacy, so you should adapt to these needs. The interface should use a minimum number of commands. This can be achieved by introducing a service for retrieving the required context by the system.

International design requires that the intelligent appliances speak the correct language and, when necessary the correct dialect. While this may seem negligible, this will bring real power to these appliances. Only if it adapts to the person using it on the language level will it become really useful. And dialects are a means to make things more enjoyable and accessible. In case of text interfaces, the correct scripts and alphabets need to be taken into account as well.

When using graphical signs, it is important to make sure that you do not use visual puns (e.g., a picture of a key to signal keyword searches, a little table to represent a table of numbers, a wooden log to represent a log file). Instead, use icons that look like a universally recognized object or represent a universally understood process. Where you cannot find culture-free icons, you will have to implement different icons for each culture. When you look for inspiration for your icons, get inspired in your target locales, not your local country.

Make sure that you respect other people's cultures in your design. You would demand the same. Avoid using numbers except to convey numerical information, as the number 13 means bad luck in some countries and good luck in others, for example. Hand gestures are notoriously different from culture to culture. Therefore gesture-based interfaces should be always checked for a specific locale before introducing them to that market.

There are many more things you need to take care of when designing international products, which can fill a complete set of books. Please consider this section as a hint and not as a complete listing of all issues that may arise. It is a complex subject, but worth studying when developing a new appliance or service.

4.5.5 Accessibility

While not directly connected to globalization, accessibility is a related issue. Accessibility solutions (for the physically challenged) can be easily built if we stick to the design criteria we have developed in this chapter. Most of the user interface concepts we've described are essential for successfully addressing people with physical handicaps of one sort or another. The number of such people is huge and growing, and governments are requiring that products usable by be everyone regardless of physical limitations. The United States has already implemented regulations, and the European Union is following suit. In Germany, all governmental Web sites, for example, already have to be designed in a way that allows access for everyone, but especially for physically challenged.

Traditionally, accessibility solutions have been oriented to assisting external devices that could be connected to standard computer systems to overcome accessibility issues. Nowadays, following the design for all principles, efforts are mainly directed towards including accessibility aids in standard systems (hardware and software) in such a way that everyone will be able to effectively use an off-the-shelf computer system regardless of his or her disabilities.

As a result, most hardware and software manufacturers have to invest in accessibility solutions over the next few years. Therefore, me-centric products would need to be invented at this time, just to do a good job on the accessibility issues. IBM[12], Apple[13], and Hewlett-Packard[14], for example, have already introduced accessibility policies for all future product developments.

4.6 Conclusion

The design and development phase is essential in creating successful me-centric solutions. While this is true for all product development, it needs to be emphasized that product development, no matter whether it is a software service or an intelligent appliance, needs to focus on the user. The reason why so many computer programs are difficult to use is they have been designed, developed, and tested by programmers.

---

[12]http://www-3.ibm.com/able/
[13]http://www.apple.com/disability/
[14]http://www.hp.com/accessibility/

In many cases, even the documentation is written by the programmer, making it even less likely that a typical user's viewpoint will be addressed effectively.

This means that not only do the designers and developers need to change their way of doing their work, but also the result needs to change dramatically. Technical people need to work with the end users, but also with psychologists and sociologists to create compelling products. Me-centric computing development has moved beyond computer science. Me-centric computing can only be successful if cross-cultural and cross-scientific teams work together on the design and development.

As you can see, me-centric devices need to integrate a variety of flexibilities in design and implementation. This is required to enable these products to work well in diverse cultures and locales and to provide users affordances they find natural. This requires an architectural approach that can help us create and deliver a large number of diverse products from a finite, manageable set of components.

The next chapter introduces the architecture for me-centric component technologies, which are independent of a specific solution and can be used as infrastructure ingredients in all me-centric solutions.

Part III

Principal Technological Components

Chapter 5

ME-CENTRIC
ARCHITECTURES

5.1 Introduction

As mentioned in Chapter 2, today's computing architecture is built according to the OSI model,[1] which focuses on the hardware and supporting technologies rather than the user. In order to realize a true me-centric computing environment, machines must understand users, not the other way around.

Have a look at Figure 5.1. Here you can see how the future computing model should look. It centers around the user. Through smart human-computer interfaces, users will communicate with intelligent appliances that were built for a specific purpose. Depending on the machine's capabilities, a given task can be executed by the appliances autonomously or can pass on certain subtasks to Web services on the Internet. The connection between the Internet and the appliances is handled by the intelligent network that is the networking infrastructure for me-centric computing.

The basic idea of the me-centric computing architecture is easily summarized: First, make computers disappear into intelligent appliances that everyone finds easy to employ. Second, have the appliances take on human work and accept delegated responsibilities, rather than asking humans first to divide tasks into those parts that they will do themselves and those parts that they must steer the computers to do. Then coordinate and combine the results coming from the myriad parts.

The me-centric computing model holds that inexpensive, microscopic processors and radio transceivers are embedded in everyday things,

---

[1]http://www.cisco.com/univercd/cc/td/doc/cisintwk/ito_doc/introint.htm#xtocid5

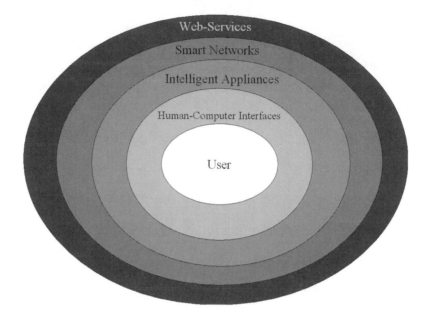

Figure 5.1. Future Computing Model

thus making everything "invisibly" intelligent. Today, we already find them in phones, television sets, cameras, cars, thermostats, and credit cards. Tomorrow, we will find them also in business cards, note pads, desks, keys, doors, shoes, and wall paint. The result is an intelligent environment that integrates computing seamlessly into work and life.

The components in such domain-specific architectures are generic and interact with one another through standardized interfaces termed interconnections. As needed, the generic components may be parameterized to simplify customization for particular applications. Specific implementation components can be saved in and retrieved from a repository, and advanced technology may be used to generate particular implementation components more or less automatically from requirements. This approach to composing application systems from a collection of modular components and standardized interconnections is called *domain-specific software architecture*,[2] and the most frequent reusable multi-part structures are termed *patterns*.[3]

Behind this simple idea of reusable architectures is a range of assumptions and beliefs that provide a fuller context and rationale. El-

---

[2]http://www.htc.honeywell.com/projects/dssa/dssa_whatis.html
[3]http://www.enteract.com/ bradapp/docs/patterns-nutshell.html

ements in this context include the assumed development process, the key resources that are required, and the principal sources of leverage. Furthermore, it is necessary to understand the key constraints, sources of variation and controls, and flexibilities and exceptions. You also need to understand relationships to other methods and standards. Each of these is discussed briefly.

Computing devices already cover a wide range of platforms, computing power, storage capacity, form factors, and user interfaces. We expect this heterogeneity to increase over time rather than decrease, as new classes of devices such as pads or car computers become widely used. Today, applications are typically developed for specific classes of devices or system platforms, leading to separate versions of the same application for handhelds, PCs, or cluster-based servers.

Furthermore, applications typically need to be distributed and installed separately for each class of devices and each processor family. As heterogeneity increases, developing applications that run across all platforms will become exceedingly difficult. As the number of devices grows, explicitly distributing and installing applications for each class of devices and each processor family will become unmanageable, especially in the face of migration across a wide area. Therefore, a new computing architecture needs to be put in place.

5.2   Overview of Architecture-Driven Approach

5.2.1   Development Process

The development processes for creating me-centric applications can be manifold, as we learned from the last chapter. Although we do not want to impose any development methodology on you, we think it is important to notice that user-centric development processes provide a higher quality result in me-centric computing.

The application systems should be developed in two basic steps: First, for each application, customer-specific requirements must be elucidated and any changes in the reference requirements (deviations from standardized requirements presupposed in the architecture) must be understood; second, specific implementation components must be selected to meet the specific requirements of each customer. This two-step process greatly simplifies many smaller steps and a wide range of alternative sequences that may be possible.

Additionally, various policies may be imposed to require particular intermediate products and decisions. Nevertheless, the architecture process is one of adapting a generic solution to fit a particular problem by understanding the unique requirements of the customer at hand and selecting or customizing solution components to fit.

5.2.2 Key Resources

Our approach depends on a reference architecture, reusable components, and tools for adapting a reference architecture to meet requirements of particular customers. A variety of techniques can enhance the quality of these key resources and the processes by which they are developed, applied, and maintained. These resources constitute the principal intellectual capital for a product line and are the appropriate concern of a product line manager. The cost of technology components and interconnection resources needs to be kept low, because only with cheap ingredients is it possible to expand the deployment of the basic architecture into every aspect of life.

5.2.3 Principal Sources of Leverage

Our approach can provide enormous leverage on hardware and software affordability, program predictability, and mission performance. These benefits result from from accumulating and exploiting software components that can be configured to meet the specialized requirements of each customer-specific application derived from the architecture's generic solution.

This approach, moreover, can make software development predictable, by eliminating or simplifying design, development, and testing. By reusing a solution repeatedly, confidence increases in its suitability while incremental errors are reduced in frequency. Finally, better software quality translates directly into higher performance of critical missions, because the software functions correctly and does what the user intends it to do. Furthermore, because this approach makes software easier and cheaper to obtain, it means that more of the critical functions customers need will be provided. This, in turn, means that more ambitious and challenging missions will be accomplished with a greater range of capabilities provided. This success will translate directly into reduced losses and improved outcomes, at lower cost.

5.2.4 Key Constraints

For our approach to work, several constraints must be satisfied. First, reference architectures must be reused over several applications, networks, and appliances. The benefits of reuse require both experience from reuse and opportunities for reuse. A product line manager must be able to adopt and enforce adherence to a reference architecture, and other stakeholders must comply. The affected stakeholders can include users, component developers, system integrators, maintainers, system operators, and even standards-setting bodies.[4]

Each architecture defines a potential common approach to achieving interoperability and interchangeability that buyers and suppliers can exploit within a certain domain. A critical proportion of these participants must agree to the approach for it to prove practical.

5.2.5   Sources of Variation and Flexibility

One reason why software reuse and systems integration are difficult is that independently developed software components often embed different assumptions about the context in which the components will be applied.

Our approach attempts to avoid this problem by providing enough specificity in open interfaces so that independent developers can produce plug-and-play components. The reference architecture must make explicit the context assumptions so that all developers can treat these consistently. Descriptions of components must make explicit which types of variations are permitted and must rule out others. Certain variabilities can be anticipated in a reference architecture and supported explicitly, giving the reference architecture "built-in" flexibility.

For example, different transaction rates might be supported in various ways, including replicating processes and dynamically balancing workload across multiple processors. Typically, this kind of flexibility is supported by setting parameters for architecture components or by specifying a range of possible values for capabilities required of component implementations.

Exceptions to a reference architecture should be possible as well, but each of these will generally reduce predictability and reusability of the affected components. In addition, by using a non-compliant component within an application, the manager increases the likelihood that subsequent efforts to plug in new or modified components will fail. Such interoperability failures are traceable generally to incompatibilities introduced by the non-compliant component.

---

[4]Standards can be determined either by consensus committee processes or unilaterally by market-dominating vendors. While the former might be more "open" than the latter, the importance of standards to the architecture-driven approach is the same: standards assure that components interface, interconnect, and interoperate as expected. Thus, architectures incorporate standards by *reference* to them, and a *reference architecture* is a pattern that goes beyond formal standards by citing generic or specific solution components.

5.2.6 Relationship to Other Methods and Standards

A reference architecture might be considered as a kind of "standard" for a particular application-specific community. The reference architecture specifies standard component interfaces, and the domain model provides a reference model showing how an application fits into its application context and environment. Furthermore, generic components of the reference architecture typically make assumptions about what capabilities they get from their implementation environment and which capabilities they must provide to other components.

These are the same concerns addressed by various standards. In short, each architecture should harmonize with other important standards that affect the same stakeholders. For example, standards for distributed computing and desktop presentation managers apply to many architectures. Although standards are always in flux, each architecture will either be consistent with particular standards or incompatible with them. Compatibility is preferred.

5.3 Key Ideas

5.3.1 Introduction

Based on the idea that the user is in the center, a new interaction model is required. At the top of the model is the user who interacts with the intelligent appliances through human-computer interfaces. The interfaces and appliances can be considered an integrated system. The interfaces convert the human input into an XML data stream, which any device and service that adheres to the same XML standards can understand. When a device or service outputs information, the interface will convert the XML data stream back into a human understandable format, such as voice, images, or text.

Have a look at Figure 5.2, where you can see the three major modules of the me-centric computing architecture. At the lowest level, you can see the infrastructure and Web services, which reside on the smart network. The connection between these modules and the intelligent appliances is handled through different types of network connections. This can range from simple land-line dial-up connections to the Internet, WLAN access, or mobile connections. The architecture is independent of the network connections; ideally, it will allow the appliance to select the most appropriate connection and allow seamless roaming between different network connections.

To support highly dynamic and varied human activities, the architecture needs to be pervasive, meaning that it should be everywhere,

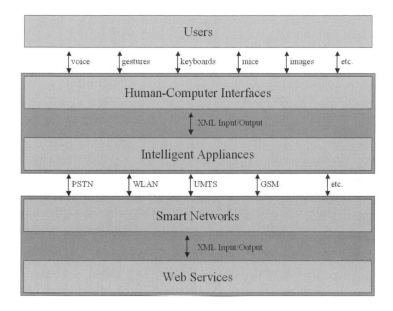

Figure 5.2. Architecture Overview

with every portal being able to reach into the same information base, either directly or indirectly. While this may be a bit constraining, we think that the architecture needs to support universal interoperability at the semantic level. This means that it should be able to be federated (built with different components, standards, and implementations), but be able to work across those seams. In that sense, the ideal architecture is comprehensive at the level of semantics of interoperation, but not necessarily imposing that it be realized by uniform parts or a single information base.

To be embedded into the lives of everyone involved, just like wearing a wristwatch or using a mobile phone, this architecture needs to be pervasive and invisible, but highly intelligent and able to sense the context and do things automatically. One of the key features of the architecture is that it needs to support nomadism, meaning that users and intelligent appliances are allowed to move around freely, according to their needs. The architecture needs to be adaptable, as it must provide flexibility and spontaneity in response to changes in user requirements and operating conditions.

In order to be efficient, it needs to free itself from constraints imposed by bounded hardware resources. Instead, it should address system constraints imposed by user demands and available power or communication bandwidth.

To make it easier for humans to use, the whole solution needs to support intentions. It therefore needs to be able to interpret the user's intentions in a given context, as opposed to interpreting strictly what the user is expressing. For example, a user may ask "Where is the best Italian restaurant in town?". The system must be able to determine if the user is really looking for the restaurant's address ("Where") or decide if the user intended to ask "What is the best Italian restaurant in town?" and respond accordingly.

Most important, the whole architecture should be designed in such a way that it must never shut down or reboot. Single components of the architecture may come and go in response to demand, errors, and upgrades, but the architecture as a whole must be available all the time.

This is achieved through a combination of specific user and system technologies. Speech and vision technologies enable us to communicate with the Web services as if we're interacting with another person, saving much time and effort. Individualized knowledge access and collaboration technologies help us perform a wide variety of tasks—what we want to do in the ways we like to do them.

5.3.2 Smart Programming

There are a number of ways that intelligent appliances can interoperate with a system, but it really comes down to one simple question: Will the computing device generally be connected to the network or not? This one question will help to determine whether only the presentation is pushed to the appliance or if processes will have to execute on the appliance as well. If the device will be connected to a server at all times, or if reviewing cached static data is sufficient, the device needs to manage only the presentation services layer.

To make me-centric computing as economic as possible, it is necessary to reuse as much as possible; therefore, the presentation characteristics and the form factor of intelligent appliances need to be taken into account. They are often quite different than the 1024×768-pixel browser most Web applications are designed for. The Web today can be characterized by HTML, JavaScript, and streaming audio and video. This set of technologies assumes that the underlying device has all the hardware and software resources of the personal computer platform, including display, keyboard, mouse, infinite backing store, high-speed processor, and constant connection at high bandwidth. This won't work in the me-centric world. Therefore, it is important to introduce a new concept that is an intelligent, render-device-oriented translation mechanism. This concept is called transcoding.

The problem is simple to express but difficult to resolve. It requires that all business-processing systems be as deployment-transparent as possible. If users access these systems via a personal computer with high resolution and rich color, the system should take advantage of that. Conversely, if the users access the systems via voice recognition systems or mobile phones, the input and output needs to be transcoded accordingly.

Today, the de facto standard for achieving this level of presentation independence is XML. This type of independence would move the presentational elements to the client device. XML files will only contain structured data, which can be rendered by the appropriate output device.

A rich component specification will help significantly in this scenario. It could be used as input to a transcoding engine for use as a template in defining the source material. Using advanced UML[5] concepts, it is possible to export those specifications. This allows the component specification to be extracted into a machine-parsable format. The transcoder is now able to understand the format and behavior of the interfaces and its operations. Provided the intelligent appliance is interested in simply executing operations of a given interface and viewing the results, minimal additional work is required. If the appliance is better served by the implementation of more involved processes, then script code can be written to facilitate the collaboration of multiple operations or components, with the results provided to the transcoding engine in an expressive fashion.

The software architecture needs to support both networked and standalone application capability. Therefore, an intelligent caching mechanism needs to be implemented that allows networked applications to run standalone. These caches need to be implemented in all devices that are part of the network to make it possible to accommodate for loss of device connectivity or network services.

5.3.3 Smart Appliances

Intelligent appliances such as PDAs, mobile phones, and cars will become popular within the next few years; new cars will be equipped with navigational assistants, for example. Because these appliances are fairly technical, it is clear that the additional technology will be

---

[5]Unified Modeling Language (UML) is a standard notation for the modeling of real-world objects as a first step in developing an object-oriented design methodology.

assimilated without much trouble by the user. The challenge that lies ahead is to introduce intelligent agents and smart services in areas that have been non-technical in the past. If we can overcome this challenge, me-centric computing will have established itself as the major paradigm in computing.

PDAs and mobile phones are fairly well developed and widely adopted. Enhancing them will make usage even easier, but there are natural limits that will inhibit growth, just as we see today with personal computers. Not everyone is willing to buy one, has the need for one, or can afford one.

Therefore, smart appliances need to become cheaper and need to enter domains that were not considered yet. Especially in low-tech areas, there is lots of potential for low-cost appliances. You can find a selection of scenarios in Chapter 2, and in Chapter 8 more information on how to design good intelligent appliances.

One of the biggest challenges in intelligent appliances is creating good human-computer interfaces. Only if these interfaces are easy to use can it be expected that many people will use them. A well designed interface also allows access to information and services for people who cannot read, for example, because the appliance allows for alternative input and output streams.

5.3.4   Smart Infrastructure

Besides the appliances that are responsible for the interaction with the user, the smart infrastructure needs to make sure that everything that needs to be connected is connected in the right way. Therefore, the network itself needs to be intelligent in connecting the appliances and Web services whenever needed through the appropriate means. One big issue that needs to be addressed is quality of service (QoS). Depending on the type of application you want to run on your appliance, different requirements may apply. Game players using their next-generation Game Boys will have the game on the appliance, but will require a low-latency network connection to play against others. Probably they won't need much bandwidth, but the response time needs to be very high. Other applications such as streaming video or audio do not require a fast response time, but do need a high throughput. Depending on the requirements, the appliance needs to negotiate with the network which type of connection is the most suitable for the type of application.

New automatic networks based on technologies such as Bluetooth, ZigBee[6], UMTS, and IEEE 802.11 help to achieve this goal. In addi-

---

[6]http://www.zigbee.org/

tion to this, roaming software will help nomadic users switch from one type of connection to another without losing the connection and, more importantly, without losing the application context. The goal is to create ubiquitous local networks that require no human intervention or even knowledge, for example, to wirelessly connect the components of a stereo system.

ZigBee, formerly known by several other names, including HomeRF Lite, is a wireless technology focused on low-cost, low-power applications. It will run at speeds ranging from 10 kbps up to 115.2 kbps, which at the top end is about twice the speed of a dial-up modem, but only a fraction of the speed of Bluetooth. ZigBee has a range of 10 meters to 75 meters, longer than that of Bluetooth. As for power consumption, ZigBee's wireless modules are expected to last between six months and two years if powered by a pair of AA batteries. More information on these technologies can be found in the book *Internet Future Strategies*, which discusses these and other technologies in more detail.[7] So far, no decision has been made as to which standard will be used in the future, but most probably there will be multiple standards that will interoperate with each other seamlessly.

To establish the connection of the intelligent appliances, it is necessary to introduce point servers. They are used to integrate a mix of user and embedded devices in a localized automatic network. Point servers will be surrounded by all kinds of intelligent appliances, which will vary widely according to each setting. The point server is a very simple but powerful general-purpose device that does more than simple access points. It provides the necessary logic for connecting the right devices and services with the appropriate means.

Me-centric computing does not automatically mean wireless connections; it can include wired connection to the Internet.

DSL and cable modem connection on the wired side of the Internet and mobile data networks such as CDPD, UMTS, GPRS, CDMA2000, and W-CDMA will play an important role in accessing the Internet and Web services. This area, whose goal is ubiquitous Internet connectivity at broadband data rates, is just beginning its mass-market rollout.

Besides these local-area network connectivity technologies, there are also wide-area application infrastructure technologies such as RFID, telemetry, and GPS. The goal is to create ubiquitous network nodes, and many vendors are now providing technology to enable this vision. The space includes technologies that extend enterprise systems beyond user terminals to devices and objects in the supply chain or the field, and enable real-time business modeling and decision making.

---

[7]Daniel Amor (2001). *Internet Future Strategies*. New York: Prentice Hall

5.3.5 Smart Services

Web services are a key property of the computing ecosystem that empowers me-centric appliances. These appliances know how to access and employ Web services to perform the tasks and subtasks that collectively accomplish the master's objectives. They are the foundation of the automated service in the background that is necessary to make the me-centric solutions work. Web services are component services that run on the Internet and can be combined on the fly to create personalized me-centric services for the customer. Depending on the needs of the user and the devices used, Web services will provide the right information, communication or transaction capabilities to the users. Web services are not necessarily Web-based solutions, so the name is a bit misleading, as not all services will be visible on the Web. Probably, most services will run behind-the-scenes in an automated way.

The key to success with Web services is their integration via agents. These agents can act on behalf of a user, an appliance, the network or another Web service. Agents are used to communicate more intelligently and do things autonomously. This means that a Web service can start a query for travel prices from Stuttgart, Germany to San Francisco, California. The Web service requires this information as part of a travel service that it is offering to smart appliances used by travelers. The agent is tasked with this query and will now try to find as much information as possible about this query. The advantage of this technology is that the instructions to the agent are standardized, meaning that different companies can create agents that perform the same or a similar task. The communication between agents and other intelligent components is always the same, making it easy to task several agents at the same time. Another important feature of agents is that they work autonomously. This means that in our example the Web service can ask the agent and continue with other work, while the agent collects the required information. Once the agent has finished its work, it reports the result to the Web service that can include it into a bigger context and provide it to the intelligent appliance that will format the information in the appropriate way.

5.4 Conclusion

This chapter offered an overview of the building blocks that are required for a me-centric computing architecture. As you will discover, the building blocks are at different development stages while the networking infrastructure is well developed; the appliances and interfaces are just about to be rolled out. On the Web services side, things look even more distant. The reason for these differences is the length of time that the different fields have been researched. While networking has been researched for decades, appliances have been researched for only a few years, as the cost for appliances dropped only in the 1980s, and the quest for a good Web services infrastructure started only at the beginning of the 1990s.

To make me-centric computing successful, it is necessary to have all three areas of development integrated into a single framework. But one of the strengths of the me-centric computing paradigm is that while a networked infrastructure is desired, the components can also work without any connectivity to the network or other intelligent components. Therefore, we will see point solutions appearing in the near future that will grow together naturally with the introduction of new and better solutions. Another advantage of this approach is that it will make it possible to connect intelligent components with differing development stages. That means that there is no need to start an infinite update spiral as with today's software on personal computers. If a certain intelligent component, device, network node, or service does not provide a certain feature, the other components will know how to handle it.

The architecture needs to make sure that the following features are enabled: compound applications, delivery mechanism, and loose coupling. The compound applications will enable the integration of different data sources, ranging from local files to databases on the Internet. The delivery mechanisms enable the data to be passed between compound applications easily, and the loose coupling makes it possible for the applications to run even though networks or other resources are not available.

This end-to-end architecture allows service providers and application programmers to develop and deploy network-based applications to address a range of devices with similar user interface requirements, while allowing content providers to create content in a device-independent format, insulating the content from device evolution.

In the next chapters, we will explore in more detail the technologies that are required to run a me-centric computing environment and see what is presently available. We will also show how these technologies are integrated today and how integration can be improved in the future.

Chapter 6

WEB SERVICES

6.1 Introduction

6.1.1 Definition

Web services are a key property of the computing ecosystem that empowers me-centric appliances. These appliances know how to access and employ Web services to perform the tasks and subtasks that collectively accomplish the master's objectives. They are the foundation of the automated service in the background that are necessary to make the me-centric solutions work. Web services are component services that run on the Internet and can be combined on the fly to create personalized me-centric services for the end customer. Depending on the needs of the user and the devices used, Web services will provide the right information, communication, or transaction capabilities to the users. Web services are not necessarily Web-based solutions, so the name is a bit misleading, as not all services will be visible on the Web, but probably most services will run behind the scenes in an automated way. Web services liberate an organization's critical information assets. By orchestrating Web services, companies can integrate and access diverse and incompatible software systems in an automated manner.

Web services represent a discontinuous innovation. It is a total paradigm shift that could signal the end of software as product and a new wave of software as service. Perhaps even more telling is that virtually every technology industry market maker is moving aggressively to support the concept. This is one of the major reasons to introduce Web services. We won't all use the same operating system, programming language, distributed object system database, or other application. This has created lots of problems in integration. With Web services, we can join different types of applications, services, and devices without having to bring everything to the same product-centric, implementation-dependent, proprietary standards.

In the long run, Web services make it possible to move away from monolithic, custom-coded applications to choreographed, scripted components. These services enable companies to move from tightly coupled systems to loosely coupled ones, based on a well-defined programming model for connecting businesses via the Internet.

The term "Web services" has been around for a while now, but each vendor, standards organization, and marketing research firm defines it in a slightly different way.

The following Table offers some of the more popular definitions of web services, with the W3C organization coming to agreement on the official working definition shown in the table.

Company	Definition
Forrester Research	Automated connections between people, systems, and applications that expose elements of business functionality as a software service and create new business value.
Gartner Group	A software component that represents a business function (or a business service) and can be accessed by another application (a client, a server, or another web service) over public networks using generally available ubiquitous protocols and transports (i.e., SOAP over HTTP).
Hewlett-Packard	Assets—information, business processes, computing resources, applications—made available via the Internet as a means of driving new revenue streams and creating efficiencies. In the emerging technology landscape, any object, device, infrastructure, or "thing" with an embedded chip can be tracked electronically, called on to perform a task, or serve as a link to services.
W3C	A web service is a software application identified by a Uniform Resource Identifier (URI), whose interfaces and binding are capable of being defined, described, and discovered by XML artifacts, and supports direct interactions with other software applications using XML-based messages via Internet-based protocols.

Company	Definition
IBM	Web services are self-contained, modular applications that can be described, published, located, and invoked over a network, generally, the World Wide Web.
Microsoft	Programmable application logic, accessible using standard Internet protocols.

Although there are many opinions as to what constitutes a "web service," each definition shares some common ground: markup language components transported over the Internet via HTTP. Each definition supports the Internet standards, such as SOAP and UDDI, which will be discussed later in this chapter.

Through Web services, companies can encapsulate existing business processes, publish them as services, search for and subscribe to other services, and exchange information throughout and beyond the enterprise. Web services will enable application-to-application e-marketplace interaction, removing the inefficiencies of human intervention.

Dynamically generated HTML content works well in Web browsers, but can be a nightmare for anyone trying to utilize that data with other programs. For example, you can easily view an auction site in a browser, but an application would require a complex HTML parser to read the status of your bid from the same site. Worse, you would need a different parser to track a different auction site, and the simplest redesign of either site could throw off your program.

In the early days of personal computing (mid-1970s to mid-1980s) and client/server development, object-oriented technology (OOT) was invented. Providing a metaphor for creating a mental model of software as discrete objects, OOT advocated creating comprehensive hierarchies of classes in which classes often inherit common functionality and attributes from their parents. OOT is a set of techniques for performing object-oriented analysis (OOA), object-oriented design (OOD), and object-oriented programming (OOP). Many of the popular languages still in use today are object-oriented languages, including Java and C++.

Reuse is essential for me-centric computing, as many services will contain the same base components on different operating systems and hardware platforms. OOT delivered on the promise of reuse, but primarily at the coding level. However, as it turns out, the code reuse requires a substantial amount of investment in initial development and mastery of low-level details. For example, one class can inherit from another class only if they're both written in the same language. In many cases, it must be the same release of the same language. Consequently, reuse in OOT is possible; at most, however, it's limited to a departmental level or divisional level and requires a fairly well-trained IT staff.

Few companies have achieved reuse at an enterprise level with OOT. And this is where Web services fit into the picture. Web services surpass the primary goal of OOT, but without the extended learning curve and costly infrastructure.

Web services solve these problems with a consistent and easy method for accessing online information. As more online services are offered, new applications can be built to interact directly with them. For example, that Web-based auction site could let you write software that automatically updates your bids based on the status of a bid on a different auction site. Or you could edit your Web log with your favorite word processor if the site and application were both speaking the same human language. Web services could potentially create a whole new type of Web.

Although Hewlett-Packard has been preaching its "e-services" for years now, the reality of Web services began with the introduction of SOAP and, subsequently, its adoption by the industry. To date, despite being touted as the next "Big Thing" for the enterprise, most Web services exist as simple operations (e.g., stock quotes, currency conversions, etc.) or short-cuts (e.g., single sign on, site links). Microsoft while trying to promote its .Net technology, has recognized that it may even be too early for end customers to use Web services.

Web services make application functionality available over the Internet in a standardized, computer-accessible manner. Applications that could not be accessed except by following rigid proprietary protocols are now accessible over the Internet using the same infrastructure that has enabled the widespread use of browsers. What is more—for the first time—applications/programs can "talk" to each other regardless of the language in which they were developed, the platform they were developed for, or the object models and internal protocols they use.

6.1.2 Advantages

Web services are a good solution because once you build them, they allow ubiquitous access from any platform. This means that you do not have to worry anymore about having several teams working in parallel on the same implementation of a given service. It will not matter anymore if you use a Windows-based PC, a mobile phone, a television, or any other device.

Another important feature is that you can mix and match them while building a new application without worrying about which platform was used to build them. The interfaces of Web services are predefined and standardized, making it easy to connect existing modules with new applications, add new features without hassle, or replace a certain feature with a better one.

Incremental development using Web services is natural and easy. This makes upgrade and updates also painless, as people can enhance the system without having to test the whole solution again. It should suffice to test the module that they modified, as each module is self-contained and can also work on its own. This paradigm does not call for the modification of parts of an application that are not needed at the current time. This allows for flexibility, risk reduction, and cost savings while developing new functionality.

Web services allow for true encapsulation, isolating components so that only the business-level services need to be exposed. Many Web services built today are designed for internal use only. They are either used for internal services or for the connection to partners and suppliers. These Web services can be exposed for external use without changing any code.

This means that the basic business processes of a company can be built on Web services and then made available in different forms to customers, partners, and suppliers without having to touch the code again. This allows for true decoupling between application components serving different business needs. A system is less prone to break down when an application component implementation changes (and they will change).

Implementing Web services becomes easier, as all new versions of the major development toolkits support the Web services paradigm of development. This also means that finding trained talent to develop Web services-based software is easier and cheaper than finding people with knowledge about proprietary systems.

In the Web services methodology, the service description is defined in a human readable format, which allows for easier understanding by developers. Coupled with the higher granularity of Web services-based system components, this makes for a less complex solution with all its associated savings, risk reduction, and deployability.

By introducing the component-based development methodology, a single stakeholder can create a Web service unilaterally, because it does not disturb the status quo of the IT infrastructure. Once the Web service is deployed, it can be tested and analyzed by a user community that may be both external and internal. This is in contrast to other approaches that need all or most stakeholders to agree on a standard before development even starts.

In short, Web services promise more of the benefits of modularity, encapsulation, and interoperability that have always been high on the priority list of organizations dependent upon computer applications. While no technology by itself is a panacea for the problems faced in integrating and rationalizing diverse computer-based organizations and processes, Web services will greatly advance our ability to provide universal access to effectively integrated computer-based solutions. Web services is one of those "order of magnitude" improvements that create a qualitative change in our environment.

6.1.3   Business Needs

Web services are not a universal remedy that can solve all possible problems. They will not fit all possible applications that one can imagine today. Some applications may need to be developed that are highly interactive, highly coupled, and require fine granularity control. These applications will continue to be developed by conventional means. This does not mean that some aspect of the functionality of this kind of application is not amenable to being exposed as a Web service. Some guidance is needed in order to select the projects that provide the best return on investment while using the Web services paradigm.

Web services can be a good choice for applications that are based on a source of time-sensitive, parameterized data about which internal or external users want to query or be notified. In this case, the user application can connect to the Web service and express the parameters of the query. This would be the easiest way for the user to connect to the application. This also means that only the core function is a Web service. The front-end application could be a Web site or a Windows-based fat-client, but no matter which client is used, it would always show the latest version of the data.

The same rule also applies for applications that use complex algorithms. Supply chain optimization is one good example for an application with a complex algorithm. Once implemented, they are easy to use, so the difficulty lies in implementing them. If implemented as a Web service, end-user applications can easily exchange information and services with the supply chain optimization service without requiring the user to understand the details of this complex algorithm.

In many large organizations, a need exists to aggregate several smaller services to create a higher-level service. If all services are implemented as Web services, it is easy to create a good solution. Imagine our supply chain optimization example. If the whole supply chain is

designed as component Web services, it is easy to introduce a new optimization component that will affect the whole supply chain without
having to change the code for all other components. Users of the optimization engine are only interested in a complete solution that includes
a complete plan with both the logistics and manufacturing pieces.

Another good example of how Web services can play an important
role is in partner integration at the business process level. In many
cases, visibility into partner applications is needed at the business
level. This view into these applications can then be composed into a
new application that seamlessly integrates partner applications into a
unified business process.

Web services can also play a great role in infrastructure services,
such as storage, validation, or calendaring. By implementing these services as Web services, they can be used from a variety of applications
without a need for reprogramming. This means that a word processor
or a database management system could use the storage service, and
the e-mail and weather forecast service could use the calendaring service. The advantage is that not only can the service be re-used, but
even more important for the user is the reuse of the same data in all
applications. It makes sense to invoke Web services over the Internet
in a structured fashion rather than rebuild these applications for each
Web application.

This requires processes to be streamlined when the information
is created. Redundant work needs to be eliminated. This is easily
achieved by basing the information publishing process on the XML
standard. This is especially important for companies that distribute
information of great value, such as medical, legal, and business organizations.

Because XML is format-independent, it is possible to easily generate multiple outputs. A document written in XML is able to generate documents for formats such as CD-ROM distribution, Internet
delivery, help systems, and printed documentation. If information is
collected from multiple sources, the integration becomes much easier
than if only one format is used.

6.2   Web Services Networks

6.2.1   Definition

A Web services network (WSN) makes the deployment of Web services
practical. Web services networks provide the infrastructure and services that the requesters and providers of Web services require in or-

der to conduct business. These business-class services include non-repudiation of messages, guaranteed delivery, once-and-once-only delivery of messages, encryption of messages, and authentication of requesters and providers. In addition, Web services networks facilitate the connection of requesters and providers of Web services to each other and provide the ability to manage, control, and monitor the machine-to-machine (or application-to-application) interactions that are part of the Web services protocol.

The creators of Web services, using tools and platforms from companies such as IBM, Hewlett-Packard, BEA, and Sun, use the Web services network as a seamless part of their infrastructure, similar to how businesses today use telephone networks. Ideally, a WSN should not require any rework of code written to service-enable applications.

Web Services Infrastructure

The following are infrastructure components of Web services:

- **Service Provision**—An application that provides services that are useful to business entities both within and outside an enterprise.

- **Service Toolkit**—A toolkit that exposes the useful business service in a standardized, Internet-accessible format.

- **Application Server**—A server that enables communication to the application and provides a run-time environment for the Web services aspect of the application.

Table 6.1. Web Services Infrastructure

If we look at the infrastructure components of Web services in detail (an overview can be found in Table 6.1), we can see three major components that need to be available in every case: a service provision, a toolkit, and an application server. An example of a service provision (as defined in the table) might be an application that tracks the inventory level of parts within an enterprise. This can provide a useful service that answers queries about the inventory level. These applications usually already exist within an enterprise (in the form of legacy applications) or may be developed from scratch using a Web services toolkit.

Web services toolkits are available from many companies. IBM[1] provides the Web services development environment, and Microsoft[2] provides its Visual Studio .NET toolkit. These toolkits can be used to expose the inventory-level query service as a Web service that can be accessed over the Internet by any other program. While IBM, Sun, and most of the others use Java for the development of Web services, Microsoft is using Visual Basic and C#. The toolkit also ensures that the service provides a standard set of interfaces, which are accepted by all the applications that want to use it.

As for application servers, there are many different types available. Most of them are built on Java technology, except for Microsoft. You can choose among Tomcat[3] server from Apache[4], Websphere from IBM, and Weblogic from BEA[5], just to name a few.

6.2.2 Advantages

So far, no vendor of toolkits or Web services platforms has supplied solutions for providing the full spectrum of business-class Web services. Indeed, they can't supply these solutions because their model is to sell platforms at a customer's site that then connect to another platform (paid for by the second customer) on another site. The connection itself is point-to-point, and the quality of service provided is negotiated and provided by each platform at each end of the point-to-point connection. However, we live in a networked world; we want to connect to dozens, if not hundreds, thousands, or tens of thousands of such platforms. The "edge," or the platform at one end of the connection, cannot supply the solution that is valid across the entire network of connections.[6] Platform providers are tied to the so-called hub-and-spoke model[7], which is by necessity a proprietary solution.

In a many-to-many world, they have a difficult time scaling to meet the needs of the new Web services ecosystem. The cost of creating a hub and then connecting the spokes is much higher compared to the cost of

---

[1]http://www.ibm.com/

[2]http://www.microsoft.com/

[3]http://jakarta.apache.org/tomcat/

[4]http://www.apache.org/

[5]http://www.bea.com/

[6]Grid computing is the solution for this set of problems. It is a largely non-proprietary approach to connecting vast numbers of computers into a pool of shared resources. Arising out of scientific research communities, Grid computing portends a flattening of the computational resources hierarchy, not unlike the flattening in organizational communications hierarchy caused by wide adoption of email.

[7]The hub-and-spoke model consists of the hub being a central or regional service center and the spokes being the services that could be integrated in such a center.

plugging into a network like a Web services network. The ease of use both in deployment and in the operation of the Web services network is unmatched by platforms.

Web services are cross-departmental and cross-enterprise. They pose unique challenges in deploying since the monitoring, tracking, and reporting of Web services interaction is not within the domain of a single department or enterprise. There is a need for an entity that is able to see the interactions at both ends of a Web services connection, both at the Web service provider's end and at the Web service requester's end. The functionality needed has been detailed in the section above. A Web services network meets all these needs.

As the use of Web services grows, enterprises require the ability to manage how their Web services are consumed, and the users of these Web services require the ability to manage and orchestrate their interactions with Web services. A Web services network that has visibility into both sides and can manage interactions is the best solution for an enterprise's needs.

6.2.3   Quality of Service

A successful infrastructure makes it quick and easy for authorized users to access the appropriate information and services while it remains well protected from intruders or unauthorized personnel. Businesses that fail to bolster their infrastructure to handle rising IP traffic can count on big problems, such as frustrated customers and business partners. Building an IT infrastructure that can handle current and future e-business demands has become a strategic initiative.

Building a stable infrastructure, however, is one of the greatest challenges IT managers face. Reconstructing the enterprise to meet demands of e-business will also be important over the next few years. Investments will go toward building combined voice/data networks that use high-bandwidth technologies such as Gigabit Ethernet, and integrating network management platforms, storage area networking, and wireless communications. Once these high-bandwidth networks are in place, businesses will focus on finding ways to make them perform better.

To ensure that the most critical applications receive the infrastructure services they need, companies increasingly are looking to two emerging technologies: Quality of Service (QoS) and policy management. These tools are designed to work around the "best-effort" performance that is an inherent quality of IP networks such as the Internet.

Without QoS, all services on the Internet are treated as equal—there is no way to allocate bandwidth or guarantee high performance for specific applications. This results in unpredictable and unreliable performance for all services, which could severely limit its growth and use, not to mention the development of future networked applications.

Web services networks can provide QoS guarantees and make the use of Web services (which may extend out to thousands of users) manageable. These QoS guarantees can be provided in security, reliability and manageability.

When a network and an application both incorporate QoS protocols, the application is able to request and receive predictable bandwidth or priority service. Policy management describes the use of rules, or policies, set by the enterprise to establish the level of service that will be granted to particular users or types of traffic. Companies that offer policy management technology include Lucent[8], Cisco[9], and Orchestream[10].

These infrastructure technologies use different methods to meet the same goal: getting the best-possible performance out of an increasingly crowded Internet. And while content management—an additional technology—doesn't directly affect network performance, it is being integrated with caching, load balancing, and policy management systems with increasing frequency because it is a critical piece of the e-business infrastructure puzzle.

Delivering rich media content such as live presentations or video broadcasts further stresses the network infrastructure. These kind of media especially require high levels of QoS to avoid breaking the visual or auditory experience, i.e. to prevent "stuttering."

6.2.4 Security

One of the biggest concerns with Web services is security. Many people fear that these personalized and automated services can create privacy issues by releasing information to the wrong people and services and without the consent of the user. Microsoft and its Passport service are probably best known for this situation. Microsoft offers the ability to store personal information, such as addresses and credit card information, on its servers, which can be pulled from online shops to reduce the need for retyping the information each time. While in theory a good idea, it means that Microsoft controls the information flow of these vital pieces of information. Many consumer advocates and service providers have balked at this prospect.

---

[8] http://www.lucent.com/
[9] http://www.cisco.com/
[10] http://www.orchestream.com/

Communication via the Internet is, by default, open and uncontrolled. This conflicts with the needs of businesses and customers, which require privacy, confidentiality, and integrity in their transactions. The growing demand raises the awareness of security issues and concerns about conducting secure business via the Internet. News reports on Internet security are hypercritical and increase the fear that business on the Internet is dangerous. Network-based fraud is growing dramatically and has made Internet security a business issue, not just a technical issue, to be resolved in the IT departments of companies considering an Internet business strategy. Not surprisingly, as society becomes more dependent on network systems, information security will become even more of an issue.

A major problem is the identification of the users. In a real shop, a customer is identified by his or her appearance, but on the Internet everyone looks the same. Although it is possible to pretend to be someone else in real life, it is even simpler online. Nobody can be sure about the identity of the other person without deploying additional technologies. Neither is it possible to identify a single person or a company reliably. To make me-centric computing successful, it is necessary to automate many things, among them the identification of the communication partner. Only if this can be established does it make sense to create Web services that exchange information automatically.

To enforce information security, unauthorized access to electronic data on the business-critical systems of a company or the private systems at home must be prevented. Unauthorized access can result in the disclosure of information and the alteration, substitution, or destruction of content. Individuals and organizations that use computers can describe their needs for information security and trust in terms of five major requirements: confidentiality, integrity, availability, legitimate use, and non-repudiation.

Confidentiality is necessary to control who gets to read the information and to conceal the information from all others. Integrity assures that information and programs are changed only in a specified and authorized manner, and that the data presented is genuine and was not altered or deleted during transit. Availability ensures that authorized users have continued access to information and resources. Legitimate use means that resources cannot be used by non-authorized persons or in a non-authorized way. Repudiation is defined as "the rejection or refusal of a duty, relation, right, or privilege." If an electronic transaction is viewed as a binding contract between two parties, a repudiation of the transaction means that one of the parties refuses to honor its obligation to the other as dictated by the contract. Thus, non-repudiation can be defined as the ability to deny a false rejection or refusal of an obligation with irrefutable evidence.

These five requirements may be weighted differently depending on the particular application. In some cases, integrity is more important than legitimate use; in other cases, confidentiality is very important, while the availability of the system is not a problem. A risk assessment must be performed to determine the appropriate mix of requirements. A number of different technologies can be used to ensure information security. These technologies exist, but need to be implemented in a wider security strategy, as the processes around security are probably even more important than the technology itself.

6.2.5 Reliability

Reliability refers to the fact that a Web service works in the way that it is intended to work for a business in all reasonable circumstances. The messages passed back and forth during a Web service life cycle should be delivered to the right receiver(s), in the right amount of time, in the right order, and the right number of times under all reasonable circumstances. If for some reason any message is not reliably delivered, then the sender, receiver, or manager of the Web service should be alerted to the fact. The Internet does not even try to guarantee this reliability.

Web services networks have to guarantee reliability building on top of standard Internet protocols. They should impose no special requirements on applications while doing so. The most important aspects of reliability are guaranteed delivery, non-repudiation, and once-and-once-only delivery.

A Web services network should provide the guarantee that once a message is sent over the Internet as part of a Web services interaction, it reaches the intended recipient. Time-outs and resends should be handled automatically and transparently. The capability to queue messages to be delivered when the receiver is able to accept them should be provided. Guaranteed delivery implies that an application can make a request to send a message and not have to write state-keeping routines that check whether a message has reached its intended destination with the intended results.

Once a Web services network is able to implement guaranteed delivery, in conjunction with its authentication capabilities and the keeping of records within the network, it can guarantee that a recipient cannot repudiate a message that the recipient received and also that a sender cannot repudiate a sent message. The customer order information can be kept within the network, in the scenario above, so that even if the customer's systems do not record the sending of an order via the Web service at the manufacturer's site, the network will be able to prove that was indeed the case.

A Web services network has to guarantee that a message that is intended to be delivered once should be delivered (guaranteed delivery) and should not be delivered more than once. If a message is delivered more than once, it could have a major impact on the reliability of the service. Imagine a bank that would execute a money transfer five times instead of once or an online shop that would send you seven books instead of one.

6.2.6 Manageability

Once Web services are deployed throughout an enterprise, managing access to them, tracking their usage, logging the services performed, and potentially billing the users for the service all become problems that need a solution. Web services networks provide a network solution that manages all the Web services and the connections between Web services and requesters of those services. This is a very important function that can have a huge impact on the ROI of Web services deployment.

If these deployments can be managed at low cost and low risk, then the ROI will be as intended. Cost overruns will inevitably hit projects that do not plan for these management tasks while deploying their Web services. Web services networks provide low-cost, seamless, low-risk solutions to this management problem.

First of all, it is important to make sure that everything is logged. This means that every event happening at the user end, the service provider end, and in between while invoking a Web service has to be logged and easily visible to the managers of the Web service. Web services networks need to provide the logging facilities and the reporting facilities over the logs; otherwise, it is almost impossible to find out if something went wrong.

To make sure that all anomalies are found, it is necessary to introduce monitoring services. Web services need continuous visibility into the performance metrics of Web services requests/replies, endpoint states, and message delays. Web services networks should provide this functionality, again without altering the standards-based Web services interactions in any way. In this way, it is easy to identify problems and make sure that they can be followed up.

In case something goes wrong, it is very important to be able to track down the problem. Real-time knowledge of the state of a user request and the reply from a Web service is required. The importance of tracking increases when messages are queued asynchronously for delivery. Web services networks should provide tracking functionality that is easy to use and does not interfere with the normal functioning of a Web service.

From a security point of view, it is very important to implement access management on the Web services network level. While deploying Web services, categories of users are allowed various access levels to different Web services. This setup and the management of the access given needs to be implemented by a Web services network. A new user being allowed to enter orders would need to be allowed to access the Web service; this should happen transparently through the actions of the Web services network without effecting the functioning of the Web services in any way.

6.3 Extensible Markup Language

6.3.1 Common Problems of the Web

In order to move on to do *real* e-business on the Web, it is necessary to understand why this is not possible using current technologies. This especially refers to the HTML standard that hinders the development of new applications on the Internet, as it was not designed to do anything but present documents in a Web browser. E-business has requirements other than displaying documents. Among other requirements, documents need to be displayed, processed, rearranged, stored, forwarded, exchanged, encrypted, and signed. Using HTML, it is difficult to express the hierarchical relationship of data values (known from database records and object hierarchies). HTML reflects structure and presentation, but conveys nothing about the meaning of the marked-up document.

Today, most applications are tied to the browsers, but many corporations have applications installed that are not able to display the information in HTML, yet need to exchange the information over the Internet. Many customers also want Internet applications to have the look and feel of their applications, and this can be achieved by launching external applications from within the browser. The best solution is to have Web applications that understand the Internet protocols, such as HTTP and TCP/IP, that do not require a Web browser. This allows existing applications to be extended to talk to other resources, such as databases and applications over the Internet. While the Internet protocols help to establish the communication, XML enables the exchange of data between applications that usually have totally different data formats.

In order to create intelligence on the Web, search engines need to understand the content of Web pages, but so far they are not able to. In searching for a certain piece of information, it is highly likely that you get one good result and at least 100 incorrect ones (some search engines are even worse by a factor of 10 to 100). The problem is that search engines normally only index a set of words, document titles, URLs, and metatags, but do not know anything about the structure of the document. A search engine cannot decide if a document is a news article or a thesis, for example. There is no way to mark up the significant portions of a document to focus on the important parts and ignore the noise (such as copyright statements, navigational bars, and design elements). This would allow a much finer granularity of control over search engines. By adding additional attributes to Web elements, this can be achieved. Let's say you are researching information on a singer who also acts and writes (such as Cher or Madonna). It would be good to have a classification of the function of the person on the Web site. If tags like <singer>, <actor>, <author> could be used in HTML, the number of direct hits would be much higher. With XML, these tags can be easily defined and used.

Another common problem on the Web is the collection of related pages and saving them to your hard disk or printing them out. The current method is to save or print them on a page-by-page basis, which can become really annoying if there are more than ten pages. In many cases it is also difficult to identify the other parts of a particular collection, as the document that links all resources together is not known to the person who looks at a particular page. Often a link is not provided, as the owner of the link is aware that the document is part of a larger collection. In order to express the interrelationship, special metadata[11] should be attached to the documents, making it easier to find the other documents related to the topic of a particular search. Although adding metadata is possible in HTML, the information is restricted to the whole document, not to only parts of it that may be of interest for a particular search. Using XML, it is possible to create metadata for all text elements.

6.3.2 Moving to XML

XML is an ISO-compliant subset of the Standard Generalized Markup Language (SGML), a system for organizing and tagging elements of a document. XML is extensible because it is a metalanguage, which en-

---

[11]Metadata is information about information and is an established standard for HTML pages using the tag <meta>.

ables someone to write a document type definition (DTD) like HTML 4.0 and define the rules of the language so the document can be interpreted by the document receiver. XML is like an alphabet for building new languages and gives companies a way to start with a common foundation and a common alphabet. Every industry is able to define the specific terms they use.

Unlike HTML, the layout is not defined in the XML file, nor is the sequence of the text on the screen. The semantics and the structure of the data is preserved. The data is organized as in an object-oriented database. XML is about creating, sharing, and processing information. The purpose of XML is to provide an easy-to-use subset of SGML that allows for custom tags to define, transmit, and interpret data structures between organizations. These tags look like HTML tags, but describe the meaning of the information in a format that is predictable and precisely defined.

The widespread introduction of XML into Internet applications will change the way we experience the Web today and remove two constraints that are holding back Web development: its dependence on a single, inflexible document type (i.e., HTML) and the complexity of the full SGML, whose syntax is very powerful but extremely complex. XML reduces the complexity of SGML and enables the development of user-defined document types on the Web. Some say that XML provides 80 percent of the benefits of SGML with only 20 percent of the effort.

Although HTML will continue to play an important role for the content it currently represents, many new applications require a more robust and flexible infrastructure. E-business on the Internet will work only if the information that is transported is not restricted to one make or model or manufacturer. Information can also not cede control of its data format to private hands. In order to save time and effort, the information needs to be provided in a form that allows it to be reused in many different ways.

The presentation of XML documents can be implemented by using the Document Style and Semantics Specification Language (DSSSL)[12], Cascading Style Sheets (CSS)[13] specification, or the Extended Stylesheet Language (XSL). While DSSSL is not widely used, and CSS is mainly used for display on the Web, XSL is becoming the predominant way of representing XML on different platforms.

---

[12]DSSSL is a standard for the processing of SGML (Standard Generalized Markup Language) documents. It describes how such a structured document might be presented visually, or converted, or processed in some other way

[13]CSS specifies the possible style sheets or statements that may determine how a given element is presented in a Web page.

6.3.3   XML Applications

XML is slowly finding its way into Internet applications. Although mostly invisible to the end user, many XML applications have already been created to simplify the processing of documents by moving from application-specific data formats to XML.

XSL

Similar to CSS, XSL separates the content from representation. It specifies the formatting characteristics of XML documents on the Web, while CSS specifies the formatting characteristics of HTML documents.

While CSS has its own proprietary syntax, XSL itself has been written in XML and can be extended through JavaScript, scripting language for the manipulation of HTML and XML documents. The formatting model is the same as in CSS and the highly complex DSSSL.

Although it is possible to use CSS for formatting HTML tags, it is not necessary, as all HTML tags have a predefined representation in a Web browser. XML tags are highly dynamic, and none of them has a predefined representation in a Web browser. A designer may create the tag <box>, which is perfectly valid in XML, if defined in a DTD, but no browser will know how to format this tag. XSL is able to add the missing style information to the XML tag.

Although CSS can also format XML documents, it can only be used for rather simple documents. But XML has been invented to create highly structured and data-rich documents. Unlike CSS, XSL can also transform XML documents, moving an existing document in a form to another document in another form. XSL is able to dynamically render a page when elements need to be rearranged, while CSS can represent the data only in the form in which it was originally placed in the file. XSL can be used, for example, to rearrange Web content for printing to fit better on a printed page, without the need of downloading another version of the same document.

Although XSL is extensible through JavaScript, many developers feel that its features can be replaced by JavaScript and the Document Object Model (DOM), which specifies how objects in a document (text, images, headers, links, etc.) are represented.

SMIL

Based on XML, the Synchronized Multimedia Integration Language (SMIL, pronounced "smile") has been created by the W3C[14] and is a

---

[14]http://www.w3c.org/AudioVideo/

powerful way to synchronize any type of media (e.g., audio, video, text, and graphics) and build time-based, streaming multimedia presentations without having to learn a complex programming language.

Until now, it was necessary to use either programming languages such as Java to implement complex TV-like content or multimedia applications such as Macromedia's Director.[15] Using simple instructions that are similar to HTML, you can build complex animations. By using an interpreted language, the time needed to download multimedia content decreases dramatically.

The major difference between SMIL and Director is that SMIL does not create one large file that needs to be downloaded. Instead, images, sounds, and animations are downloaded one after the other in the order of appearance in the presentation. If components are used in several multimedia presentations, the browser may have some already in the cache, reducing the download time even further. The customer is able to see the beginning of the multimedia much earlier and is able to decide if it's worth waiting for the rest of it.

Just as with HTML pages, replacing components is easy and does not require you to rebuild the complete page. With SMIL, you can replace components and use the presentation in an instant, without interrupting the service for your customers. The authoring process can be simplified by using SMIL. It also supports hyperlinks in order to offer interactivity.

SMIL was developed to complement other Web technologies, such as Dynamic HTML (DHTML) and DOM. Although Microsoft initially supported the SMIL initiative, the company now contends the technology is no longer compatible with its media player. Perhaps because they developed their media player at the same time, most other technology companies are jumping onto the SMIL bandwagon.

SMIL is not meant to be a replacement for existing multimedia technologies. It is possible to join the media formats and create an even richer experience.

RDF

Another very interesting application is the Resource Description Framework (RDF),[16] which has been developed by the W3C. RDF adds metadata to Internet resources, whereby a resource can be any object on the Web, such as a Web page, image, or sound. The metadata can be used to find a resource by adding a detailed description and keywords

---

[15]http://www.macromedia.com/
[16]http://www.w3c.org/RDF/

to the metadata, to rate the content, and to digitally sign an object on the Internet.

The problem with the metadata of HTML pages is that computers are not able to understand the information. If the description of two Web pages is similar and points to the same type of information, such as "Germany is a country in Europe" and "Germany is a European country," a computer will not be able to detect this without extensive programming. RDF associates unambiguous methods of expressing these statements so that a machine can understand that they have the same meaning.

Although RDF is able to improve search results on the Web, it is not restricted to this application. It is able to describe individual elements and the relationships between them.

Therefore, the W3C has developed a data model and a syntax for the RDF. The difference between RDF and similar frameworks is that RDF has been developed especially for the Web. The syntax for RDF is based on a special data model that defines the way properties are described. It represents the properties of a resource and the values of the properties.

Although RDF has been developed independently of XML, it can be easily represented in extensible markup language. Therefore, the names of the properties and the values are not predefined, but can be chosen by those responsible for the Internet object. The creator of an RDF record can choose which particular properties or sets of properties will be used. In order to ensure the uniqueness of every RDF record, it uses the namespace mechanism, which is also used in XML and the Internet. The namespace is the set of names in a given naming system.

RDF is already used on the Internet. Netscape uses RDF to index site content in order to allow users to find information more quickly. The feature "What's Related" in Netscape Communicator 4.5 (and above) uses RDF to display related sites within the browser. Millions of users worldwide are using this feature, and it is so far the most popular XML application.

WSDL

As communications protocols and message formats are standardized in the Web community, it becomes increasingly possible and important to be able to describe the communications in some structured way. The Web Services Description Language (WSDL) addresses this need by defining an XML grammar for describing network services as collections of communication endpoints capable of exchanging messages. WSDL service definitions provide documentation for distributed systems and serve as a recipe for automating the details involved in applications communication.

WSDL files are a subset of the registries in UDDI[17] and ebXML[18]. It is an XML vocabulary that provides a standard way of describing service IDLs.[19] It provides contact information, descriptions of the Web services, their location, and specification on how to invoke them.

WSDL is the resulting artifact of a convergence of activity between NASSL (by IBM[20]) and SDL (by Microsoft[21]). It provides a simple way for service providers to describe the format of requests and response messages for remote method invocations (RMI).

A WSDL document defines services as collections of network endpoints, or ports. In WSDL, the abstract definition of endpoints and messages is separated from their concrete network deployment or data format bindings. This allows the reuse of abstract definitions: messages, which are abstract descriptions of the data being exchanged, and port types, which are abstract collections of operations. The concrete protocol and data format specifications for a particular port type constitute a reusable binding. A port is defined by associating a network address with a reusable binding, and a collection of ports defines a service.

The UDDI registry is broken down into industry categories and geographic locations. A WSDL file is often generated from another information source, like a Component Object Model (COM)[22] IDL or Common Object Request Broker Architecture (CORBA)[23] file or Enterprise Java Beans (EJB)[24] class definition. The current WSDL specification details how to map messages and operations to HTTP GET/POST, SOAP v1.1, and MIME, a specification for formatting non-ASCII messages.

It is important to observe that WSDL does not introduce a new type of definition language. WSDL recognizes the need for rich type systems for describing message formats and supports the XML Schemas specification (XSD) as its canonical type system. However, because it is unreasonable to expect a single type system grammar to be used to

---

[17]http://www.uddi.org/

[18]http://www.ebxml.org/

[19]The Interface Definition Language (IDL) is the prevalent language used for defining how components connect together.

[20]http://www.ibm.com/

[21]http://www.microsoft.com/

[22]COM is Microsoft's framework for developing and supporting program component objects. It is aimed at providing similar capabilities to those defined in CORBA.

[23]http://www.corba.org/

[24]http://java.sun.com/products/ejb/

describe all message formats in the present and future, WSDL allows the use of other type definition languages via extensibility.

In addition, WSDL defines a common binding mechanism. This is used to attach a specific protocol or data format or structure to an abstract message, operation, or endpoint. It allows the reuse of abstract definitions.

WSFL

To compose more complex services out of existing service components, it is necessary to provide a means for describing the workflow. The Web Services Flow Language (WSFL) is an XML language for this particular task. WSFL considers two types of Web services compositions:

1. **Usage Patterns**—Describes workflow or business processes.

2. **Interaction Patterns**—Describes overall partner interactions.

In Chapter 2 we provided a series of example scenarios where WSFL would play a key role. If you look, for example, at Figure 2.6, you can see the need for several workflows. The different services that are available on the market are brought into a specific context to form a dedicated service for construction sites.

6.3.4   Other Applications

XML applications are developed not only by the W3C, but also by companies and other organizations. The W3C is offering a standard set of applications, but every company is free to develop new and innovative applications based on XML, which can be for private, internal use only or can be made public for external review and use. For example, engineers at NASA[25] plan to use XML to develop an instrument control language for infrared devices on satellites and space telescopes. The XML syntax will be used to describe classes of infrared instruments, control procedures, communications protocols, and user documentation. Computers will parse the tagged data and generate instrument control code, most likely in Java.

Siemens[26] is using a system that allows employees to submit their timecards and lets managers approve them online. Each timecard submission and approval is tied to basic human resource (HR) data such as name, serial number, and employee type. The timecard validation depends on pay code rules and frequency tables. Managers have the

[25]http://www.nasa.gov/
[26]http://www.siemens.com/

ability to temporarily delegate approval responsibilities, and the entire system interfaces to the corporate-wide directory service database as well as to the payroll system.

In order to achieve this goal, the data between the different systems needs to be interchanged. Therefore, a data format is required that can be shared among the applications. XML serves as the data interchange format in a time and attendance system and enables the integrators to reuse interface code, extend and modify data structures to accommodate personalization and internationalization, and design the system without worrying about limitations imposed by data sources. Data fields can be added without disrupting the existing structure and applications. Global development and the different holiday schedules of each country can be easily implemented with XML. The developer can use the same pay-period DTD, but just drop in a new holiday attribute. XML makes the localization of an application easy, maximizing code and data model reuse. Many other companies have started to use XML to integrate their existing applications and exchange data between different platforms and database systems.

6.3.5   Business via XML

XML has become the industry-neutral standard for information exchange. XML is used throughout the industry in a similar paradigm as Electronic Data Interchange (EDI)[27] to exchange information in a very structured and predefined way. The difference between EDI and XML is that EDI had a limited set of structures that were accepted, and a new information structure needed months or even years to go through all instances to become a new industry standard. XML allows anyone to create new data structures on the fly. While this is great for communication between two parties, it poses a problem for industry-wide exchange of information. If every company develops its own XML standards, this could lead to incompatibilities and additional overhead for converting the data. The problem is less the different order of information and more that some companies may omit data or add information that other companies will not be able to process.

To automate the value chain and the intercompany business processes, it is necessary to define XML data structures that contain all information for a certain industry with the option of omitting or adding information for the exchange of data. Many fear that the independent software vendors will drive incompatible versions of XML that best fit their own product strategies.

---

[27]EDI is a standard format for exchanging business data.

XML has been integrated by PeopleSoft, Oracle, and Baan into their Enterprise Resource Planning (ERP) systems. SAP is integrating XML into its Business Application Programming Interfaces (BAPI), which give developers access to the internal workings of the company's R/3 software. If the manufacturers of ERP software agree on a common XML format, developers will gain a standardized, vendor-neutral way to access human resources, financial, and manufacturing data stored in these systems. But if the software manufacturers are not able to find a common standard, XML will not resolve the problem of proprietary Application Programming Interfaces (APIs), which made life difficult in the past.

Today, vertical XML vocabularies have already been implemented, which enable single industries to exchange information. So far, these vocabularies have been introduced for the financial sector, the content management industry, air traffic control, and the footwear business. Although this helps each single industry, there still needs to be cross-industry standards within the business software products. Having several XML flavors accepted may still be valuable, but it would also be limiting and would not achieve the actual goal of reducing costs and increasing automation.

While the independent software manufacturers need to adopt a generic XML standard, at the same time, each industry needs to develop an XML schema. For example, it is necessary to define data structures for types of computers, reseller locations, configuration restrictions, and pricing models. These XML schemas are developed by standards bodies, such as the W3C, Commerce.Net,[28] RosettaNet,[29] and the Organization for the Advancement of Structured Information Standards (Oasis).[30] They are defining links within and between industries in a vendor-neutral way. E-business, supply chains, and other areas have already been addressed.

6.3.6 Standard XML Schemas

To ensure interoperability between systems, standard XML schemas are a must. The problem is that all the standards bodies are developing different standards for the same areas. For some time, it looked like the usual competitors would start a new standards battle over XML schemas just as we have seen battles over the right way to interpret HTML or the split in the industry over how Java should evolve.

---

[28]http://www.commerce.net/

[29]http://www.rosetta.net/

[30]http://www.oasis-open.org/

Two portals have been set up that represent the two industry camps that want XML to follow their ways. The first is XML.org,[31] which has been developed by Oasis and is backed by software makers such as IBM, Sun, Novell, and Oracle. The portal has been established since 1998.

On the other side of the fence, Microsoft launched its BizTalk[32] initiative in May 1999, which has been established as an XML design clearinghouse, developer resource, and repository for XML schemas. To make BizTalk a success, Microsoft is backed by ERP software manufacturers such as SAP, e-commerce software and service providers such as Ariba,[33] and partners in the industry such as Boeing.[34]

The XML portals provide a forum for XML schemas that have been designed for specific industries, such as the financial sector, health care, and insurance companies. Microsoft's BizTalk portal has raised suspicion among competitors that fear that Microsoft wants to take over the XML software application industry by defining its own standards without the consensus of the rest of the industry. Parts of the industry fear that this initiative could splinter the XML market.

Fortunately, Microsoft reconsidered its position regarding XML and joined Oasis in June 1999 to reduce the fears of the market. Microsoft's decision to back Oasis has eased several industry fears and made it possible to develop a common framework for XML applications on the Internet.

6.3.7 ebXML

The ebXML standard (Electronic Business XML) was developed by Oasis[35] and UN/CEFACT[36] to help make XML the worldwide language for electronic data transactions, much as English has become the standard vernacular for international business transactions. "The ebXML architecture begins with a business process and information model, maps the model to XML documents, and defines requirements for applications that process the documents and exchange them among trading partners." As with the UDDI registry, the ebXML registry lists a company's capabilities in a standard profile, allowing businesses to find one another through the registry, define agreements, and exchange XML messages that facilitate business transactions. "The goal is to allow all

---

[31]http://www.xml.org/
[32]http://www.biztalk.org/
[33]http://www.ariba.com/
[34]http://www.boeing.com/
[35]http://www.oasis.org/
[36]http://www.unece.org/cefact/

these things to be performed automatically, without human intervention, over the Internet."

6.4   Web Services Technologies

6.4.1   Introduction

While XML is probably the best-known technology, there are several other technologies in the Web services area that play an integral role in making the services work and making them accessible over the network. In this section, we give a brief overview on SOAP, UDDI, and HTTPR. While SOAP is used for encapsulating messages between heterogenous systems, UDDI is used for the definition of services. While the technical details are not so important for the theme of this book, it is important to know on a high level how they work and what their role is. HTTPR is a new transport protocol, developed by IBM to make the transport more reliable.

6.4.2   SOAP

The Simple Object Access Protocol (SOAP) is a standard for encoding inter-machine function calls in XML so they can be passed among heterogeneous systems. It enables any client application to call a function on any server machine, no matter what operating system each is running or what language each is written in.

SOAP is a lightweight protocol for exchange of information in a decentralized, distributed environment. It is an XML-based protocol that consists of the following elements:

- **Envelope**—This defines an overall framework for expressing what is in a message, who should deal with it, and whether it is optional or mandatory.

- **Header**—An optional element that contains header information.

- **Body**—The body element contains call and response information.

- **Fault**—An optional element that provides information about errors that occurred while processing the message.

SOAP can potentially be used in combination with a variety of other protocols. IBM's SOAP Security Extensions add an XML Digital Signature for messaging authentication, element-wise encryption for confidentiality, and attribute certificates for authorization.

A SOAP envelope marks the beginning and ending of a SOAP message. It can also specify encoding rules for serializing or marshalling the data over the wire. A SOAP header might contain a mail-to address or addresses, a payment code, or information about an RPC-style[37] interaction. There may be several headers in a SOAP envelope or none at all. The SOAP message body carries the data formatted as either a self-describing structure or as an RPC-style interface.

Although these components are described together as part of SOAP, they are functionally orthogonal. In particular, the envelope and the encoding rules are defined in different namespaces to promote simplicity through modularity.

6.4.3 UDDI

UDDI (Universal Description, Discovery, and Integration) is a consortium formed by Microsoft,[38] IBM,[39] and Ariba[40] for creating a standard for the description, registration, and discovery of Web services.

Within a more distributed model of the business part of the Internet, a flexible, open, yet comprehensive framework is required to embrace this diversity, encouraging agreement on standards, but also stimulating the innovation and differentiation that fuel the growth of e-business. The framework also needs to allow businesses to describe the business services that their Web sites offer, and how they can be accessed globally over the Web. A global solution must go beyond traditional directories, to also define standards for how businesses will share information, what information they need to make public, and what information they choose to keep private.

The resultant UDDI framework is "a set of databases where businesses can register their Web services as well as locate other Web services."[41] Applications use SOAP APIs to read or populate WSDL company profiles associated with UDDI. UDDI is a global, platform-independent, open framework to enable businesses to discover each other, define how they interact over the Internet, and share information in a global registry that will more rapidly accelerate the global adoption of e-business.

The UDDI specification provides a common set of SOAP APIs that enable the implementation of a service broker. The UDDI specification

---

[37]RPC is a protocol that one program can use to request a service from a program located in another computer in a network without having to understand network details.
[38]http://www.microsoft.com/
[39]http://www.ibm.com
[40]http://www.ariba.com/
[41]http://www.metagroup.com/cgi-bin/inetcgi/search/displayArticle.jsp?oid=22261

was outlined to help facilitate the creation, description, discovery, and integration of Web-based services. The motivation behind UDDI.org,[42] a partnership and cooperation of more than seventy industry and business leaders, is to define a standard for Business-To-Business (B2B) service interoperability.

UDDI has been organized as a sort of Yellow Pages for the Web, accessed via WSDL (a template for company information). WSDL supports ebXML registry features, which are similar to those of UDDI. In addition to competing with UDDI's database features, the Web services part of ebXML was once considered in competition with the SOAP standard. Fortunately, that debate was settled when OASIS brokered an agreement to integrate SOAP into ebXML. Today, these protocols are both overlapping (UDDI and ebXML) and complementary (SOAP and ebXML).

The solution is the creation of a service registry architecture that presents a standard way for businesses to build a registry, query other businesses, and enable those registered businesses to interoperate and share information globally in a distributed manner, just as the Internet was intended to be used. A Web services framework and public registry will enable buyers and sellers and marketplaces around the world to share information, connect Web services at low cost, support multiple standards, and prosper in the new digital economy.

UDDI is also a framework for Web services integration. It contains standards-based specifications for service description and discovery. The UDDI specification takes advantage of W3C and Internet Engineering Task Force (IETF) standards such as XML, HTTP, and Domain Name System (DNS) protocols. Additionally, cross-platform programming features are addressed by adopting early versions of the proposed SOAP messaging specifications found at the W3C Web site.

6.4.4 HTTPR

As HTTP unfortunately does not provide any QoS, an extension protocol is required to support the reliable transport of messages from one application program to another over the Internet, even in the presence of failures either of the network or the agents on either end. HTTPR is such a protocol. It is layered on top of HTTP. Specifically, HTTPR defines how metadata and application messages are encapsulated within the payload of HTTP requests and responses. HTTPR also provides protocol rules that make it possible to ensure that each message is delivered to its destination application exactly once or is reliably reported

---

[42]http://www.uddi.org/

as undeliverable. Smart agents can use the HTTPR protocol and some persistent storage capability to provide reliable messaging for application programs.

Layering HTTPR on HTTP in this way has the additional benefit that HTTPR can be used for reliable messaging with enterprises whose only presence on the Internet is a Web server behind a firewall admitting only Web-related traffic. Given the asymmetries of HTTP (client connects to server, client sends request, server sends response), it will be convenient to use the terms "client" and "server" even though messaging agents may, in other senses, regard themselves as peers. The agent initiating an HTTPR interaction does so by sending a POST command, in the HTTP sense, including with it a payload that identifies itself, specifies an HTTPR command and, if the command asks the server to accept messages, includes a batch of messages.

The server sends back a response, whose payload includes status information and, if the client requested, a batch of messages intended for that client. The messages, and any accompanying meta data, are uninterpreted bytes as far as HTTPR is concerned and are assigned no other meaning by it.

Each batch is assigned an identifier by its sender (either client or server), which is sent along as HTTPR metadata with the batch. Correctly functioning messaging agents will, in accordance with the specification, store this identifier and the state of their processing of that batch of messages, in stable storage at the appropriate times. In the event of a failure, this information can be recovered from stable storage and used by the messaging agents, through specified interchanges of that state information, to resolve the status of the batch of messages, thereby achieving exactly-once delivery.

6.4.5   BEEP

BEEP (Blocks Extensible Exchange Protocol) is an Internet standards-track protocol framework for Internet applications. BEEP can be considered a turbocharger for Internet applications that offers advanced features such as a standard application layer that supports dynamic, pluggable application "profiles." It has peer-to-peer, client-server, or server-to-server capabilities, and supports multiple channels over a single authenticated session. It also provides support for arbitrary MIME payloads, including XML.

BEEP gives network developers what they've long needed. It is a standard toolkit for building protocols quickly and conveniently. This means that new standard protocols can be easily developed and introduced. If you need to design a protocol that really fits your application,

BEEP can create it. BEEP provides a readily available set of building blocks for use in designing network protocols, solving common issues and letting developers focus on the specifics of their own protocol rather than reinventing the wheel.

6.4.6 Summary

If you look at the different applications based on XML, you can see how they lay the foundation for me-centric computing by providing a lot of base services that are required to support the service and information exchange on a platform-independent level.

6.5 Solution Stack

6.5.1 Introduction

While the full architecture is a work in progress, we explain what the building blocks are that need to work together. Delegating work, which is one key focus, depends on the "system" understanding the kinds of goals people have and how these can be performed by plans or processes that achieve those goals. Much of everyday life will be characterizable in this way. Individuals will have tailored user profiles that describe how they vary from standardized approaches with nominal defaults. This will require efforts to standardize the semantics of processes and how they can be achieved.

With Web services, information sources become components that you can (re)use and mix to enhance networking applications ranging from a simple currency converter, stock quotes, or dictionary to an integrated, portal-based travel planner, procurement workflow system, or consolidated purchasing system with processes across multiple sites.

For these reasons, the architecture of a "Web services stack" varies from domain to domain. The number and complexity of layers for the stack depend on the service it provides. Each stack requires Web services interfaces to get a Web services client to speak to an application server, or middleware component, such as CORBA, Java 2 Enterprise Edition (J2EE), or .NET. To enable the interface, SOAP is often used, as well as SOAP with Attachments (SwA), and Java RMI, among other Internet protocols.

Thus, starting with XML and Web standards, we will have to fill out the semantics of tasks, people, goals, resources, etc., so that devices from various manufacturers can work with services provided by various service providers to get work done. HP's e-speak concepts laid out much of this. UDDI and Web services are putting down the foundations for service-centric computing, service discovery, and service invocation. Much of the user interface experience will be all that users notice or care about, but behind the covers everything will have been rearranged to make possible delegation of work to agents.

Although XML has achieved universal acceptance as a standard format for exchanging data between disparate systems, developers still lack an equally accepted protocol for secure process-to-process communication. Several standards bodies, including the IETF[43], the W3C, OASIS and the UN/CEFACT, are addressing this challenge. Their goal has been to develop a set of specifications to allow any business of any size in any industry to do business with any other entity in any other industry anywhere in the world.

Agents will need to communicate with one another and be able to monitor, control, and report on their results. Users will want to reinforce the "system" for doing the right things and, perhaps punish it or criticize it for doing undesired things. Adaptive learning processes will need to convert this feedback into improved performance. Network economics should be exploited to get multiplicative effects from allowing all the knowledge-based elements to interact with others, so that when new areas of task competency are developed, they can immediately augment and combine with the other areas of competency a user already exploits.

Every single capability required for the future depicted thus far exists today somewhere in the IT labs of the world, and most of the capabilities have been at an adequate level for practical deployment for at least five years. The challenges can be divided into three different levels:

1. **Component capabilities**—such as speech understanding or text to speech.

2. **Agent architecture**—including task knowledge.

3. **Service economy**—including especially Web services.

The current capabilities and remaining challenges in each of these areas are described elsewhere in this book. 1 is discussed in Chapter 3, 2 in Chapter 7, and 3 at the beginning of Chapter 6.

To describe services, information, and processes in a software- and hardware-independent way, it is necessary to introduce a data exchange standard that is capable of being on all platforms and within all solutions. It has become quite clear that this standard will be XML,

---

[43]http://www.ietf.com/

which was introduced a few years ago and has become the *de facto* standard for the exchange of information.

Although there are a variety of Web services architectures, XML can be considered a universal client/server architecture that allows disparate systems to communicate with each other without using proprietary client libraries. This architecture simplifies the development process typically associated with client/server applications by effectively eliminating code dependencies between client and server, and the interface information is disclosed to the client via a configuration file encoded in a standard format (e.g., WSDL). Doing so allows the server to publish a single file for all target client platforms.

Figure 6.1 gives you an overview on the solution stack that will be discussed in the next section in more detail.

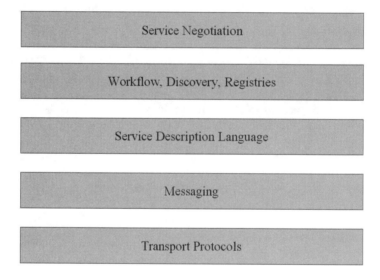

Figure 6.1. Solution Stack

6.5.2   Service Negotiation

If we look at the solution stack (Figure 6.1), we can see that Service Negotiation is the top layer. On this layer, the two parties involved in a certain transaction can negotiate and agree on the protocols that should be used to aggregate Web services. This layer is also referred to as the Process Definition layer, covering document, workflow, transactions, and process flow (see also Figure 6.2). The protocols that are negotiated are not only about the data formats and how they are transmitted (e.g., XML and Corba), but typically also the security parameters and quality of service parameters are negotiated in this step (e.g., only encrypted traffic and 256 kbps minimum throughput).

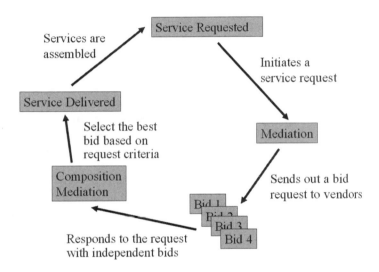

Figure 6.2. Service Negotiation Diagram

It is important to note that the service negotiation layer should not require a manual intervention, but should work autonomously and hidden from the user. It should support rapidly changing user requirements, for example, if a user wants to start a video session or an application requires a database update. It should also be possible to support changing network capabilities; a network should be able to tell the user of costs on a new link, for example. And it should support network-to-network negotiation.

6.5.3 Workflow, Discovery, Registries

The WDR (Workflow, Discovery, and Registries) layer is used to create workflows using Web Services Flow Language (WSFL) and Microsoft XLANG, which are XML languages to describe workflow processes and spawn them.

WSFL specifies the interfaces of Web services. It determines whether the Web services should be treated as an activity in one workflow or as a series of activities. While WSFL complements WSDL, XLANG is an extension of WSDL. WSFL supports the flow and global models. The flow model describes business processes that a collection of Web services needs to achieve. The global model describes how Web services interact with one another. XLANG, on the other hand, allows orchestration of Web services into business processes and composite Web services. WSFL provides a better model presentation, while XLANG is better with the long-running interaction of Web services. Web services can be declared as private to avoid the exposure of details to public applications.

Web services that can be exposed may, for example, get information on credit validation activities from a public directory or registry, such as UDDI. There are many directories that can be used in conjunction with Web services for business-to-business (B2B) transactions in a complex Enterprise Application Integration (EAI) infrastructure under certain conditions. ebXML, E-Services Village, BizTalk.org, and XML.org are probably the best-known directory services. Web services is still primarily an interfacing architecture, and it needs an integration platform to which to connect. The integration platform covers the integration an existing applications that cannot work as Web services yet.

Hewlett-Packard, IBM, Microsoft, and SAP launched implementation of their UDDI sites that conformed to the latest specification, including enhanced support for deploying public and private Web service registries and the interface (SOAP/HTTP API) that the client could use to interact with the registry server. In addition to the public UDDI Business Registry sites, enterprises can also deploy private registries on their intranets to manage internal Web services using the UDDI specification. Access to internal Web service information may also be extended to a private network of business partners.

6.5.4 Service Description Language

The Web service description language (WSDL) is required to connect to a Web service. The WSDL is used to describe the communications in some structured way, based on standardized communications protocols and message formats. It addresses this need by defining an XML grammar for describing network services as collections of communication endpoints capable of exchanging messages. WSDL provides documentation for distributed systems and serves as a recipe for automating the details involved in applications communication.

With it, service requesters can search for and find the information on services via UDDI, which, in turn, returns the WSDL reference that can be used to bind to the service.

To simplify the description of the structure of data in a common format, the Web Service Conversational Language (WSCL) can help developers. The structured data is described in XML Schema, which can be recognized by customers, Web browsers, or indeed any XML-enabled software programs.

6.5.5   Messaging

The Messaging layer provides standardized technologies that act as the envelope for XML-based messages, covering message packaging, routing, guaranteed delivery, and security. Most commonly used is SOAP. Messages are exchanged based on the status of various Web services as the work progresses.

SOAP describes the data items exchanged at a high level; that is, it treats them as documents. These documents may or may not contain descriptions of their content, but they all share one common property: they are structured. Structure is given to these documents by describing them in XML format. SOAP itself is described as a sequence of XML tags, thus telling what the content of a SOAP message is. SOAP can be used to make remote procedure calls. In this way, the Body element of the SOAP message contains a tag that represents the name of the function that is to be called at the receiver side. The receiver will append the text Reply to the tag's name and return it to the sender.

6.5.6   Transport Protocols

The transport protocols layer provides mechanisms and technologies to connect systems and communicate data between these systems. These protocols include the standards ones, like Hypertext Transfer Protocol (HTTP), Secure HTTP (HTTPS), File Transfer Protocol (FTP), and Simple Mail Transfer Protocol (SMTP), new transport protocols are about to be established: DIME, HTTPR, and BEEP. DIME (Direct Internet Message Encapsulation) is a lightweight, binary message format designed to encapsulate one or more application-defined payloads into a single message construct. HTTPR is a protocol that offers the reliable delivery of HTTP packets between the server and client. BEEP is a generic application protocol kernel for connection-oriented, asynchronous interactions.

6.6 Examples

6.6.1 Cooltown

Cooltown is a vision presented by Hewlett-Packard of future mobility, connectivity, community, and transformation based on open standards and user needs. As Hewlett-Packard puts it: "In Cooltown technology transforms human experience from consumer lifestyles to business processes by enabling mobility."

In Cooltown, people, places, and things are first-class citizens of the connected world, wired and wireless. It is a place where Web services meet the physical world, where humans are mobile, devices and services are federated and context-aware, and everything has a Web presence. In Cooltown, technology transforms human experience from consumer lifestyles to business processes by enabling mobility. Cooltown is infused with the energy of the online world, and Web-based appliances and e-services give you what you need, when and where you need it for work, play, and life.

The Cooltown vision of a responsive world of mobile services requires clear, creative thinking about technology. For several years, HP Labs has been working at the intersection of nomadicity, appliances, networking, and the Web. The model for this research is one of open collaboration and partnership with others who share similar goals. In Cooltown, even a wristwatch has the capability of becoming an intelligent Web appliance.

Above all else, creating a Cooltown ecosystem requires a community of like-minded people who believe in open participation, investing in the Web, and creating real solutions that add value to people's lives. Hewlett-Packard's goal is to help bring that community together, to openly share ideas and implementations, and to make a real contribution to the Web and to the world.

In Cooltown, personalization can lead to richer, more efficient daily experiences. For instance, a variety of useful objects can sense your presence and seamlessly cooperate to give you enhanced customer service. Smart devices in your pockets become your personal remote control for Web services. On command, they can access and capture information wirelessly transmitted by devices called beacons. These beacons broadcast a URL for the object or place, pointing you to a Web presence providing product information, entertainment, advertising, or a gateway to e-services for the item or the location. Capturing information from a beacon on your mobile device is like bookmarking the physical world. In effect, your pocket device becomes a remote control for the world at large (see also the Web site in Figure 6.3).

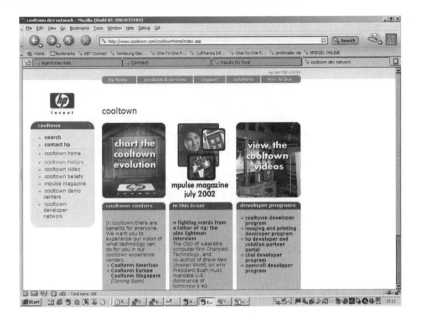

Figure 6.3. Cooltown Web Site

In Cooltown, URL bookmarks can be gathered from online interactions, messaging services, synchronization applications, etc. Once
bookmarked, URLs can be sent to remote Web locations, or beamed directly to a variety of Web appliances using a beaming technology called
"e-squirt." Using this technology, your mobile phone or handheld wireless device can "squirt" the URL, enabling you to instantly put presentations on a screen, documents on a printer, or music on a connected
stereo.

Other examples are numerous. A student may use an e-service that
can download a Spanish dictionary from her computer to her watch.
Once the program is downloaded, the young Spanish student is able to
access the knowledge stored in everyday objects via beacons—instantly
translating that information into Spanish.

In Cooltown, emergency services are made more effective through
the use of smart, connected appliances. Technology saves lives by providing a vital link to emergency medical services. Your personal portal
becomes a critical access point for service providers who need to know
the status of your physical condition. The result: fast, informed medical attention via biometric detection, personal portals, and medical
e-services.

For firemen, a Cooltown-enabled visor is actually a context-aware appliance with the ability to display real-time building and victim information. The data displayed on the fireman's visor is provided by, and accessed through, a Web-linking appliance. As he passes through the rooms, the information is updated by the space manager, which maintains the Web presence for the house.

Even the cat has a Web presence. She is linked to the environment via a location identifier that is emitted by a beacon embedded in her collar and acquired by the space manager. The cat's Web presence is automatically located in that space and made available for immediate use by the fireman's smart, connected visor.

Cooltown core technologies create a Web presence for your car that is linked to the car's electrical, mechanical, and information subsystems. The car is a rolling Cooltown space, a physical location that also provides a corresponding mobile Web presence for the vehicle, the driver, and driving-related services. To maximize safety and simplicity, the driver's interface uses multi-modal voice browsing that allows him to control interactions with the vehicle while he drives without having to reduce concentrate at the road ahead.

When Cooltown technologies are used in combination with other open-building-block capabilities such as wireless communications, GPS, short-range wireless networking, and smart handheld devices, the car is no longer simply a means of transportation. It becomes a participant in a vast ecosystem of automotive and transportation services. And the service station becomes an island of connectivity, an e-oasis where a variety of helpful transactions—from car repair to alternative transportation options—are effortlessly fulfilled.

Cooltown is more than a futuristic vision; it is also a pragmatic architectural approach for researchers and developers to create Cooltown services and environments and to participate in a community of like-minded experts.

6.6.2 .NET Passport

Microsoft .NET Passport (see Figure 6.4) is a suite of e-business services that allows purchasing goods and services online. Passport provides its members with the Single Sign In and Express Purchase services at participating sites, reducing the amount of information that has to be remembered or retyped.

The idea behind Passport is to increase sales for businesses and help build stronger relationships with customers by streamlining the purchase process and by providing a high-quality, more secure online experience for a large member base.

When members sign in to a participating site, the system sends the members' zip code, country/region, and city information. Members can also choose to provide their nickname, e-mail address, age, gender, and language preference to participating sites.

Consumers can store billing and shipping information in their .NET Passport Wallet. When using the Express Purchase service, members can see the contents of their .NET Passport, select the data to be sent, and then send their encrypted information to a participating merchant site with a single click.

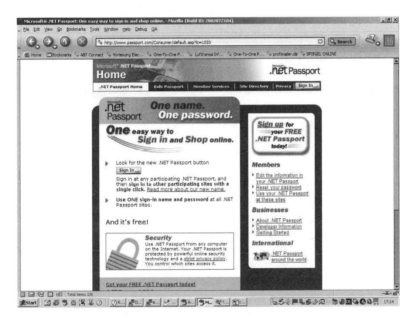

Figure 6.4. Passport Web Site

Besides these two services, the Microsoft Kids .NET Passport service is an example of providing children with a positive, safe online experience. Kids .NET Passport helps parents protect their children's privacy online by allowing parents to decide whether their children can use services provided by participating Web sites that collect and/or disclose personally identifiable information. These services can include newsletters, discussion groups, pen pal programs, wish lists, and contests.

While Passport sounds like a great solution, many privacy groups fear that too much information about users is handed over to Microsoft. On one hand, it is not clear what Microsoft will do with the data. On the other hand, Microsoft is the number one target for hackers due to the security holes in the software that they provide, making it a security risk to leave these services openly available on the Internet. Hackers could try to steal the information and reuse it for their own benefit.

6.7 Conclusion

The way Web services are envisioned, companies acquire publishing information from a registry (such as ebXML or UDDI), build an implementation that meets the requirements, and then publish their services to the registry. Other companies then discover a service listed in the registry, comply with the established standard, and conduct business. Once agreed-upon standards and rules of engagement have been met, applications can take over, removing human interaction from the overhead of transacting business. In this model, using existing infrastructure, applications may exchange information regarding services that a company wants to provide and consume. Moreover, applications may continue to poll the registry for other applications (companies) that provide identical services under more favorable terms.

XML is about enabling remote access to services through a standardized approach to laying out data and service requests using a lingua franca for machine-to-machine intercommunication. With such an alphabet, we can get on with the task of asking what kinds of interactions people want their machines to undertake for them. We can determine how machines might be constrained to behave so that they will tend to achieve their masters' objectives within appropriate resource, time, and security constraints. And finally, we can determine appropriate ways of dealing with outages, violated expectations, delays, inconsistencies, etc., that would normally make machine-to-machine interactions too brittle for everyday users to rely upon for highly personalized (low volume, specialized, customized) services.

The next chapter provides information on agents and how they can be of use for the me-centric environment.

Chapter 7

AGENTS: IGNITING MACHINE-TO-MACHINE WORK

7.1 Software Agents

7.1.1 Introduction

Software agents are probably the key technology in me-centric computing, and they act as the glue for the whole architecture. Software agents are used for communication between intelligent components of the network, and they represent users on the network. With intelligent agents, it becomes possible for the first time for people who use computers to reduce their workload, because they can offload it to these agents. People can do more without having to work more. Therefore, it is very important to understand what agents are and how they work.

Recent trends have made it clear that software complexity will continue to increase dramatically in the coming decades. The dynamic and distributed nature of both data and applications requires that software not merely respond to requests for information, but intelligently anticipate, adapt, and actively seek ways to support users. Not only must these systems assist in coordinating tasks among humans, they must also help manage cooperation among distributed programs.

In response to these requirements, the efforts of scientists from several different fields have begun to coalesce around a common broad agenda: the development of software agents. In software development, several levels of abstraction have taken place to make programming more efficient and easier. Software developers and system designers use high-level abstractions in building complex software to manage complexity and to make programming more natural. An abstraction focuses on the important and essential properties of a problem and hides the incidental components of that problem.

It started out with methods and functions, and went on to objects and agents. An object is a high-level abstraction that describes methods and attributes of a software component. An agent, however, is an extremely high-level software abstraction that provides a convenient and powerful way to describe a complex software entity. Rather than being defined in terms of methods and attributes, an agent is defined in terms of its behavior. This is important because programming an agent-based system is primarily a matter of specifying agent behavior instead of identifying classes, methods, and attributes. It is much easier and more natural to state desired results (give objectives, propose goals, delegate tasks) than it is to tell one *how* to accomplish them or what behaviors should be done. This is the necessary and sufficient condition for delegating work: Tell the agent what you want the conditions to be (at the end, along the way, etc.), and leave the agent to figure out how to achieve them. Agents provide a new way of managing complexity because they provide a new way of describing a complex system or process. Using agents, it is easy to define a system in terms of agent-mediated processes.

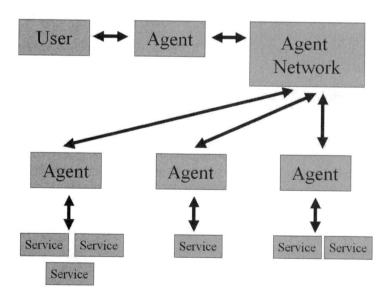

Figure 7.1. The User-Agent Relationship

If you look at Figure 7.1, you can see how the relationship between user and agent works. There you can see a user, an associated agent, and a set of agents that are communicating with the personal agent through the agents network. Work is delegated by the user, accepted by the associated agent and partly delegated to the other agents. These agents execute their tasks and report back to the associated agent, which in turn reports back to the user. The agents interact with legacy systems, such as payment systems and order entry systems. The key difference to today's computing paradigm is that you do not tell the agent how to do the work, but you ask the agent to accomplish something.

A software agent has a common set of features: It is autonomous, communicative, and perceptive. This means that the agent is capable of operating as a standalone process and performing actions without user intervention. It can communicate with the user, other software agents, or other software processes, and is able to perceive and respond to changes in its environment.

While software agents must be autonomous, communicative, and perceptive, they can have different levels of competence as determined by their programs—that is, their task specifications. If the competence is limited by the task specification, that would be a failure of the user's to ask for the right thing. If the agent were, on the other hand, given a good and effective task specification but seemed incompetent at accomplishing it, that would be a reflection of ignorance, limited problem-solving ability, or some other inherent weakness.

The goal is to make software agents as useful as possible, which in turn requires that we be able to task them in the most natural possible way. Just as we would task an assistant or a craftsman. That in turn requires that they understand the kinds of aspirations we have, the way we communicate those to them, and what they would need to do to ensure correct interpretation of the inferred tasks and effective and efficient accomplishment of those tasks. If we could easily tell them what we wish and they could always get it right and do the right thing, we'd find them almost super-natural, like an extraordinary personal assistant.

The system developer no longer has to design communication protocols and message formats. The agent provides this capability as part of the basic agent mechanism. Agents have the inherent capability to build models of their environment, monitor the state of that environment, and reason and make decisions based on that state. The software developer simply needs to specify what the agents are to do in any given situation.

Consider, for example, the system design issues involved in building a content management application that ties together content editors, content managers, designers, and Webmasters, and automates much of the content approval process. Building this system using current technology is a complex and difficult task, because the system decomposition forces the developer to deal with relatively low-level concepts (e.g., content input form, layout, approvals) when defining the overall system architecture.

In addition, significant design time must be dedicated to defining the communications protocol and interfaces that will allow the company to exchange data with external contributors for text and images. In an agent-oriented system design, the system solution might include a text collection agent, a workflow agent, an approval agent, etc. The focus is placed on the behavior of each of these agents and communication between agents. The problem is made much easier because the level of abstraction is much higher and the programming problem becomes one of specifying agent behavior. Business people, for example, can easily control the process, as they understand what is happening. They do not have to deal with source code or application interfaces anymore.

Software agents provide an ideal mechanism for integrating legacy systems with new data systems. Agents can be used to perform data translation and implement data systems interfaces that meet a wide variety of requirements (see also Figure 7.2). In many applications, system developers have legacy code that performs some unique function that is needed in their new applications. A software agent can be used to invoke and execute this legacy code, leveraging the value of the existing code base.

Through agents, it is possible to delegate work. To delegate work, it is necessary to be sure that this work is done properly and on time. However, by definition, delegation implies relinquishing control of a task to an entity with different memories, experiences, and possibly agendas. Thus, by not doing something ourselves, we open ourselves up to a certain risk that the agent will do something wrong. This means that we have to balance the risk that the agent will do something wrong with the trust that it will do it right. This decision must be based on both our internal mental model of what the agent will do (hence, how much we trust it) and the domain of interest (hence, how much a mistake will cost us).

A very important feature of agents is the graceful degradation in case of problems. When communicating with an agent, a communications mismatch or domain mismatch can occur. This means that either

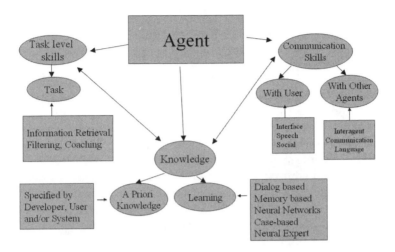

Figure 7.2. The Agent Model

the two parties do not understand each other very well or the parties are talking about the same task, but in different environments. So if the agent is not sure what to do, it should only fulfill the subtasks it is sure about and request another communication round with the user, before executing the rest of the subtasks. This is generally a better outcome and gives the user more trust in the agent's performance.

The user and the agent are essentially collaborating in constructing a contract. The user is specifying what actions should be performed on his or her behalf, and the agent is specifying what it can do and providing results. This is often best viewed as a two-way conversation, in which each party may ask questions of the other to verify that both sides are in agreement about what is going on. As such, the two parties interact more as peers in agent-oriented systems; in non-agent-oriented systems, the user typically "commands," through some interface, a particular action, and is probably never asked a question about the action unless something goes wrong. In a strictly agentless situation (e.g., a text editor), the feel of the interaction is different than when an agent is present, primarily due to the discourse-oriented nature of the interaction with the agent and the more "stimulus-response" or "non-conversational" feel of the text editor. Once the agent has understood what the user wants it to do, the agent can start the same contracting with other agents, services, devices, or other humans to make sure that the task is executed in the way agreed upon by the original contract between the initiator and his or her agents.

7.1.2 Typical Use of Agents

Software agents can be used in a variety of environments and applications. They reduce the complexity of formerly highly complex systems, but not in all cases. Software agents cannot simplify every type of problem. Agents can be used, for example, in applications that involve distributed computation or communication between components. They can also be used in applications where the software agents need to analyze messages or objects coming from the network and need to respond in an automated manner. Agents are, therefore, well suited for most Internet applications (see Table 7.1).[1]

In applications that can be automated, agents can play an important role, as they maintain a description of their processing state and the state of the world around them. These agents can operate without input or intervention of a user. Today, these agents are already used in applications such as process automation, workflow management, and robotics.

Since agents have the ability to draw inferences, they can easily perform sequences of complex operations based on messages they receive, their own internal beliefs, and their overall goals and objectives.

7.1.3 Software Agencies

Software agents can work on their own, but show their power when working together with other software agents. In this way, it is possible to create a highly competent answer from a set of simple agents. A collection of software agents that communicate and cooperate with each other is called an *agency*. System designers using agents must consider the capabilities of each individual agent and how multiple agents can work together.

The agent-based approach allows the system designer to implement the system using multiple agents, with each agent specialized for a particular task. For example, an electronic commerce application might have buyer agents, seller agents, stocking agents, database agents, e-mail agents, etc. All of these agents need to communicate with each

---

[1]For more information, see also: Anderson, R. H., and J. J. Gillogly, *Rand Intelligent Terminal Agent (RITA): Design Philosophy*, Rand Corporation Technical Memorandum R-1809-ARPA, February, 1976.

Agent Systems

Agents are ideally suited for a wide variety of applications, but they are particularly well suited for the following types of applications:

- **Process and Workflow Automation**—In companies, these agents can reduce human interaction across the supply chain, for example.

- **Electronic Commerce**—Agents can find the lowest price, the fastest delivery, or the best product on behalf of the buyer.

- **Distributed Problem Solving**—When trying to solve a problem, agents can swarm out to other systems either to find a solution or to use the CPU power of that system to solve the problem.

- **Internet Applications**—Business-to-Business (B2B) applications, for example, which involve complex workflows with partners and suppliers, can be handled through agents.

Table 7.1. Agent Systems

other and must have the capability of working together to achieve a common set of goals.

7.1.4 Competence Levels

Agents can be constructed with a wide range of capabilities. One of the advantages of the agent-based approach is that many times a complex processing function can be broken into several smaller, simpler ones. Since each individual agent can be crafted to be an expert in solving a specific problem or performing a particular task, you can build systems that exhibit complex behaviors by using a collection of relatively simple agents.

Sometimes, however, we do need to build agents that are quite smart. With the agent-based approach, you can implement agents with sophisticated intellectual capabilities such as the ability to reason, learn, or plan. In addition, intelligent software agents can utilize extensive amounts of knowledge about their problem domain. This means that the underlying agent architecture must support sophisticated reasoning, learning, planning, and knowledge representation.

Sophisticated software agents can be very difficult to build if you are building them from scratch. You will need specialized skills and knowledge in a variety of areas including agent architecture, communications technology, reasoning systems, knowledge representation, agent communication languages, and protocols. If you want to add machine learning or machine planning capabilities, you will need skill in these areas as well. If you don't possess these specialized skills and knowledge, you should use an agent construction toolkit. Agent construction toolkits allow software developers without agent expertise to quickly and easily build software agents.

7.1.5 Trust

We expect it will take quite a while for people to trust that their agents will do the right thing (see also Table 7.2). For example, in the United States in June 2002, TiVo recorded a replay of a baseball game rather than the World Cup match that viewers had requested. This seriously affected customers' trust in the system. The reason was that ESPN decided to put the show on its premier channel ESPN, rather than ESPN2 as it had advertised and which was listed in the online schedules. TiVo was, in fact, blameless.

So each agent and all agents will have to earn our trust through demonstrated reliable performance and a sense of responsibility to get the right result, whatever it takes. The day after the World Cup match, users received an e-mail (see excerpt in Figure 7.3) from TiVo that explained what needed to be done in order to record the right game. A really good service would have communicated not back to the user but to the user's delegated agent (on the TiVo box), and made the appropriate change in behavior on time.

In the United Kingdom, TiVo played even more with the users' trust by recording a show that was paid for by the production company, so every user of TiVo found this show recorded on his or her device, no matter whether this was desired or not.

To increase the trust in agents, the agent technology needs to verify the results of previous activities if required and needs to put updating agreements with service providers in place, in case of changes. If the TiVo agent and the TiVo service had put updating agreements in place, people would have seen the right program. On the other hand, agents should do what the user wants and should not be doing things other people want.

Agent Trust Building

Agents can do their job well only if the user trusts them. Therefore, the agent needs to build a trustworthy relationship through
the following actions:

- **Understand User's Intent**—The agent should paraphrase
  the intent of the user, so the user gets a feeling that the agent
  really did understand what was requested.

- **Understand User's Context**—The agent should demon-
  strate understanding about the user's context and values
  (e.g., money, time, concern for privacy, concern for relationships, attitudes and manners of speech, value of other people's time, resources, etc.).

- **Provide Reports**—The agent should provide intermediate
  reports and results to the user to "keep the relationship
  warm" with the user.

- **Possess Reasonable Reaction to Errors**—The agent
  should provide a reasonable and caring reaction to errors
  and exceptions

- **Ask for Help**—In truly novel circumstances, where the
  agent does not have any experience, it should ask the user
  for support.

Table 7.2. Agent Trust Building

7.2 Mobile Agents

7.2.1 Introduction

The ultimate goal of me-centric computing is to allow fast and pervasive access to information and services, through desktop machines at
work, school, and home, through televisions, phones, pagers, and car
dashboards, from anywhere and everywhere. Mobile code and mobile
agents are essential for allowing such access.

Mobile agents are programs that can migrate from host to host in a
network, at times and to places of their own choosing. An agent is an
autonomous, intelligent, collaborative, adaptive computational entity.

```
Message-ID: <200206210136.g5L1aMY11395@sjsapqa.engr.tivo.com>
From:  TiVo Customer Care <tivocare@tivo.com>
To:  rick@radicalsimplicity.com
Subject:  Last minute change to World Cup schedule
Date:  Fri, 21 Jun 2002 03:36:22 +0200

Dear TiVo subscriber,

This is an important announcement for World Cup fans.  Effective
June 20, 2002, ESPN has changed the station for the quarterfinal
matches between USA/Germany and England/Brazil.  They have both
changed from ESPN2 to ESPN.

Due to the short notice of this station change, TiVo will not be
able to update your program guide information prior to the game.
To ensure that this match is recorded:

...
```

Figure 7.3. Excerpt from TiVo E-Mail to Customers

Here, intelligence is the ability to infer and execute needed actions, and seek and incorporate relevant information, given certain goals. The state of the running program is saved, transported to the new host, and restored, allowing the program to continue where it left off. Mobile agent systems differ from process-migration systems in that the agents move when they choose, typically through a "jump" or "go" statement, whereas in a process-migration system, the system decides when and where to move the running process (typically to balance CPU load). Mobile agents differ from "applets," which are programs downloaded as the result of a user action, and then executed from beginning to end on one host.

Mobile agents are an effective choice for many applications, for several reasons, including improvements in latency and bandwidth of traditional client-server applications and reducing vulnerability to network disconnection. Although not all applications will need mobile agents, many other applications will find mobile agents the most effective implementation technique for all or part of their tasks.

Although we believe that current trends in Internet technology and usage lead to the use of mobile agents, several technical and non-technical hurdles must be addressed along the way. These hurdles represent significant but not insurmountable challenges, so we predict that many major Internet sites will accept mobile agents within a few years. If we look at mobile agents, they are built on the same feature set as immobile software agents. They are autonomous, which allows them to pursue an agenda independently of its user. This requires aspects of periodic action, spontaneous execution, and initiative, in that the agent must be able to take preemptive or independent actions that will eventually benefit the user.

Agents also need to be personalizable. This allows agents to support people to do some tasks better. Since people don't all do the same tasks, and even those who share the same task do it in different ways, an agent must be able to learn new aspects of a given task. Ideally, there should be components of learning built into the agent. The typical end-user should not have to program the agent. The agent should know what to do. Some agents can already learn by looking over the user's shoulder. Another very important aspect is the memory of the agent to make sure that whatever the agent learned can be reused next time.

A very important aspect of agents is the ability to communicate with the user. The agent should be able to give some feedback to assure the user that the agent is executing the right task with the right parameters. This generally requires a discourse with the agent, a two-way feedback in which both parties make their intentions and abilities known, and mutually agree on something resembling a contract about what is to be done and by whom. This conversation may be very short, involving only a request and a response, or a higher-level discourse in which the user and the agent repeatedly interact, but both parties remember previous interactions.

7.2.2 Mobile Code

If we come back to the levels of abstraction, we can see that in the past it was difficult to exchange code between devices, operating systems, or services. In the past, mobile code was usually machine-dependent and could run only on very specific machine architectures. Also, obtaining such code involved the whole process of searching for applications on FTP sites, downloading the applications, sometimes compiling them, and then running them on the local machine.

With mobile code, the code has been encapsulated to make the movement of the code possible. Mobile code is code that traverses a network in its lifetime and executes on a destination machine. Mobile code allows for pushing or pulling code (i.e., procedures or even programs) to or from remote sites, and for executing the transferred code at these sites. Examples for mobile code systems are Java applets, remote evaluation (RPCs where the procedures are transferred before calling them), or even Postscript files (which are programs that are executed on printers, for example).

Mobile code is the basis for mobile agents. Mobile code allows distributed systems and the abstractions to be more flexible to build and use. Mobile code enables distributed systems to adapt to application needs. Rather than fixing the interface to a resource and the pattern of interaction with it, a minimal interface can be defined and code implementing higher-level interfaces placed alongside it as required.

These higher-level interfaces can be application-specific, allowing for interaction patterns that were unknown at the time the resource was made available. Sending code close to a resource can also reduce network usage because the point of interaction with it moves.

Through mobile code, a richer functionality can be given to the interaction between processes. This means that application-level operations can be done on the network. By sending higher-order language features across the network, distributed components can be tightly bound together when they communicate. At the same time, familiar distributed systems can be built using mobile code.

Mobile code helps to support user mobility. Personalized environments that support state-saving can follow a user between computers. Heterogeneous state-saving allows a user's programs to be relocated between computers. By using a mobile code system with language support for state-saving, applications can direct arbitrary component migration without priming program servers with specific support.

One big issue connected to mobile code is security. Unfortunately, not all mobile code is good, but some code comes in the form of a virus trying to destroy data on other computer systems. Viruses are a kind of mobile code and, at the most abstract level, can't be distinguished from mobile agents; therefore, it is necessary to implement some security measures to reduce the risk of a virus infection. When mobile code arrives from an unknown or untrusted source, it would be a good idea to ensure that the software is safe to run. This can be done by applying certain restrictions to this untrusted software.

Untrusted mobile code should not overwrite critical system data, thereby causing a system crash. It should also only access memory in its own address space and not memory belonging to other applications and processes. Illegal disk operations, as a default policy, should also be forbidden.

The application's safety policy is a set of restrictions placed upon locally run untrusted code to ensure that the program does not behave in a manner that is detrimental to the system or to the system security. In Java, this is called the "the sandbox model," because each agent is restricted to operate in its own "sandbox." This policy should include at least the following safety properties: control flow safety, memory safety and stack safety. This means that mobile code should never jump to and start executing code that lies outside of the program's own code segment. All function calls should be to valid function entry points and function returns should return to the location from which the function was called. It should also never be allowed to access random locations in memory. The program should only access memory in its own static data segment, live system heap memory that has been explicitly allocated to it, and valid stack frames. And last, but not least, the mobile code should be allowed to access only the top of the stack. Access to other areas of the stack should be completely restricted.

Depending on the environment in which agents should run, additional and more complicated safety policies can be put in place. Only if these policies are in place and correctly enforced should one allow mobile code to be run on its computing device.

7.3 Challenges with Agents

7.3.1 Technical Hurdles

As discussed above, agents can help in many areas, but there are some hurdles that need to be overcome before software agents can become really useful. Therefore, it is important to discuss these shortly and show how they can be overcome. Most of these challenges are more of a theoretical problem, which can be easily solved.

One of these areas is the performance issue. Current mobile agent systems save network latency and bandwidth at the expense of higher loads on the service machines, since agents are often written in a (relatively) slow interpreted language for portability and security reasons. Another reason is that agents must be injected into an appropriate execution environment upon arrival. Thus, in the absence of network disconnections, agents (especially those that need to perform only a few operations against each resource) often take longer to accomplish a task than more traditional implementations, since the time savings from avoiding intermediate network traffic is currently less than the time penalties from slower execution and the migration overhead. Fortunately, significant progress has been made on just-in-time compilation (most notably for Java), software fault isolation, and other techniques, which allows agents to execute nearly as fast as natively compiled code. These efforts should lead to a system in which accepting and executing a mobile agent involves only slightly more load than if the service machine had provided the agent's functionality as a built-in, natively compiled procedure. But the natural speed growth of networks and hardware make this point less and less significant over time.

Nearly all mobile agent systems allow a program to move freely among heterogeneous machines. For example, in Java, the code is first compiled into some platform-independent representation called byte-codes, and upon its arrival at the target machine is either further compiled into native code or executed inside an interpreter. For mobile agents to be widely used, however, the code must be portable across mobile-code systems, since it is unreasonable to expect that the computing community will settle on a single mobile-code system. Making code portable across systems will require a significant standardization effort. As Java was developed with agents in mind, it is quite clear that Java is the de facto standard for agents, so standardization is already somewhat at hand.

As discussed above, one of the biggest issues in agent technology is security. It is possible now to deploy a mobile agent system that adequately protects a machine against malicious agents. Viruses are nothing more than malicious agents. Some challenges still remain. First, a technology needs to be established that allows protecting the machines without excessively limiting agent access rights. The agent should also be protected from malicious machines that could try to infuse malicious code into the agent, and protection for groups of machines that are not under single administrative control needs to be implemented. An inadequate solution to any of these three problems will severely limit the use of mobile agents in a truly open environment such as the Internet. Many companies are presently working on solutions that will make agent technology more secure.

7.3.2   Non-Technical Hurdles

Besides the technical challenges discussed above, there remain several non-technical issues that may deter the widespread adoption of mobile-agent technology. Internet sites must have a strong motivation to overcome inertia, justify the cost of upgrading their systems, and adopt the technology. While the technological arguments above are convincing, they are not sufficient for most site administrators. In the end, the technology will be installed only if it provides substantial improvements to the end-user's experience: more useful applications, each with fast access to information, support for disconnected operation, and other important features.

One problem today in getting mobile agents to the market is to define the appropriate killer application. The "mobile agent" paradigm is
in many respects a new and powerful programming paradigm, and its
use leads to faster performance in many cases. Nonetheless, most particular applications can be implemented just as cleanly and efficiently
with a traditional technique, although different techniques would be
used for different applications. Thus, the advantages of mobile agents
are modest when any particular application is considered in isolation.
TiVo has an agent in it, for example. Anybody can create an agent using any technology he or she wants, but people aren't creating enough
of them so far and they don't work together economically and effectively
yet, because that part of the architecture hasn't matured. This argument can easily be turned around, as we are approaching a me-centric
computing environment. This environment is full of killer applications
that require agents—in fact, it will be difficult to find scenarios without
agents.

Another problem that may arise is the fact that it is unlikely that
any Internet service will want to jump directly from existing client-
server systems to full mobile agent systems. A clear evolutionary path
from current systems to mobile agent systems must be provided. Our
me-centric approach allows for easy transition.

Today "applets" (mobile code) are widely used for better interaction
with the user, and the associated commercial technology is improving
rapidly (e.g., faster Java virtual machines with just-in-time compilation). From applets, the next step is proxy sites that accept mobile code
sent from a mobile client. In all likelihood, such proxies will be first
provided by existing Internet service providers (ISPs). Since the sole
function of the proxy sites will be to host mobile code, and since the
ISPs will receive direct payment for the proxy service in the form of
user subscriptions, the ISPs will accept the perceived security risks of
mobile code. Once mobile code security is further tested on proxy sites,
the services themselves will start to accept "servlets," mobile code sent
from the client directly to the server (or from the proxy to the server).
Once servlets become widely used, and as developers address the issue
of protecting mobile code from malicious servers, services will start to
accept mobile agents.

Another critical evolutionary path is the migration of agent technology from intranets to the Internet. Mobile code technologies will
appear first in the relatively safe intranet environment. For example, a large company might find mobile agents the most convenient
way to provide its employees with a wide range of access to its internal databases. Companies with intranets tend to be early adopters of

new (useful) technology, because their administrators have more control over the intranet and the technologies used therein than over the Internet; control means that security is less of a concern, and wide deployment of agent support services can be encouraged. As the technologies mature in intranets, site administrators will become comfortable with them, and their practicality, safety, and potential uses will become clear. Then they will find their way into the Internet.

A final important hurdle is the problem of revenue flow and commercial image. If agents are used instead of Web browsers, the number of human visits to the Web pages will presumably decrease, and the advertisements will not be seen anymore. This means that many sites that offer their service for free (by showing banner ads) need to rethink their revenue streams. A payment component for agent-mediated services will be probable.

All of these hurdles are not impossible to overcome. Actually, many companies have already shown that they can overcome them. Others fail because they ignore these hurdles altogether.

7.4   Automated Web Services

7.4.1   Introduction

When looking towards the future of Web services, the breakthrough will probably come in the form of access to services and added intelligent capabilities through semantic reasoning. Agents bring the most crucial capability to turn Web services from the existing mass of information, where users need to surf and browse, into a dynamic set of capabilities deployed around and serving the user. Agents represent this great opportunity towards a new and completely different computing model, freeing humans from many chores imposed by the Internet.

Agents can turn Web services into proactive entities working as peers to serve the end users, representing them and defending their interests in a competitive world where services are negotiated and composed dynamically. Agents introduce an unparalleled level of autonomy into future systems so that users can delegate high-level tasks in a generic manner. To enable agents, they need to get mission statements, the definition of domains of competence, and a definition of autonomy through policies to be applied in these domains.

These domains and policies need to support reasoning as they might overlap in real life; for example, the policies of multi-national companies have to comply with the policies of the nations in which these companies operate. These domain and policy mechanisms permit deployment and dynamic adaptation to any situation. In particular, they allow Web services to combine without prior design, to negotiate end-to-end contracts to ensure the final result of composed Web services, and to monitor their execution on behalf of the user.

Agents will become the trusted intelligent interface between man and machine, allowing communications through speech acts and representing the interest of the user in any Web transaction at any time, like a trusted friend or broker. Hence, agent interfaces need to evolve towards ease of use, ease of delegation and monitoring of tasks, increased privacy, personalization and security, and user habits being acquired through learning.

Agents can now migrate to slim wireless appliances and evolve in a multitude of micro-worlds, typically the cells of wireless phones, malls, schools, and a community of friends; they can discover the resources and represent their user. This technology needs to be rolled out on a large scale to test the deployment capabilities as well as the usability of the technology in a mass market.

7.4.2 Machine-to-Machine Work

We've focused thus far on how components or agents can accept delegation, perform tasks on our behalf, understand what we want to do, and understand how to do things effectively to change the nature of the relationship between us and machines. But, equally profoundly, they change the nature of the way machines interact with machines. Although some degree of automation and humanless interaction occurs today, we expect to see an explosive increase of this type of activity as millions of people delegate billions of tasks to agents.

Each agent may rely on many others to do its work, and these in turn will rely on others and interact with others. This "Web" of machine-to-machine work will change the landscape of the computing infrastructure and the nature of transactions. This can provide a new level of reality that begins to approach the visions of science fiction writers. Once the machines are empowered and capable of doing real work on their own, what governance will they need and what constraints will be imposed?

Many authors have spent a considerable amount of time on how the world would change if everything is done automatically by machines or robots. Not only science fiction authors but also futurists look at this topic with a mixture of fear and desire. George B. Dyson, for example, provides visionary, long-range concepts in his book[2] and Forrester

---

[2]George B. Dyson (1998). *Darwin among the Machines: The Evolution of Global Intel-*

does some research on machine-to-machine work, which they call the X Internet.[3]

The essential points of these studies are that the Internet provides a foundation for an almost incomprehensible explosion of machine-to-machine interactions, fundamentally altering our concept of commerce and vastly expanding the range of value-added transformations that constitute the basis of our economy.

7.4.3 The Semantic Web

The easy information access based on the success of the Web has made it increasingly difficult to find, present, and maintain the information required by a wide variety of users. In response to this problem, many new research initiatives and commercial enterprises have been set up to enrich available information with machine understandable semantics. Only this enables automated machine-to-machine transactions. This semantic Web approach, which was defined by Tim Berners-Lee, provides intelligent access to heterogeneous, distributed information, enabling agents to mediate between user needs and the information sources available.

Web services deal with the limitations of the current Web. Currently, the Web is mainly a collection of information but does not yet provide support in processing this information. Web services can be accessed and executed via the Web. However, these service descriptions are based on natural language descriptions (e.g. "Find the cheapest flight to London"). To interpret these descriptions, a human programmer needs to be kept in the loop. As a result, the scalability and economic potential of Web services is severely limited. Reaching the full potential requires utilizing semantic Web technology as a basis for automating access to Web services. Machine-interpretable semantics will enable us to mechanize service identification, configuration, comparison, and combination.

Semantic Web-enabled Web services have the potential to change our life to a much higher degree than the current Web already has done. The following elements have been identified to be the minimum requirement for a well-working semantic Web: public process description and advertisement; discovery of services; selection of services; composition of services; and delivery, monitoring, and contract negotiation. These elements were described in Chapter 6 in more detail. Here, you can see how they are related to agents.

---

ligence. Cambridge, MA: Perseus Publishing.
[3]http://www.forrester.com/ER/Marketing/0,1503,214,00.html

7.5 Examples

7.5.1 Agentcities

Agentcities[4] is a worldwide initiative designed to help realize the commercial and research potential of agent-based applications by constructing a worldwide, open network of platforms hosting diverse agent-based services. The ultimate aim is to enable the dynamic, intelligent and autonomous composition of services to achieve user and business goals, thereby creating compound services to address changing needs.

The initiative will build on a wealth of innovative technologies including agent technology, semantic Web technologies, UDDI discovery services, e-business standards and grid computing. Application areas already envisaged range from e-health and e-learning to manufacturing control, digital libraries, travel services, and entertainment services.

The Agentcities network is designed to act as a distributed testbed for experimenting with agent technology and composable services. It allows the creation of a common resource for developers wishing to collaborate with each other and link up their agent systems and services. Agentcities also provides a benchmark environment to validate and test compliance to relevant technology standards and provide input to the standards themselves. It can also act as a focus for discussion of next-generation information networks as well as the development of services, technologies, and methodologies (see Table 7.3).

While infrastructure (messaging, directories, etc.) is necessary to create the network, the objective of the Agentcities project is not simply to deploy infrastructure. Many of the real challenges of deploying and using such a network lie in how diverse services can discover each other, the development and usage of a semantic framework, and how coordination can be achieved between heterogeneous systems.

The primary objective of Agentcities is, therefore, to create a rich, open environment to explore these questions. Although a number of the projects underpinning Agentcities take the area of travel, tourism, and entertainment as their application domain, there is no restriction on the applications that could be deployed in the Agentcities network.

The main example of developing a platform in the network to model the services available in a town or city (hence, the name Agentcities) simply provides a convenient domain focus to begin tackling the problems of semantics, ontology, and dynamic service composition in manageable proportions (see also Figure 7.4). Other groups are already con-

---

[4]http://www.agentcities.org/

Overview of Agentcities

Agentcities is based on these principles:

- **Consensual Standards**—Communication and interaction in the network will be based on publicly available standards, such as those developed by the Foundation for Intelligent Physical Agents (FIPA) and the W3C.

- **Open Source**—Although commercial technologies are not discouraged, Agentcities will promote freely accessible open source implementations to ensure free and open access to the network.

- **Open Access**—Any organization or individual can set up their own Agentcity in the network to host their own agent services, provide access to them and access those deployed by others.

- **Shared Resources**—People accessing agent-based services in the network, such as directory, naming, and application services, are encouraged to add their own services to extend the utility and diversity of the services available to the community.

Table 7.3. Overview of Agentcities

sidering very different application domains and how to exploit Agentcities in their own way. Interest groups that are already forming include:

- **Travel, tourism, and entertainment services**—Focal application area of the EU Agentcities research project.

- **Business services**—Marketplaces, payment systems, transactions and catalogue services.

- **Coordination technologies**—Coordination media and shared coordination methods.

- **Medical and healthcare services**—Distributed services for organ transplantation, access to patient medical records, and local emergency services linked with existing projects and new activities.

Figure 7.4. The Agentcities Web Site

- **Manufacturing and supply chain integration**—Using the Agentcities infrastructure as a substrate for coordinating distributed manufacturing processes and supply chain integration.

- **Security services**—Using the Agentcities infrastructure as a testbed for analyzing and beginning to address the security needs of such open, heterogeneous environments.

- **e-Learning**—Distributed agent-based tutoring systems.

- **Wireless applications**—Seamless interaction between wireless and wire line agents to dynamically compose service based on user location.

- **Personalization**—Dynamic composition of user services to suit individual tastes.

The Agentcities project will have a significant impact on the global deployment of agents and will provide a useful resource for the development of the next generation of networked systems. However, Agentcities is not attempting to be the panacea of agent or network programming since much hard work is involved in developing semantic frameworks and content languages for agents to communicate. Therefore, the role of the Agentcities project is to stimulate this process and encourage participants to think in an open context and to envisage their systems in the context of a worldwide environment. The process of connecting an increasing number of diverse agent systems will teach us much about which details matter when it comes to creating true interoperability, not just at the syntactic layer, but also at the semantic layer.

7.5.2 Hive

Hive is one of the first distributed agents platform built by MIT[5] to provide the integration of ubiquitous computing with wearable devices. It is a decentralized system for building applications by networking local resources. The key abstraction in Hive is the software agent: Applications are built out of an ecology of multiple agents interacting over the network.

From a programmer's perspective, each Hive agent is a distributed Java object and an execution thread, which also implements the following properties:

- **Autonomous**—Agents can be sent into a system and entrusted to carry out goals without direct human micromanagement.

- **Proactive**—Because agents have their own threads, they can act independently of other running agents. They encapsulate computational activity.

- **Self-describing**—An ontology of agent capabilities can be used to describe and discover available services. Hive agent descriptions consist of both a syntactic description (represented by the Java class of the agent) and a semantic description written in the Resource Description Format (RDF, see Chapter 6).

- **Interactive**—Agents can work together to complete a task. Hive agents can communicate both through an asynchronous event/subscriber mode and through Java RMI (Remote Method Invocation). Agent communication is completely peer-to-peer, so an agent might both send and receive at different times.

- **Mobile**—Agents can move from one physical device to another.

Along with agents, the Hive architecture defines so-called "shadows." Shadows are the low-level drivers for the physical resources of

---

[5]http://www.hivecell.net/

a particular object. For security, only local agents can access a particular shadow. All remote agents that wish to access local resources must go through local agents. Finally, Hive defines the concept of a "cell," which encapsulates a group of agents. The cell is essentially a Java process that implements an environment within which the agents operate. Generally, there will be one cell per local object or wearable computer, though this is not a hard and fast rule. A wearable computer is a computer that is subsumed into the personal space of the user, controlled by the user, and has both operational and interactional constancy. Agents are free to communicate and move between cells. Hive also provides a graphical interface to view and manipulate agent interactions. The interface is itself just one more Hive agent that receives and displays agent events.

Hive supports the discovery of new agents through two kinds of lookups. Agents can be queried both based on their syntactic description and on their semantic description. Semantic descriptions include information such as a resource's owner or the room in which it lives.

Using this infrastructure, several agents have been created to make resource finding simple for wearable computer users. MIT has created a "resource finder agent" that receives location events and produces sets of agents whose semantic descriptions match that location. These agent sets can then be winnowed further by other resource finder agents that are looking for specific services like stereo equipment or large-screen monitors. To bootstrap the initial list of cells, a resource finder agent contacts a known master cell listing agent. The creation of new agents is announced to subscribing agents in the form of events, or a special cell managing agent can be queried.

In this system, each wearable computer is simply another Hive cell in a decentralized Hive network. Sometimes, the wearable is the interface to an external service; sometimes, the wearable is a service provider for an agent in the environment (or on another wearable); and sometimes, the wearable and environment are interacting.

On Hive, several agents have already been implemented. The following provides a very short overview on their functionality. The first one is the automatic diary, which basically stores the location information about a user. Whenever the wearable user types in a note or idea, that note is automatically timestamped and tagged with the location where that note was made.

Besides the automatic diary, MIT has implemented a DJ agent, which plays the right music in a given room for a certain occasion. If a person enters the room and no music is running, the agent will look at the personal preferences of that user and select the appropriate music.

To make sure that the music does not annoy other people in the room, the DJ agent implements resource management policies to ensure fairness. In the default case, a DJ takes requests sequentially and plays one request for each agent that has a song. Thus, people's requests will be played in a round-robin fashion, one request per person.

In addition to this, a remembrance agent has been implemented. As an example, imagine a wearable that acts as a tour guide at a museum. As the visitor moves through various exhibits, extra information about each site is presented on her wearable. Because this information is location specific, it is more easily maintained if it resides in the museum databases and is sent to a visitor's wearable only when she enters the exhibit area.

Besides providing services to the user, the architecture can also make the wearable act as a service provider. The so-called "Where's Brad?" agent produces a map that shows the current location of a wearable user. This agent uses the same resource discovery tools as do the agents on the wearable, except now instead of finding agents associated with a location, they find agents associated with a particular person.

7.5.3 OnStar

OnStar,[6] which connects drivers to a 24-hour on-call center for emergency services or help finding a restaurant or hotel, is one of the new services GM is offering. It is one of the most popular in-vehicle communications system in the United States, with more than 2 million subscribers. It is a subsidiary of General Motors[7] and provides service for many car models, including GM, Lexus, Audi, Saab, and Volkswagen.

OnStar can be considered as a collection of Web services and agents that integrate in an open marketplace on a portal. The portal knows about capable resources (agents) for a certain task and can bring these into play whenever required. This portal can be seen as a concierge that would be the natural mode for me-centric access to services in various environments. The system can, for example, alert an OnStar operator when an air bag deploys, but also notify operators about accidents that did not trigger an air bag deployment and send more information about the crash. Crash sensors in the front and rear bumpers and on both sides of the vehicle can tell where the vehicle was hit and the speed and force of impact. This technology is especially helpful for accidents in rural areas, where there may not be witnesses and the victims may not be immediately discovered.

---

[6]http://www.onstar.com/
[7]http://www.gm.com/

OnStar operators can also locate a stolen vehicle, remotely unlock the doors, provide roadside assistance, perform remote diagnostics, give directions, and even make dinner reservations. Similar services have been set up by DaimlerChrysler[8] (TeleAid and Dynaps) and Fiat[9] (Connect).

In the future, the information may also be transmitted electronically to 911 centers, first responders, and hospitals using secure Internet connections. The system may also one day be able to tell how many people were in the vehicle, whether they were using seat belts, and other information that helps emergency responders anticipate injuries before they arrive at the accident scene.

7.6   Conclusion

Software agents have been around for years, but the actual implementation of intelligent agents is still in its early stages. As agents gain wider acceptance and become more sophisticated, they will become a major factor in the future of the Internet and in me-centric computing. Intelligent agents will not completely replace today's way of working on the Internet or networked appliances, but they will make information gathering much easier for users and consumers. Instead of searching through lists and lists of unwanted sites, users could ask their agents to start searching, and in a few moments, the agents will come back with just the information that is needed.

If all security-related issues can be solved in the near future, the trust in software agents will increase and they can start to take over smaller jobs for their masters. Over time, these agents will be more sophisticated and work in groups, making it possible to give them more complex tasks as well. As said during the introduction of this chapter, agents will be the glue that holds together the entire me-centric computing environment on a loose basis, as they can work even if they are not able to reach their masters all the time or communicate with others.

We have now laid most of the foundation required for building the kinds of intelligent appliances that will put people at the center of information technology. In the next chapter, we will illustrate how one builds the right appliances for a me-centric scenario. That chapter shows which technology is required and how to deploy it within an existing environment.

---

[8]http://www.daimlerchrysler.com/
[9]http://www.fiat.com/

Part IV

New Business Opportunities

Chapter 8

INTELLIGENT APPLIANCES

8.1 Introduction

The basic components of any intelligent environment are intelligent devices. Intelligent appliances will become the signature of this new era. They will do what we want, when we want, how we want, and where we want. One common perception of an intelligent device is any traditional device that now contains an embedded processor, thus providing new functionality.

Personal computers today are quite obvious. When you look at a portable MP3 player or a cell phone, you do not see a computer, you see the functionality that the computer inside is enabling. But when you look at the box that your monitor is connected to, you instantly think "computer." Intelligent appliances often cannot be seen, but their impact can be felt. They're embedded within some device, which is something very different from what most people think of as a computer.

In a recent commercial on Japanese television, a baby takes his first tentative step. The mother grabs her cell phone, captures the moment on the phone's camera, and sends it to dad. Alfa Romeo supplies its cars with navigation systems that are capable of providing additional information such as good restaurants around you or your destination. The embedded system transmits the geographical data to the Alfa Romeo call center while you talk. It's becoming more and more common for electronic devices to be enriched through such additional services.

To become truly ubiquitous, devices will need to know much about the world in general and how to do tasks well. They will also need to be able to understand our instructions and requests, as well as take feedback from us that enables them to do better. Of course, most of these appliances will be supported by knowledge-based services provided over the net. When we speak to our phone, for example, we will be exploiting advances in the handheld device as well as in the intelligent network services running on back-end servers. There will be many agents to do many tasks, and these will benefit from composing and using the capabilities of others.

The single defining characteristic of the intelligent appliance is its capacity to accept user goals or intents and responsibly carry them out in an intelligent (efficient, effective, appropriate, acceptable) manner while assuring that the human user's trust in the appliance is maintained intelligently (in ways that are efficient, effective, appropriate, and acceptable).

Intelligent appliances are networked, and they work in a distributed computing environment. Typically, they depend on interacting with other devices or network services. Three main rules must be applied. First, a compelling set of benefits must be presented. Second, the product should be easy to install and use. The device form-factor and user interaction must be optimized for the location and tasks being performed. And third, the technology must be transparent. Users should be able to focus on the tasks they are performing, rather than on the tools they are using. The users should always have the feeling that they are interacting with a single underlying system and the devices simply serve as access points to, or controllers of, that environment.

Compensation will be based on micro-payments and service contracts. Billing for services and products procured will be fully automated. Information from accounts, suppliers, and organizations we each use will be aggregated for us and interpreted. In short, the economy will expand around thousands of knowledgeable agents that can do what we want in a credible way. We will select which ones to employ based on rated performance, much the way the average pro sports franchise chooses its players. For those of us with no desire to dip into that level of choice, we will contract for services from businesses that provide a suite of intelligent agents to cover our needs. Each of these new benefits creates business opportunities, and these span the entire range of IT and service industries.

The concept of intelligent devices has become an important topic. Internet appliances must be dynamically upgradable for software replacements, software patches, and software extensions. Ease of adaptability is an important aspect of Internet appliance development. The commercial world is developing devices that can exist in an intelligent environment. Commercial products can be found that support the distribution of software components across computing resources as well as the Internet. Distributed and Internet platforms exist in abundance. The hardware components and networking infrastructure exist to support ubiquitous computing.

8.2 Infrastructure Needs Me

8.2.1 Computing Realms

Me-centric applications will be running on an aggregate computer that will consist of many distributed individual computers. In order to understand this aggregate, we need to classify these computers into realms (see Table 8.1) so we can think about the kind of software we'll need to build for them. These realms are also illustrated in Figure 8.1.

Computing Realms

We see computing being handled in roughly four realms, with different functionality appearing at each level:

- **Personal Area Network (PAN)**—The device(s) that I carry with me.

- **Local Area Network (LAN)**—Devices that are in the local physical area that I can use.

- **Metropolitan Area Network (MAN)**—Servers that are distributed regionally to handle load balancing, proxying, caching, content delivery, authorizing, etc.

- **Wide Area Network (WAN)**—Servers in large data centers carefully organized to handle large loads for specific applications.

Table 8.1. Computing Realms

The PAN includes all the devices that I carry with me. These could include a PDA and cell phone in the short term, but may end up being a richer set in the longer term as smaller, single-purpose appliances appear. These computing resources band together to serve a single person. The LAN serves devices that are in the local physical area that I can use. These may be I/O devices like large screens, speakers, and printers. They may also be computer resources, such as local data caches, media accelerators, etc. They also include connectivity resources such as access points, connectivity diversity (a combination of beacons, 802.11, cell networks, and/or wired networks). These computing resources enhance the computing for the small set of people in physical proximity.

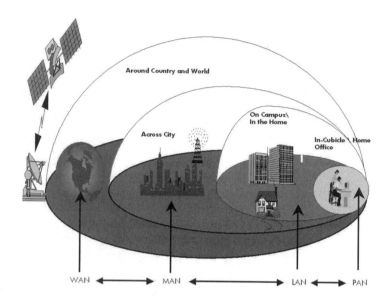

Figure 8.1. Computing Realms

The MAN includes servers that are distributed regionally to handle load balancing, proxying, caching, content delivery, authorizing, etc. These may be at an ISP, in an enterprise machine room, or at a wireless regional data center (serving several cellular antennas). These computer resources serve a large number of people based either on physical location (cellular network) or based on business relationship (ISP provider or coworkers in an enterprise). The WAN provides servers in large data centers carefully organized to handle large loads for specific applications. This is the way that most Internet and many wireless services are provided today. These computer resources are optimized to scale to huge populations, covering a measurable percentage of the worldwide demand for specific services.

8.2.2 Ecosystems

We postulate three ecosystems that are competing for dominance. They differ in how services are delivered to an individual.

- **Spontaneous**—The idea here is that appliances will form spontaneous connections to perform localized services for *me* without requiring any global Internet access. As an example, my PDA, camera, and printer may collaborate to provide a preview, crop, transcode, frame, and print service for real estate snapshots without requiring any external connection.

- **Internet**—The networks (both wired and wireless) are *stupid* and merely carry bits between my appliances and the á la carte services that I use.

- **Managed**—My wireless network and/or my portal carefully manage, unify billing, and control the quality of services I use, though they will also grudgingly allow me to get access to others through their system.

Both the managed ecosystem and Internet expect me to use WLAN (802.11) and WAN (3G) technologies[1]; they differ on business model, not capability.

There are several ways the competition between these ecosystems may turn out. One may dominate, dwarfing the other two. Or the three may coexist (as they do today). We will look at these ecosystems as being equally likely for now and, trying to hedge our bets in the technology roadmap, concentrate on those technologies that keep our options open.

For the users, it should not matter which of the three technical ecosystems they will be using. For them, it will be one unified ecosystem that will make sure that all required services will be available, no matter how they are transported to the user.[2]

8.3 Appliance Design

8.3.1 Form Follows Me

When designing smart devices, it is important to take some design issues into consideration before starting to build the device and the services around it. First, it is important to define the target groups and the related services. Based on this information, one should decide on a type of device that is adequate for this group (which could be, for example, a PDA, an Internet stereo, a refrigerator, or a Web pad). Next, it is important to understand what the related services for the product

---

[1]3G is the third generation of mobile technologies, which includes the UMTS technologies.

[2]Seamlessness of user experience is the ideal, but seams, gaps, and drop-offs between these networks are today's norm. We expect seamlessness to be a prerequisite for rapid user acceptance. Seams create friction and drag, slowing down transition to the new paradigm.

will be and in which environment it will be operated. Is it used, for example, indoors, outdoors, in a hot or cold environment? Depending on these requirements, the device will look different. Also of great importance is knowing of which context the application should be aware. Should it know its position, the outside temperature, or in which process step the user is at the moment? This will help to determine which additional sensors are required to make it easy to use. Appropriate context will make possible a great simplification of the user interface. Last, but not least, the target cost of the product should be clarified to make it commercially successful.

Currently, no one knows exactly what the customer will find useful. Manufacturers need to have adaptive designs and need to keep in touch with how the user interacts. It is important that a user does not have to learn a whole new way of interacting with the system, or it will fail (e.g., many older people who would benefit from buying a home PC are put off by an aversion to operating it). It is not enough to provide a mass of different devices for different user tasks, each connected to the network. The device must be easy, compelling, and enjoyable to use. Each device will compete others for space, mind share, and power outlets. As a consequence, some devices will be multifunctional, absorbing and displacing others.

Appliances must be designed from the perspective of the overall user experience. This includes the whole life cycle of ownership from initial advertising to purchase, installation, and use, to support, upgrade and eventual replacement.

Ergonomics play an important role in designing intelligent appliances. Only with good ergonomics will people use them. What needs to be taken into account is the human anthropometry in relation to workspace design. It is important to see how well the human and the appliance interact and how it can be improved for maximum performance. The arrangement of displays and controls needs to be verified and checked if they are to be linked properly.

Also to be taken into account are the cognitive and sensory limits of humans, which can make design unusable if the limits are ignored. Related to this, it is also important to check for fatigue and health issues that may arise from using the appliance. This is important when you design not only for the disabled, but for all users.

When designing the hardware, interfaces such as CRT and other display technologies need to checked for sensory and perceptual effects. You especially need to check legibility and display design. The interfaces need to be checked against the possible environment. These factors are even more true for speech input and output. If the device is meant to work outside, for example, you should make sure that you consider all possible weather conditions, including severe temperatures, winds, and storm conditions. You should also provide clear guidelines for its use under various environmental conditions, especially those that may be considered unsafe. If you use speech input and/or sound output, you should make sure that it can function under normal environmental noise factors and accommodate accordingly. Obviously, if you are designing a device to be used at a construction site, for example, you'll want to consider the optimal method for communicating with the device based on factors typical to such an environment. Likewise, additional care needs to be taken if you expect the devices to work in stressful or hazardous environments—make sure its design and endurance is appropriate to the situation in which it is expected to work.

Related to the interfaces, you need to make sure that the control design of the system is developed in a way that the users can use it without having to learn a lot. It means that the sequence of controlling the device is clearly structured and that you are only allowed to execute functions that are appropriate for this stage. The most favored devices will be ones that quickly acquaint themselves with their new masters, probably by borrowing knowledge and learned preferences from other appliances that have previously served the master well.

8.3.2 Technology Follows Me

Me-centric computing devices will be extremely diverse, including PDAs, set-top boxes, screen phones, in-vehicle computing platforms, smart phones, and home gateways, to name a few. As the market matures, this list of devices will continue to expand into areas that we cannot even imagine today. Described in this section are some of the requirements that must be addressed in order to build economically viable and successful devices.

Me-centric devices must appear to be appliances, not computers. This has implications such as instant on, user interfaces that match the function of the appliance, deterministic response times (even when disconnected), and clear and tight association between buttons, dials, and functions. A network-enabled set-top box's first priority is to deliver high-quality audio-visual content. The new functions associated with buttons and dials need to be as responsive as today's remote control when changing channels on a set-top box.

These devices target a broad range of price points, form factors, and hardware capabilities. Requirements vary across user interface models (including a range for both audible and small, medium, and large manual/visual), power requirements (battery life versus AC power), processor families (ARM, x86, PPC, MIPS, Hitachi SH, etc.), and network capabilities (fully connected, sporadically connected, and/or disconnected operations).

Human-computer interaction appropriate to the task and location needs to be sorted out. Liquid crystal display (LCD) touch screens, voice recognition, and text-to-speech output look like far better alternatives to the traditional PC with keyboard and mouse as methods of input and output. A consistent software user interaction model will also help achieve the wider goal of simplified learning and use. Also, it will encourage application development, thus avoiding software companies having to transfer their products to several different platforms. Existing desktop operating systems will not adapt well, as they depend on the present user input/output methods.

To be successful, it is necessary to rethink product concepts. While many manufacturers still think that the products they sell will create the profit the company wants to make, it is necessary to think of products as potential service offering platforms. These service offerings drive ongoing interaction with customers, which can become the cash-cow for the company. Eventually, it will be possible to give away the device for free, as the service fees will make sure that the company receives its share in the deal.

This has worked quite successfully with mobile phones. In Germany, the United States and Italy, for example, many mobile phones are sold for less than 1 euro/dollar or given away for free if the buyer subscribes to the phone network for at least two years. While the sale of the mobile phone would give the company a higher instant reward, selling subscriptions guarantees the company an income for the next two years.

To make this work, it is necessary to rethink existing business models. Ongoing annuity revenue becomes part of the picture, and customer relationships become a valuable asset in creating new partnerships, which build on brand recognition and trust. This creates opportunities to both offer services and to serve as a service integrator.

Through this new approach, it is possible to leverage increased customer interaction and data collection capabilities, which can lead to an increase in customer satisfaction. It also allows companies to provide improved products to the community and increases the company's partnership value and power lines.

When designing an appliance, it is important to make sure that one has the service in place before starting to design the hardware. Only this will guarantee that you reach the business goal that you are planning for (see also Table 8.2).

Creating Value in Product Design

In *Creating Breakthrough Products*, Craig Vogel and Jonathan Cagan identify seven classes of attributes that can create value by contributing to a product's usefulness, usability, and desirability, which create an experience that fulfills a consumer's fantasy.

- **Emotion**—The perceptual experience that a consumer has when using a product. It can include a sense of adventure, independence, security, or sensuality.

- **Aesthetics**—A focus on sensory perception, including the visual form, tactile interactions, and auditory, olfactory, and gustatory signals.

- **Product Identity**—A statement about individuality and personality, expressing uniqueness, timeliness of style, and appropriateness in the context.

- **Impact**—The social or environmental effects, which are connected with the customer's personal value system and can often help build brand loyalty.

- **Ergonomics**—A product's basic usability reflects its ease of use from both a physical and a cognitive perspective. It must also be safe and comfortable.

- **Core Technology**—The ability to function properly and perform to expectations. It must be reliable enough to work consistently.

- **Quality**—The durability, precision, and accuracy of manufacturing processes, material composition, and methods of attachment must all meet the customer's expectations.

Table 8.2. Creating Value in Product Design

Important for me-centric appliances is the so-called "last mile" network connectivity to support the delivery of both data and application services. These include security models, device management, user management, content formatting, and software distribution requirements. Short-range ad hoc networking technologies, such as Bluetooth,

HomePNA[3], or WLAN based on IEEE 802.11 are becoming more common. This connectivity capability has implications on the device architecture requiring seamless support for transparent, appliance-like, ad hoc collaboration among these devices themselves.

Classes of Intelligent Appliances

Intelligent appliances can be grouped into four classes that address the complete landscape of requirements.

- **Thin Clients**—Render network delivered content to the user, either visually, audibly, or both with no local state information.

- **Thick Clients**—Support applications using a programming model that is native to the device.

- **Gateways**—Interface to the "last mile" of broadband capability while simultaneously providing the ability to host network-delivered services to be used on behalf of other devices in the network.

- **Server Configurations**—Support the combination of gateway, thin terminal and thick terminal capabilities to allow, in a single device, hosted services, device-specific applications and content rendering for network delivered data.

Table 8.3. Classes of Intelligent Appliances

Typically, intelligent appliances are grouped into four classes (see Table 8.3). These four classes address the whole range of requirements that we can foresee for the moment. They include thin clients, thick clients, gateways, and server configurations. The thin terminals do not contain any business logic themselves. They are used to deliver content, either visually, audibly, or both with no local state information. They act as a relay station for information and services. The advantage is that the footprint is rather small, but unfortunately these devices rely heavily on network connectivity, as they do not work without it.

Thick clients are like thin clients, but they have a larger memory footprint allowing the device to run applications and store data lo-

---

[3]http://www.homepna.org/

cally. This means that these devices can operate if there is no Internet connection. These devices support applications using a programming model that is native to the device. In many cases, Java is used. Gateway systems act as a local cache for thin and thick clients. They provide the gateway to the "last mile" of broadband capability. At the same time, these systems provide the ability to host network-delivered services to be used on behalf of other devices in the network. A server configuration supports the combination of gateway, thin clients and thick client capabilities to allow, in a single device, hosted services, device specific applications, and content rendering for network-delivered data.

To make me-centric solutions cheap enough for everyone to use, it is important to create reusable device architectures. This includes hardware components and a set of programming models that are used across device and network types to allow for the construction and deployment of device classes across the complete range of devices.

To connect an intelligent appliance to the network (Internet and LAN), discovery protocols need to be implemented that allow the appliance to search for networks and services that surround it. Once the appliance has found a network, it can connect to other appliances through LAN technologies, such as Bluetooth, HomePNA, or IEEE 802.11. At the same time, it will be connected either directly or via another local device to the Internet. While connectivity is desired, privacy can be an issue due to the lack of security. Not every device and service should be able to see each other, so smart cards, firewalls and encryption technologies are required for the authentication and authorization of users, agents, and services.

A more technical discussion will lead to questions on how much power consumption is necessary to keep operations alive for a time that is acceptable by the user. This will lead to the question of whether you can use a rechargeable battery or whether you need to plug the device into a power socket. This will define the range of use for a certain device, which can lead to major design changes.

The application will define the hardware requirements. If complex calculations are required, a faster CPU will be required that in turn consumes more power. The same question arises about memory and networking usage. Does the device require 4 Kilobytes or 512 Megabytes of memory? Does it need a slow infrared connection or a high-speed wireless LAN connection? This will have a huge impact on the power consumption and the design of the whole device. The same is true for output and input interfaces, such as displays and microphones and for sensors that help to give context to the device, such as GPS. Many other technical questions need to be answered before the device can be built, but in all cases the device should not be built because of the technical capabilities, but because of the requirements of the users and the proposed services.

8.3.3 Software Follows Me

Me-centric devices need content to deliver value. New devices cannot wait for entirely new custom content to be created in order to be successful. A cogent content architecture must address existing devices and lower the entry barrier for future devices seamlessly for all content providers in the value chain. This end-to-end content architecture also needs to ensure that new devices can be added while still supporting the network scalability demanded by millions of connected devices. Furthermore, as devices collaborate among themselves, the content needs to be naturally sharable and reusable.

Therefore the solution needs to use open standards that are not controlled by one entity and are easy to extend. It does not mean that everything needs to be open source, but the basic communication and application standards need to ensure compatibility of interfaces.

The software architecture needs to support both synchronous user request-response and asynchronous user messaging and notification. Depending on the application you are using and the requirements the users have, they will need both. The architecture needs to provide end-to-end scalability, which allows for growth in applications and user base. Applications can become more complex over time and may require more processing power and network resources. Besides end-to-end scalability, management is a very complex and important topic that needs to be taken into account. The management system supporting the solution needs to take care of users, devices, network-delivered applications, and content. Only through the management system is it possible to detect problems in this networked system. Just imagine a Web site that does not work anymore. The reasons for it can be manifold. It could be the device that you use to display it; it could be the browser, the connection, the server, the application, the database, the firewall, or the filesystem, just to mention a few reasons why a certain Web site cannot be displayed. Finding the problem that caused the downtime can be difficult if you have to do it manually. Therefore, automated management systems are required to manage the solution.

As the solution uses open standards, it will be possible to integrate third-party components, products, and adapters through well-defined interface points. This makes it possible to create more complex solutions that incorporate a range of different products and technologies from multiple software providers. Based on this software infrastructure, it is possible to reuse end-to-end network programming models. The supporting application model is based on components. These components work together in a cohesive manner to enable the construction of a wide variety of network-connected devices to address the device capabilities outlined earlier.

When designing the device, it is important to decide which operating system will run on it. While most applications will be written in Java, the different operating systems provide additional built-in features that are not to be neglected. Such features include speech recognition, applications, tools, control panel applets, custom shell, and handwriting recognition. This feature is bound to the device you are using and should be tightly integrated. Therefore, the decision for the operating system should be based on the additional services it provides.

Another important factor that needs to be considered in design is how new application code and content is downloaded to the device. Until now, most applications are transmitted via memory card or cable to these devices, which is slow and not very flexible. As more and more public WLAN access points are set up and GSM/UMTS-capable devices appear, it becomes clear that the content is transmitted on the fly wirelessly. But in some situations, it could be useful to put information on a memory card or to exchange information via memory card, in case there is no network connectivity available. Therefore, the device should support these memory cards from a software and hardware point of view.

From here on, you can start a detailed technical discussion about the software required on the device to make it run. Besides the operating system, you need a boot loader (a mechanism to load a program), a BIOS (the initial program that is loaded), and file systems, which would lead too much into technicalities. While you do not need to know the details, you should know that there is more you need to take into account, as these software bits and pieces require RAM, CPU power, and time to execute, which all can impact the design of the device.

8.4   Examples

8.4.1   Introduction

While many people believe that the future lies in mobile computing, we present here some examples that are not mobile particularly, but still fit the me-centric computing paradigm, because these appliances are intelligent and work on behalf of the user. PDAs and smart phones may be the most prominent examples, but they will be only a very small percentage of intelligent appliances in the future.

8.4.2   Margherita 2000

While the market is still small, several companies have started building smart appliances. One of them is Merloni Elettrodomestici of Fabriano[4], Europe's third-largest appliance maker. Last year, the Italian firm sold more than 1 million networked appliances–most of them washing machines. Merloni's Margherita 2000[5] washing machine looks no different from standard washing machines except that it is more gentle on delicate clothes and can be controlled through the Internet.

The washing machine uses a capacitor to measure whether water and detergent have soaked into clothing. The machine can then perfectly time its washing cycles, wasting less water and not damaging delicate clothing. While it can be controlled over the net, the "smart" thing about the machine is that it "knows" not to damage clothing.

8.4.3   Screenfridge

Electrolux[6], a Swedish company probably best known for its vacuum cleaners, has developed the Screenfridge[7] (see Figure 8.2), an Internet refrigerator that manages your pantry, among other things. It can e-mail a shopping list to your supermarket and coordinate a convenient delivery time with your schedule.

The idea behind Screenfridge is that the fridge is considered to be one of the natural places for communication in every family. Many people post notes, postcards, and other messages on the refrigerator door. Screenfridge supports not only post-it notes (for which there is still a place) but also video-messaging between family members, as well as e-mail, on-line shopping, TV, and radio.

A touch of a button is all it takes to record a video message and post it to another family member. There is no traditional keyboard attached to the fridge, but members of the family are able to use a virtual keyboard that is displayed on-screen, similar to the virtual keyboards seen on PDAs. This means that the screen is a touch screen that accepts all entries by tapping the screen with a finger. As video-mails are possible, it can be expected that only a few people will use the text-mail option.

The virtual keyboard probably will be used more for traditional e-mail that can also be received and sent from the Screenfridge. Family members have their own mailboxes where both e-mail and video messages are stored. It creates a convenient environment, especially for

---

[4]http://www.merloni.com/

[5]http://www.margherita2000.com/

[6]http://www.electrolux.se/

[7]http://www.electrolux.se/screenfridge/

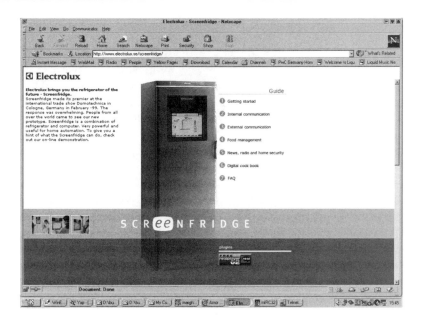

Figure 8.2. The Screenfridge Solution

people who are unfamiliar with e-mail programs, operating systems, and computers in general. The interface also allows family members to surf the Web.

Although these additional features are great, another feature directly related to the use of the fridge is called food management. This feature deals with how to store, handle and prepare food. Screenfridge can make food management easier. Not only does it provide a powerful cookbook with hundreds of recipes suitable for food stored in the fridge and tips on how to store food correctly, but you also gain valuable information on how to best handle your foodstuffs. You are even able to reorder directly from the grocery store certain foods you've used.

Screenfridge is also equipped with a TV and radio receiver. This enables you to get rid of the bulky television set in the kitchen and watch the news on the refrigerator instead. The TV can be connected to a DVD player, to a surveillance camera that watches your garden, or to a baby-cam that looks after your little baby in the crib.

8.4.4   E-Espressopoint

Another company that has already introduced intelligence into their
products is Lavazza[8], the world's biggest maker of espresso machines.
The Italian company has already manufactured more than 10,000 of
their E-Espressopoint machines and shipped them to their largest customers. This first generation is only able to send e-mails back to Lavazza providing information about servicing and reordering of espresso
coffee. By having this regular feedback, Lavazza is able to learn more
about the use of the coffee machines. These results are used by Lavazza
to create machines that serve coffee drinkers even better in the future.
The next generation of espresso machines will contain not only feedback e-mails to Lavazza, but also a full Internet connection and a touch
screen to allow the users to go online. The idea was actually developed
by E-Device[9], a small startup company that worked with Lavazza to
realize it.

8.4.5   Intello@chef

LG Electronics[10] sells a microwave called Intello@chef, which uses a
modem and a touchscreen to connect to the Internet. This allows the
consumer to download information about cooking and the usage of the
microwave. In addition to this, the system allows the user to download
upgrades to the operating system and applications installed on the microwave. Applications in this case are recipes, cooking times, and the
control of the microwave power. LG Electronics plans to cooperate with
big supermarkets to allow online ordering through the microwave.

8.4.6   MIT

MIT's Media Lab[11] has some working prototypes of smart appliances.
We will just mention two of them here. First, they have designed and
built an oven mitt that can tell whether food is still cold, is hot but
not cooked, or has cooked all the way through. It will also tell the
wearer either to put the casserole back in the oven, to serve the meal
already, or to pull out the fire extinguisher. Second, they have created
a refrigerator named Minerva that can tell what's sitting on the shelf
with 80 percent accuracy. If you have a few tomatoes, an onion, and
some pasta, Minerva might suggest that you make spaghetti for dinner.

---

[8]http://www.lavazza.it/
[9]http://www.edevice.com/
[10]http://www.lge.com/
[11]http://www.media.mit.edu/

8.5 Conclusion

Designing intelligent appliances is not very complicated, if you always keep the human in the center. The biggest issue is to design an appliance that is cheap enough for many people to afford, but powerful enough to attract a large audience. At the same time, it needs to be easy to use and adapt itself to the needs of the user.

As the hardware gets cheaper, and prices for memory and CPUs are constantly falling, it becomes easier to get the price right and the power right. The further you look into the future, the faster the devices will be and the more memory they can hold for the same price. At the same time, the power consumption is going to be reduced and rechargeable batteries will become better (where necessary), making it possible to increase the longevity of the service and the appliance. The hardware should be only the container for the me-centric services and agents and should be used for input/output purposes in a special situation. The appliance, fundamentally, does the work for a person, and to do this, it "knows" something task-specific that permits the user to delegate decision making and acting authority to the appliance.

The customer, ultimately, is valuing the ability of the appliance to perform tasks, i.e., to render services, or "accomplish transactions in the real world." Thus, the new appliances are really service performers; this means customers are buying service performers, paying for services, and valuing the ability of the appliances to become better over time.

Improvement in service performance is most likely to come from updating the software (from central casting) or, even more likely, the appliance learning and improving how best to satisfy its users in the particular tasks they do most often and in the way they most prefer to have them done. This new class of appliances will be a major breakthrough in efficiency for business and leisure activities.

Now that we know which components are required to implement a me-centric solution, Chapter 9 provides some thought on the impact of these new technologies on society.

Chapter 9

RESHAPING EVERYDAY LIFE

9.1 The Multifaceted Me

9.1.1 Supporting a Whole New Life for Each of Us

Each individual has multiple relationships with others and various groups or organizations. In some sense, each person is many people and also a member of many activities. The physical world largely separates these roles in time and space. Well-conceived me-centric computing unifies these facets into one holistic context, aggregates the experiences into a me-centric stream, and allows us to be more people, in more places, even all at once.

This isn't likely to be a small change. It's likely to make us feel both more powerful and more connected, and at the same time more liberated from the physical anchors of the past. Combining both the multifaceted integration of diverse roles with the power of delegation through automated agents, we should expect that many individuals will both feel and actually attain great positions of leverage, power, mobility, and personal effectiveness.

Although it's unlikely that most people will use this to reduce the amount of time they engage in productive activity, it's almost certainly the case that productivity in terms of work, social, political, and intellectual activities will soar. This could take the economy as a whole into an era of unprecedented productivity.

Me-centric computing will change the way we work and live. From a technical point of view, it will be a transition rather than a revolution. Just as the telephone did not replace direct human communication and the television did not replace the cinema, me-centric computing will not replace completely current computing technologies. Desktop computers will probably still be part of everyday life, but they won't be hot technology anymore; they will simply be a commodity. The big business will move on to new paradigms, technologies, and devices.

Technology has changed society over centuries. Without technology, we wouldn't have been able to build up democracies and the kind of lifestyle we are living today. All big cultures in the history of mankind were successful because of their inventions. Their downfall always came at a time when the culture could not re-invent itself anymore. But it proves that such success was possible before the Internet and other high-tech gadgets. Look at Greece more than 2,000 years ago. They were able to build up democracies. We often hear people say that the Internet will guarantee a democratic world, but we don't believe so. The Internet is just a technology, by itself neither good or bad. But just like all technologies, the Internet is able to amplify any effort you put into something. And the same will be true for new me-centric technologies and services.

If you look at the technology presented in this book, you will recognize two major trends: automation and mobility. These are not new trends, but me-centric computing is pushing them onto a new level. While automation of processes has worked well in manufacturing in the past, the Internet and especially me-centric computing allows for process automation in every job. This relieves many people from repetitive tasks, but unless we focus on simplifying these technologies, it also requires that end-users have a better education to be able to use them.

To make sure that everyone can participate, it is necessary to create an easy-to-use technology. It needs to become invisible; only then does it have a chance to reach all groups within a society. The kind of technology we are talking about needs to become embedded so that humans experience the function or benefit rather than the mechanisms that make it work. Automobiles are not invisible, nor are most parts of the mobile platform that make them behave. Instead, the automobile presents us only with a veneer associated with the parts of it we need to access (what Don Norman calls the "affordances" in *The Design of Everyday Things*). We need a way to specify mode (park, forward, reverse), a way to specify faster or slower (accelerator, brake pedal), and a way to elect where we choose to sit (doors) and where we choose to store miscellaneous things (trunk, back seat).

Have a look at the relationship the Japanese have with a cell phone. To them, the wireless phone is as intensely personal as a watch or a purse. It's an extension of the body, often with designer leather straps, World Cup flags, rhinestones, or little animal figures dangling off the end. The screen is customized with a screensaver, the ring tone with a song of the user's choice. In the United States, this affinity to the mobile phone exists on a much lower scale.

A hopeful by-product of this expanding technology will be increased opportunity for everyone, not just the best educated among us.

9.1.2   Changes in Workers' Lives

Two big categories of changes will occur. First, workers, like consumers, can delegate work and specify how to deliver value to them. This increases their productivity enormously. Along with that, their devices support mobility, so they are untethered and can be more effective more often. The second category of changes results from the integration of their lives as workers with all the other roles in their lives: parent, coach, driver, cook, financial manager, etc. They no longer need different devices to switch contexts, and the stream of events that flow to them can be integrated, aggregated, and to a large extent reduced, since many events requiring routine processing can be delegated and dispatched automatically. Companies can thus help their employees be happier, more productive, and more flexible, while at the same time addressing additional possible objectives such as me-centric training.

Through the automation of standard business processes, the amount of work as we know it today will be reduced significantly. This poses a huge problem for many people who build their lives around simple work tasks. For the next generation, the importance of work to make enough money to live a decent life is decreased. In an automated business world, products and services will be available at a fraction of the current costs, making them available to virtually anyone who desires them.

There are a couple of very real concerns that need to be addressed from a social as well as a political viewpoint. For one thing, an automated world may create psychological dependencies on networked communication, thus reducing the demand for relationships in real life. The Internet allows people to hide their identity every time they connect. People may associate more freely online because they are not bound to geographical or temporal limits. This shift in social behavior —whether for the positive or the negative, it could be argued either way—will affect both our work lives and our personal lives. Human-to-human interaction will probably become more important to some people, and less important to others.

Additionally, imagine the consequences of shifting a large percentage of work tasks from humans to computers. It remains to be seen whether the reduced amount of work will be distributed evenly among the entire work force or whether it will become a status symbol for the new information elite. It's certain that there will still be work to be done, but it's clear that just as automation in factories and other industries resulted in large employee cutbacks, one can imagine unemployment rates increasing as more and more essential tasks are delegated to devices. In a positive future, this will put more emphasis on meaningful work, such as scientific research, sports, agriculture, and the arts. There will still be a demand for innovation in these fields that can never be fully realized with technology alone. More generally, physical work will continue in importance, with little prospect that me-centric computing will affect it significantly.

9.1.3   Coordinating Business and Social Activities

Assuming we live long enough to see it, there will be a transformation of everyday life made possible by me-centric computing. It will manifest itself in many ways, but some overarching characteristics will stand out. First, computers will seem to disappear into the physical environment, being capable of interacting with people in natural ways, in a wide variety of contexts. People will be able to tell these devices what they need and will receive useful assistance from them.

The reach of humans will be greatly extended, because they will be able to start transactions easily, and these transactions may in turn cause more transactions to happen without additional human intervention. More importantly, the computing field will need to shift focus from giving more applications and tools to users to off-loading unpleasant tasks from people. Even simple things like coordinating social and business activities will become far easier when each of us can have "my assistant call your assistant." Will this, in fact, enable people who have been way too busy to start interacting a whole lot more? We suspect so.

Mobility will also change how society will behave. Many things that take time and effort now will be done on-the-fly in the future. People will be able to do their work from anywhere they want; instead of walking into an office building everyday, many people will do their work from the beach or from home. This will significantly change the way society works. Walking into an office building and staying there from 8 a.m. until 5 p.m. provides a frame around the workspace. With pervasiveness, this frame is gone. Leisure and work will not be easily separated anymore. People will move away from a society that had strict rules on when to work and when to rest. Everyone will be able to individualize his or her week. The advantage is that people will have the freedom to plan their week however they want, but the disadvantage is that social contacts with friends and family become much harder to coordinate.

This may lead to a situation where nobody has time for anyone else, because work and leisure shifts are so different that they always collide. Mobility will also enable people to be wherever they want to be. This adds a spatial problem to the timing problem, meaning that even if people would have time to see each other, they may not be very near each other. In the worst case scenario, it could lead to a society of individuals who do not know anything about each other anymore, which makes the individuals unhappy as a result.

But, in fact, technology almost never goes monotonically in the direction of antisocial behavior. People find new ways to use technology for socializing. So e-mail supplants letters, but people communicate more now that ever before. Cell phones enable workers to be isolated from offices, but the entire family and all the kids' friends are racking up huge cell phone bills because they just have to chat all the time. Web cams don't quite make it for business meetings, but they get all kinds of use in personal situations. See Figure 9.1 for a Web cam of Viareggio in Italy.

Figure 9.1. Web Cam

So we believe that me-centric appliances will increase independence, mobility, and autonomy (as most technologies have done for workers), but will be employed to enhance and increase frequency of social engagement. My agents, for example, will make it easier for me to get reservations at hard-to-get-into restaurants and coordinate schedules with friends so that we socialize more, not less often. We will be able to get our kids enrolled in appropriate programs more often with less aggravation and effort, and as a result I will have more time to apply to myself, my activities, and my friendships. These are just some examples of how these new technologies can enhance the social life of every human.

9.1.4 Information Literacy

Me-centric computing will become the major form of communication for educational institutions and businesses all over the world. Governments are catching up fast, and we need to ensure that everyone will get access to me-centric computing. In today's computing paradigm, everybody needs to have the right hardware, the right software, and the necessary knowledge to make use of the content and services. This type of knowledge is called *information literacy*.

Print literacy is still a major problem around the world. In many countries, many people cannot read or write. Today, these people have almost no chance to use a computer, because they cannot read. Today's computing paradigm is an elite information infrastructure, accessible only to those who have the resources, skills, and knowledge. This increases the gap between the rich and the poor.

To ensure global access to the me-centric computing architecture, the education standards around the world do not need to be raised (although this is always a good idea). New paradigms of accessing information will be implemented that allow the less fortunate to access the basic services via graphical symbols, for example. Just as you don't have to be literate to drive a car (because the affordances are physical), you don't have to be literate to communicate with an intelligent appliance (you talk and it talks).

Moreover, as we mentioned previously, me-centric (intelligent) interfaces are a perfect antidote to physical handicaps (such as blindness, deafness, or paralysis), because they can provide alternate affordances. We believe literacy can provide a higher floor for exploitation, but me-centric intelligent interfaces can use existing human skills (e.g., natural language) as an alternative to previous requirements for literacy.

9.2 Revisiting Computing and IT

9.2.1 Where Are We Now, and Where Are We Going?

Computers have followed a long evolutionary path thus far, and most of this has been badly predicted. Powerful mainframe computers were the original model, although even national experts were unable to foresee much demand for these machines. These machines primarily performed numeric computations, such as accounting and specialized computations for military applications. Subsequently, time-sharing machines and then personal computers made possible interactive computing, where each user could interact with one or more computer programs in real time.

This made possible much of what we think of as computing today: text, graphics, gaming, spreadsheets, and the like. As the Internet gained widespread acceptance, various kinds of data sharing and limited communications occurred, as exemplified by e-mail, chat, file transfer, and Web access. Thus, today we have reached the end result of the first philosophical era, namely computers as tools. This has had the consequence of increasing the load on us to be effective tool users. The most productive knowledge workers today are those who have learned to make the tools useful, although this has taken great skill and enormous amounts of time on the part of the tool users.[1]

We are about to change eras, and with this will come a new period that should prove a renaissance in everyday life, because computers and communication are so ubiquitous and can affect each of us. Soon, each of us will have five to ten or more devices directly working for us. These will interact with hundreds or thousands of other computers over the Internet. Every day, we will have hundreds of tasks we can usefully delegate to our intelligent agents.

This, in turn, will make us feel liberated from many of today's ordinary tasks. Productivity will soar because we will actually be getting time back, rather than squeezing more and more tool-using activity into every waking hour. As machines begin to understand human desires and intent, they will become empowered to do things we care about and do it in combination with other machines. This will stimulate the development of what will ultimately prove to be one of the dominant aspects of the future, machine-to-machine intelligent cooperation. Rather than being a science fiction horror story, in this scenario the machines take over the teamwork that directly achieves the desires of every man, woman, and child.

---

[1] Even among high-educated, computer-literate, techno-savvy people, it's extremely common to hear stories of serious problems installing a new application on Windows or upgrading one version of system software to another. The technology is too complex, and usage is gated by users' abilities to learn how to master each new and improved tool. This has decreasing returns, for all involved. A different paradigm would be required to combat this trend, if me-centric computing were not already waiting in the wings to take the stage.

9.2.2 Reshaping the IT Industry

The IT industry is significantly shaped every decade. Stalwarts and dominant companies come and go. Some catch the next wave; some do not. We see the following disruptive technologies as creating conditions around which the industry will be reshaped: wireless, mobility, intelligent devices, natural language communication and multimodality interfaces, semantics, agents, and the e-service economy.

While you can't predict which companies will prevail in this or which new companies will emerge, you can already see that companies are investing across this range of technologies. Several companies, such as IBM[2], are investing in all of these areas. A decade from now, more money will be made from people getting work done by their machines than was ever made from people doing work on machines.

If the information technology is to serve the average consumer, the technology companies need to become market-driven, task-driven, and driven by the real activities of users. Alas, this is a change so drastic that many companies may not be able to make the transition. The very skills that made them so successful in the early stages of the technology are just the opposite of what is needed in the consumer phases.

9.2.3 IT Becomes a Utility

Tapping into computing resources with a simplicity equal to plugging a lamp into an outlet has been a goal of pervasive computing efforts from the start. Known as utility computing, the idea is to provide unlimited computing power and storage capacity that can be used and reallocated for any application, which is billed on a pay-per-use basis.

Already present in a variety of capacity-based pricing models, utility computing is poised to expand throughout the enterprise as various key technologies grow together, such as Web services, grid computing, and provisioning. Growth of utility computing in the enterprise will deliver to the industry not only equal access to supercomputing resources, but also new revenue streams for commercial data centers, new application pricing models based on metered use, and an open computing infrastructure for companies with little or no standing IT maintenance budget.

Already today, companies such as IBM, Hewlett-Packard, and Sun offer services in which additional servers, storage devices, and printers are placed on-site with customers. The customer is charged for the gear only when it is turned on and used. By pooling large numbers of servers connected over the Internet, these computing companies envision a fu-

---

[2]http://www.ibm.com/

ture in which customers don't have to worry about the headaches of administering complicated computers, just as they don't have to know how to run a power plant today.

This means that we are moving towards a grid-like computing environment, where all infrastructure capabilities like storage, databases, or special equipment will all be available in the grid, and anything a customer needs will be available on demand across the grid.

Utility computing on a global scale will require the continued evolution and convergence of core technologies spanning Web services, grid computing, broadband, storage virtualization, automatic provisioning, change management, and security.

Web services will be the driver of utility computing, as there will be lots of machine-to-machine interaction without human intervention. And the utility computing model is perfectly suited for the computing required to support the massive amount of processing that is going to be needed to enable Web services.

Hewlett-Packard[3], for example, has been advancing its UDC (Utility Data Center) initiative for several years, and is currently focused on auto-provisioning technology that will enable utility computing. IBM[4], as another example, began offering a service that lets customers buy Linux computing capacity from Big Blue in much the same way they buy kilowatt hours of electricity from the power company.

9.3   Conclusion

Advances in technology will always influence society, but not merely in a positive or negative way. Me-centric computing offers huge opportunities for the world to concentrate on the important things in life and forget about the boring daily work that is done better by computers.

While technology advances, people should always think about how to simplify the use of technology and make the technology the slave and not the master. Operating a VCR today is often a very complicated mission, as is changing the time on the car stereo. Technology should enable everyone to use it, not just the highly educated specialists. A mobile phone is a good example of a simple-to-use technology that hides all the complexity from users. But furthermore, the technology (intelligent agents, devices, and services) should do work on behalf of the people. This would be a major breakthrough in the history of technology, as until now technology has been an efficient tool, but was not considered a replacement for a manual task.

---

[3]http://www.hp.com/
[4]http://www.ibm.com/

Technology in the past has replaced manual labor with mechanical power, for example. Most tools automate some previously mechanical work. But generally, responsibility for task performance (setting objectives, controlling the tools, monitoring progress, interceding to deal with exceptions, etc.) has remained 100 percent with the human. Thus, the real change is occurring in three dimensions, some quantitative, and collectively to a qualitative effect. First, the scope of what can be automated is growing to include everyday tasks, requiring a multi-step process, with needs for both knowledge of and controlled interactions with the environment and other actors/systems in the domain. Second, the control of the automatons is moving up to a level of intent, often conveyed in natural language or other high-level ways. Third, there is the transfer of responsibility for correctly interpreting intent, understanding values, and performing work to accomplish objectives. This includes transferring responsibility for monitoring behavior throughout the process, from a human to an intelligent assistant that is a computer-based agent. Robots like those in the Jetsons will become reality, maybe not so sophisticated in the near future, but we will see them.

From the perspective of a world where me-centric computing is pervasive, the introduction of the Internet will look like just a small piece of a mosaic that led to the revolution. But getting there will not happen overnight. We are still seeing the effects of the introduction of the Internet in many areas, and a me-centric computing world still requires some very creative inventions and designs over the next few years. Maybe even more important is that companies create successful businesses that are based on me-centric computing business plans, architectures, and technologies. Companies in the IT and telecommunications world are already working on such business plans. But to have a truly me-centric computing environment, all industries need to adopt this paradigm.

We hope that through this book we have provided you with some business ideas and architectural building blocks that will lead to some new insights about how the world may be tomorrow and how you can participate in forming the future.

Part V

Appendix

Appendix A

GLOSSARY

This appendix contains a list of all the buzzwords and acronyms used throughout the book. You can use this glossary while reading the book or keep it as a future reference. You can also find an electronic version of this glossary on the book's home page.[1]

3G The acronym stands for third (or next) generation of wireless technology beyond personal communications services. The World Administrative Radio Conference assigned 230 megahertz of spectrum at 2 GHz for multimedia 3G networks. These networks must be able to transmit wireless data at 144 kilobits per second for mobile user speeds, 384 kbps for pedestrian user speeds, and 2 megabits per second for fixed locations. See also *UMTS*.

802.11 The Institute of Electrical and Electronics Engineers standard for wireless local area network interoperability.

AAA See *Authentication, Authorization, and Accounting*

Abstraction A concept in a person's mind that relates to a machine. A high-level abstraction is one in which a machine or part of a machine is thought about in a way that is quite distant from the detail of the actual machine. A low-level abstraction concerns the detail of some aspect of a machine.

ACID An acronym and mnemonic device for learning and remembering the four primary attributes ensured to any transaction by a transaction manager (also called a transaction monitor). These attributes are: Atomicity, Consistency, Isolation, and Durability.

Active X Software technology developed by Microsoft that helps designers include applications in HTML pages. Its lack of security causes many people to prefer Java over Active X.

---

[1]http://www.radicalsimplicity.com/

267

Address An address on the Internet is described as a URL, or Uniform Resource Locator, which can be used for any type of addressing, such as email (mailto:info@gallery-net.com), Web pages (http://www.news.com/), and FTP sites (ftp://ftp.netscape.com/pub/). Instead of using domain names, it is also possible to use IP addresses. See also *Electronic Mail, File Transfer Protocol, Transmission Control Protocol / Internet Protocol, Uniform Resource Locator*.

Address Resolution Protocol (ARP) Used primarily with the Internet Protocol. A network layer to resolve addresses.

Advanced Research Projects Agency Network (ARPANet) A network that was developed in the late 1960s by the U.S. Department of Defense to allow communication in a postnuclear war age. Predecessor of the Internet. See also *Internet*.

AFK Net language for "away from keyboard."

Air Interface The standard operating system of a wireless network; technologies include AMPS, TDMA, CDMA, and GSM.

Agent A piece of code with some autonomy and purpose. See also *Intelligent Agents*.

Agent-to-Agent Negotiation In the me-centric world, agents can execute processes autonomously, so they need to be able to negotiate with other agents on prices, for example. First, the agent requests a bid or contract, and then it starts the contracting phase with one or multiple parties. Once a party has been selected for a particular purpose, the agent needs to monitor that it gets the expected result. If this is not the case, it needs to renegotiate the contract.

AI See *Artificial Intelligence*.

American Standard Code for Information Interchange (ASCII) A standard for the representation of upper- and lowercase Latin letters, numbers, and punctuation on computers. There are 128 standard ASCII codes that are represented by a 7-digit binary code ($2^7 = 128$). The other 128 bit codes are used differently on most computers. To display non-Latin codes, Unicode is used in most cases. See also *Unicode*.

American National Standards Institute (ANSI) The primary organization for fostering the development of technology standards in the United States. Computer standards from ANSI include ASCII and SCSI. See also *ASCII* and *SCSI*.

ANSI See *American National Standards Institute*.

API See *Application Program Interface*.

Applet Java programs that are embedded into HTML pages. Applets are restricted in such a way that they are, for example, not allowed to read and write to the user's hard disk without explicit permission. See also *HyperText Markup Language*, *Java*, *Servlet*.

Appliance An appliance or "network appliance" is a term used to denote a relatively low-cost PC designed for network access and specialized business use.

Appliance Computing An Internet-based computing architecture where software applications reside on a Web server rather than on the end-user's workstation. The workstation, or appliance, is a thin client. The appliance typically has only an operating system and a connectivity program, such as a Web browser, which allows the appliance to connect to the server in order to access applications that the end-user needs. The purpose of appliance computing is to make remote management easier and more cost effective.

Application A program that is self-contained and that executes a set of well-defined tasks under user control.

Application Program Interface (API) Interface that allows the communication between programs, networks, and databases.

Application Service Provider (ASP) A service provider that makes applications available on a pay-per-use basis. ASPs manage and maintain the applications at their own data center and make the applications available via the Internet to subscribing businesses.

Archie Software for finding files on anonymous FTP sites. It searches only for filenames, and has been replaced by more powerful Web-based search engines. See also *File Transfer Protocol*.

Architecture In terms of data processing or information technology, a general term for the structure of all parts of a computer system (hardware and software).

ARPANet See *Advanced Research Projects Agency Network*.

Articulatory Distance The gap between the semantic representations used at an interface and the physical form of the expressions used in an interaction.

Artificial Intelligence (AI) A branch of computer science that studies how to endow computers with capabilities of human intelligence.

ASCII See *American Standard Code for Information Interchange*.

Asimov's Laws of Robotics Science-fiction author Isaac Asimov is often given credit for being the first person to use the term "robotics" in a short story composed in the 1940s. In the story, Asimov suggested three principles to guide the behavior of robots and smart machines. Asimov's Three Laws of Robotics, as they are called, have survived to the present: 1) Robots must never harm human beings. 2) Robots must follow instructions from humans without violating rule 1. 3) Robots must protect themselves without violating the other rules.

Assistant (also referred to as "Expert" or "Wizard") A tool designed to help users create programs (e.g., databases).

Associative Learning The second stage of learning a skill in which connections between the various elements of the skill are strengthened. See also *Cognitive Learning*.

Asynchronous Transfer Mode (ATM)   A   dedicated-connection switching technology that organizes digital data into cell units and transmits them over a physical medium using digital signal technology.

@ The commercial a—also referred to as the "at" sign. It has become a symbol recognized the world over as a separator in email addresses.

ATM See *Asynchronous Transfer Mode*.

Authentication The process of verifying that a person is who he or she claims to be.

Authentication, Authorization, and Accounting A framework for intelligently controlling access to computer resources, enforcing policies, auditing usage, and providing the information necessary to bill for services. These combined processes are considered important for effective network management and security.

Authorization The process of allowing system access to a person.

Auto PC An in-vehicle combination AM/FM radio, Windows CE-based computer, compact disc and CD-ROM player, wireless phone, and navigational system. The units are about the size of a typical car stereo.

Automatic Vehicle Location (AVL) Combining a location-sensing device (such as a GPS receiver) with a wireless communications link to provide a home office or dispatcher with the location of a vehicle or mobile asset (such as a trailer or heavy machinery).

Avatar 2D or 3D representation or digital actor of a customer in a Web shop or chat room.

AVL See *Automatic Vehicle Location*.

Backbone The top level of a hierarchical network. Major pathway within a network offering the highest possible speed and connecting all major nodes. The main pipes along which data is transferred. See also *Network*, *Node*.

Back-end The "side" of a client/server program that supplies data (typically, a database server). See also *Front-end*.

Bandwidth The maximum amount of information that can be sent through a connection at a given time. Usually measured in bits per second (bps). See also *Binary Digit*, *Bits Per Second*, *T-1*.

BASIC See *Beginners All-purpose Symbolic Instructional Code*.

Baud Commonly used in the same way as bits per second. See also *Binary Digit*, *Bits Per Second*, *Modulator Demodulator*.

Beginners All-purpose Symbolic Instructional Code (BASIC) Invented at Dartmouth University, a computer language that is easy to learn and highly flexible.

Benchmark A point of reference by which something can be measured. For example, in a Web site usability evaluation, a benchmark can be the measurement of a participant's performance on a set of predetermined tasks, such as time to complete task. See also *Benchmark Completion Time*.

Beta A pre-release of an application that is made available for the purposes of testing.

Binary Mathematical base 2, or numbers composed of a series of zeros and ones. Because zeros and ones can easily be represented by two voltage levels on an electronic device, the binary number system is widely used in digital computing.

Binary Digit (Bit) A single digit number in base 2 (therefore 0 or 1). The smallest unit for computerized data. See also *Byte*, *Kilobyte*, *Megabyte*.

Biometrics The science and technology of measuring and statistically analyzing biological data.

Bit See *Binary Digit*.

Bits Per Inch (BPI) Describes the data density on magnetic media in bits per inch.

Bits Per Second (BPS) A unit for measuring the data transmission rate, for example, the transmission path of a modem. The fastest modems operate today at 56 KBPS. An ASCII letter consists of 8 bits; theoretically speaking, a 56 K modem can transfer 7,000 characters (nearly 2.5 pages of standard letter-size pages) per second. See also *Bandwidth*, *Binary Digit*.

Bluetooth The Bluetooth consortium introduced the open Bluetooth standard 1.0 (available as a PDF file from www.bluetooth.com) in 1999, led by the founding companies Ericsson, Nokia, Toshiba, IBM, and Intel. Bluetooth was developed especially for economical, short-range, wireless links between PDAs, laptops, cellular phones, and other (mobile) devices. Bluetooth devices are capable of detecting each other automatically and setting up a network connection. Using a modulation frequency of 2.4 GHz, data is transferred from one adapter to another, whereby the signals do not have a predefined direction and can, in principle, be received from any other device. Bluetooth functions with spread-spectrum modulation, combined with frequency hopping (1600 frequency hops per second). There are 79 usable hopping frequencies available between 2.402 GHz and 2.480 GHz spaced at 1 MHz. A unique ID plus data encryption ensures that only "authorized" devices can communicate with each other. The maximum data rate is 750 Kbps, and the range is limited to 10 meters. However, the standard also permits 100 meters with increased transmission power. Bluetooth also enables devices to communicate with each other on the basis of JINI technology without being connected by cable. Many of the typical Bluetooth fields of application overlap with those of the IrDA standard for infrared data transmission. The first hardware and software products equipped with Bluetooth were introduced at the end of 1999. Experts predict that by 2005, nearly 700 million of these devices will be in use.

Bookmark A file that contains references to Web pages that you have already visited, which then can be organized and used to return to a particular page.

Boolean Search A search allowing the inclusion or exclusion of documents containing certain words through the use of operators such as "AND," "NOT," and "OR."

Boot To startup or reset a computer. When a computer is booted, the operating system is loaded. There are two different ways of booting a computer. A cold boot means that the computer needs to be powered up from an off state, and a warm boot means that all data in the memory is erased and the operating system is loaded from start. See also *Operating System*.

Bot Net language for "robot." A piece of software, usually run from a shell account. Most bots are harmless and simply keep channels open for their owners while they are not on IRC. There are some malicious bots, however, made to take over channels, etc. A popular and usually friendly bot series is called "Eggdrop." See also *IRC*.

BPI See *Bits Per Inch*.

BPS See *Bits Per Second*.

Broadband Describes a communications medium capable of transmitting a relatively large amount of data over a given period of time. A communications channel of high bandwidth.

Brokering The general act of mediating between buyers and sellers. In the universal network world of the future, brokering technologies, such as E-Speak, will enable universal service-to-service interaction, negotiation, bidding, and selection. See *E-Speak*.

Browser Client application that is able to display various kinds of Internet resources. See also *Client, Home Page, Uniform Resource Locator, World Wide Web*.

BSIG Bluetooth Special Interest Group, with over 1,500 member companies and organizations.

BTW Net language for "by the way."

Bug A programming error that causes a malfunction of the computer software or hardware. Not synonymous with *Virus*.

Building Automation Describes the sum of all automating measures in buildings (including rented housing and private homes). Building automation makes it possible to control and regulate technical systems to ensure efficiency, primary energy savings, productivity, and comfort.

Business-to-Me-Commerce (B2Me) The trillion-dollar shift from e-commerce to a second-generation "me-centric" intelligent and personalized commerce via any media: store, phone, browser, personal digital device, or Web.

BWOTD Net language for "bad word of the day."

Byte There are eight bits in a byte, which is used to represent a single ASCII character, for example. See also *Binary Digit*.

Cache A small, intermediate memory area for exchanging or transferring data, for example, between the hard disk and central processing unit. A cache accelerates hard disk access. A cache is typically used to reduce latency.

Capture Error A type of error that occurs when a sequence of less familiar actions is "captured" by another, more frequent or better learned sequence, for example driving to work on the weekend when one intended to go somewhere else.

CBT See *Computer-Based Training*.

CEBus See *Consumer Electronics Bus*.

Central Processing Unit (CPU) The main chip inside every computer that is used to run the operating system and the application software.

CERN European Laboratory for Particle Physics in Geneva, Switzerland, the birthplace of the World Wide Web.

Certificate Authority (CA) Issuer of digital certificates; used for encrypting communication and signing documents. See also *Digital Certificate*.

CGI See *Common Gateway Interface*.

Chai A product-family name for a group of HP products supporting intelligent interaction among embedded devices through the use of the Java programming language and today's Web standards.

Chat Direct communication over the Internet with multiple persons. Unlike e-mail, responses are made in real time. See also *Internet Relay Chat*.

Checksum A special calculation applied to validate the transmission of a piece of information. If the information is transmitted and the calculation achieves the same result, then the transmission was successful.

Chip Term for complex, integrated circuits that can contain several hundred thousand semi-conductor circuits (transistors or diodes, for example). By creating structures as small as one thousandth of a millimeter, higher levels of integration can be achieved.

Class In object-oriented programming, a category of objects, or the applet file itself. For example, there might be a class called shape that contains objects that are circles, rectangles, and triangles.

Client Application that resides on the customer's computer and contacts a server to communicate, such as IRC clients or Web clients. See also *Internet Relay Chat*, *World Wide Web*.

Client/Server Databases in a network often administered from a central location by a server. Client software installed on the user's computer retrieves required data from the server.

Clipboard A piece of memory that stores information temporarily.

CODEC Program or device that COmpresses/DECompresses digital video.

Code Division Multiple Access (CDMA) A spread-spectrum air interface technology used in some digital cellular, personal communications services, and other wireless networks.

Cognitive Complexity A measure of the demands made on the user's cognitive system, in terms of, for example, complexity of information presented to the user in the interface, complexity of layout, demands made on short-term (working) memory, variability of the interface, pace of interaction, etc. This is one of the most important criteria measured in a usability test. See also *Cognitive Overload, Usability Testing*.

Cognitive Overload Excessive demands made on the cognitive processes, in particular, memory.

Cognitive System The mental apparatus that translates inputs from the perceptual system into outputs to the motor system through the use of memory processes.

Cognitive Walkthrough An evaluation method, similar to a heuristic evaluation, whereby an expert evaluates the usability of a design. The evaluator constructs task scenarios from a specification, and then role-plays the part of a user. Potential problems are evaluated against psychological criteria.

Collaborative Filtering A filter is applied to information from different sites to select relevant data that may apply to the specific e-commerce experience of a customer or specific group of customers.

Common Gateway Interface (CGI) A standard that describes how a Web browser passes information to a Web server. CGI programs read the information, process it, and pass the results back to the Web browser.

Common Object Request Broker Architecture (CORBA) An architecture and specification for creating, distributing, and managing distributed program objects in a network. It allows programs at different locations and developed by different vendors to communicate in a network through an "interface broker."

Compiler A program that translates a programming language into machine code.

Compression Technology to reduce the size of files and save bandwidth. See also *Bandwidth*.

Computer-Based Training (CBT) A way of learning that uses a computer and a software package as the delivery mechanism, offering information on a certain subject and a test for the pupil.

Concept Search Instead of searching for documents that contain a given keyword, a concept search will search for documents related conceptually to a given keyword.

Conceptual Model Refers to the knowledge that a person has about the system and the way it should work.

Constraints A Boolean relation, often an equality or inequality relation, between the values of one or more variables (often two). These relations check certain conditions at the table level, for example, whether a particular range of values was violated for numerical fields. E.g., x¿3 is a constraint on x.

Constraint Satisfaction The process of assigning values to variables so that all constraints are true.

Consumer Electronics Bus (CEB) A communications standard for home networks developed by the Electronics Industry Association (EIA) and the Consumer Electronics Manufacturer Association (CEMA).

Content Information that has a tangible aspect because it has been collected and contained in a content object. Content can be unstructured (usually text) or structured (in a database). Content can be collected at differing levels of granularity.

Content Management The process of developing, maintaining, organizing, and deploying Web content to efficiently support the collaborative activities of content creators, site administrators, and users.

Context Environmental information that is part of an application's operating environment and that can be sensed by the application.

Context of Use A description of the actual conditions of which the system is under assessment, or will be used in a normal day-to-day working situation. Examples of conditions include: the users, tasks, equipment, and the physical, social, and organizational environments in which the system is used.

Continuous Speech Recognition A computer-based speech system that can recognize a string of spoken words.

Control Prog/Monitor (CP/M) Operating system created by Gary Kildall in the 1970s.

Controlled Vocabulary A predetermined list that specifies the acceptable terms that can be used to describe a particular information resource. Control of these terms is necessary to solve two common problems: (1) Users employ different terms to describe the same resource (oil, petrol, petroleum, gas), or (2) a term can have multiple meanings (musical pitch, pitch the ball, sales pitch, etc.).

Cookie Piece of information that is stored in the browser and can be retrieved by the server that placed the information there. This piece of information can be used to identify a user.

CORBA See *Common Object Request Broker Architecture*.

CP/M See *Control Prog/Monitor*.

CPU See *Central Processing Unit*.

CRC See *Cyclical Redundancy Check*.

Credentials What must be presented to an agent, service or system that accepts your requests to delegate, and what you might need to show others down the line.

Credit Card Processor Service provider for electronic and non-electronic businesses to process credit card transactions and verify credibility of customers.

Cross-post A message that is sent simultaneously to several newsgroups. See also *Newsgroup*.

Cyberculture A collection of cultures and cultural products that exist on and are made possible by the Internet, along with the stories told about these cultures and cultural products.

Cyberspace First used in the book *Neuromancer*, by William Gibson, published in 1984. It is used to describe the Internet. See also *Internet*.

Cyclical Redundancy Check (CRC) Checksum for correcting errors that occur during data transmission.

Daemon A background process waiting for a client to start up the service, such as the POP3 daemon, which runs continually, but is activated only when people retrieve e-mail using an e-mail client.

Data Dictionary Area of memory in which all information on a database and the accompanying programs are stored and managed. This includes information on tables, triggers, constraints, relations, and indices.

Database A term with several meanings: refers to a DBMS (Database Management System) as well as a file that contains, for example, customer addresses or other data. A database can combine several tables into one file. Often, only one table is allowed per database file for PC databases. In this case, the user can still create a link to other tables from various files (see *Referential Integrity*).

Data Encryption Key (DEK) A string used to mathematically encode a message so that it can be decrypted only by someone with the same key.

Data Encryption Standard (DES) Encryption scheme developed by IBM in the 1970s.

Data Header Data structure at the beginning of a data packet header.

Data Packet Data is generally transmitted within networks in the form of data packets. These packets contain the header, the actual data (user data), and redundant data (CRC) for error correction on the receiving end.

Data Rate Also known as data transfer rate. Indicates the number of data units per specified time interval in bps (bits per second).

Data Record Combines all the data for a specific table entry into a logical entity. Using a file-card box as an analogy, a record would be the equivalent of one file card.

Data Throughput Transmission rate of the actual user data (excluding redundant data for error correction or data for delimiting individual data blocks, e.g., header). Specified in cps (characters per second).

DCOM See *Distributed Component Object Model*.

Decryption The reconstruction of encrypted data.

Delegation In a me-centric world, tasks can be completely delegated to intelligent agents and appliances that will work autonomously to get the desired result. See also *Intelligent Agent, Intelligent Appliance*.

Demilitarized Zone Zone in multilayered firewalls that contains public Internet services.

DES See *Data Encryption Standard*.

Descrambling See *Decryption*.

Description Error A type of slip that occurs when information is misinterpreted, resulting in an incorrect action. These errors tend to occur when different actions have similar descriptions.

Device A machine designed for a purpose. In a general context, a computer can be considered a device.

DHCP See *Dynamic Host Configuration Protocol*.

DHTML See *Dynamic HyperText Markup Language*.

Digerati The digital elite; invented by *Wired* magazine. Derived from the word *literati*.

Digital Certificate File containing information about its owner that can be used to identify the owner. See also *Certificate Authority*, *Secure Sockets Layer*.

Distributed Component Object Model (DCOM) A set of Microsoft concepts and program interfaces in which client program objects can request services from server program objects on other computers in a network.

Distributed Model The theory that people have neither purely functional nor purely structural models of devices, but, in fact, have knowledge that is distributed between the mind (where such knowledge may be functional, structural, or a combination of the two) and the world.

DMZ See *Demilitarized Zone*.

DNS See *Domain Name System*.

Domain In an Internet address (or URL), the domain names separated by dots are listed according to the protocol and service (such as "http://www"). An example is "ebusinessrevolution" (second level domain) and "com" (top-level domain). The top-level domain can contain a country code ("fr" for France) or an abbreviation indicating the type of server (for example, "com" for commercial companies, "org" for organizations, or "edu" for educational institutions).

Domain Name The name of a computer connected to the Internet. The domain name is used to form a URL. See also *Uniform Resource Locator*.

Domain Name System (DNS) Database that links IP addresses and domain names. See also *Domain Name, Transmission Control Protocol / Internet Protocol.*

Domotik Widespread industry solution designed to connect products such as security, telecommunications, household appliances, and heating systems by means of an integrated residential wiring system. All electrically controlled devices are networked via the European Installation Bus (EIB) and controlled by a multimedia PC. Domotik can also be operated with the HomeAssistant multimedia program used for entering the various functions. HomeAssistant runs on standard multimedia PCs. The user-friendly graphical interface is, to a large extent, self-explanatory.

Download Information (e.g., PDF files) or programs can be copied from a server (e.g., the Internet) to the computer's hard disk or other data media. Common examples of downloaded data include drivers for hardware components or updates for software applications.

DWIM Net language for "do what I mean."

Dynamic Host Configuration Protocol (DHCP) Internet standard, based on RFC 1541, for the automatic allocation of IP addresses.

Dynamic HyperText Markup Langauge (DHTML) An extension to HTML that allows for better user interaction and introduces dynamic Web page creation.

E911 911 service becomes E911 when automatic number identification and automatic location information is provided to the 911 operator.

EBCDIC See *Extended Binary Coded Decimal Interchange Code.*

E-Cash See *Electronic Cash.*

ECC See *Error Correction Code.*

ECMA See *European Computer Manufacturers Association.*

EDGE See *Enhanced Data GSM Environment.*

EDI See *Electronic Data Interchange.*

EHS See *European Home System.*

EIB See *European Installation Bus*.

EIBA See *European Installations Bus Association*.

EIDE See *Enhanced Integrated Drive Electronics*.

E-mail See *Electronic Mail*.

Electronic Cash Electronic money that can be exchanged on the Internet for goods, information, and services. It is mostly used for micropayment solutions. See also *Micropayments*.

Electronic Data Interchange (EDI) A standard for the interorganizational computer-to-computer exchange of structured information.

Electronic Mail Exchange of digital documents via the Internet.

Emoticon Sideways "face" that expresses emotions without words on the Internet using special characters on the keyboard. The best-known emoticon is the smiley :-). If you can't see the face, turn your head to the left and look again. Other emoticons include the smiling pirate .-) and the sad person :-(.

Encryption Procedure to render a message illegible to anyone who is not authorized to read it.

Enhanced Data GSM Environment (EDGE) A faster version of the Global System for Mobile (GSM) wireless service designed to deliver data at rates up to 384 Kbps and enable the delivery of multimedia and other broadband applications to mobile phone and computer users.

Enhanced Integrated Drive Electronics (EIDE)   An advanced development of the IDE standard offering higher data transfer rates and support for newer drives.

Episodic Memory The storage of autobiographical experience, for example, the objects, events, and people who have been personally encountered. In psychological experiments, episodic memory is tested using sets of words and pictures.

EPOC Operating system designed for small, portable computer-telephones with wireless access to phone and other information services. EPOC is based on a well-known operating system from Psion, the first major manufacturer of personal digital assistants (PDAs).

Error Correction Code (ECC) Redundant data that helps detect errors and eliminate them through recalculation. ECC on-the-fly means that hardware error correction for hard disks takes place while the data is being transferred.

E-service An electronic service available via the Internet that completes tasks, solves problems, or conducts transactions. E-services can be used by people, businesses, and other e-services, and can be accessed via a wide range of information appliances.

E-Speak The universal language of e-services. To accelerate the creation of an open e-services world, HP has engineered E-Speak technology. The E-Speak platform provides a common services interface, making it easier and faster to create, deploy, manage, and connect e-services. Through the process of dynamic brokering, E-Speak lets an e-service discover other e-services anywhere on the Internet and link with them on the fly—even if they were built using different technology. See also *Brokering*.

ESPRIT European Strategic Program for Research and Development of Information Technology.

Ethernet Networking standard for connecting computers on an intranet, also known as IEEE 802.3. See also *Bandwidth*, *Intranet*.

European Computer Manufacturers Association (ECMA) The European Association of computer manufacturers with the goal of defining common standards.

European Home System (EHS) Created under the auspices of the EU project ESPRIT (European Strategic Program for Research and Development of Information Technology). It uses electrical wiring as the installation bus and offers a data throughput of up to 2.4 Kbps. A separate two-wired cable can also be used instead of an electrical cable. This increases the potential data throughput to a maximum of 48 Kbps. EHS and EIB are to be united into a common standard.

European Installation Bus (EIB) Network technology for residential wiring. EIB is designed for two-wire cable only. EIB versions for electrical cables as well as wireless systems for radio and infrared (as a functional prototype) have recently become available. The Siemens "Instabus" complies with the guidelines of the EIB standard, as well as Domotik developed by Bosch. The version EIB.net can also use normal data networks in accordance with

IEEE 802.2, with transfer rates of up to Ethernet 10 Mbps. The extension EIB.net "i" allows forwarding, for example, via the normal IP router and thus the EIB connection via the Internet. Maximum EIB data transfer rate is 9.6 Kbps.

European Installations Bus Association (EIBA) The EIB Association is a widespread manufacturer association dedicated to establishing the EIB standard. Over 100 manufacturers and more than 8,000 licensers throughout Europe offer nearly 5,000 EIB components.

Expert System A database of knowledge in a particular scientific or technical speciality, maintained by speciality experts and capable of reasoning according to predefined rules.

Extended Binary Coded Decimal Interchange Code IBM's 8-bit extension of the 4-bit Binary Coded Decimal encoding of digits 0-9 (0000-1001).

eXtensible Markup Language (XML) A flexible way to create common information formats and share both the format and the data on the Internet.

Extranet Extended intranets used to share information with business partners over the Internet in a very secure way. See also *Intranet*.

Familiarity The degree of correlation between the user's existing knowledge and the knowledge required for effective interaction with a system.

FAQ See *Frequently Asked Question*.

Fast-SCSI Transmission protocol compliant with SCSI-2 that allows data transmission of up to 10 Mbyte/s on a 8-bit bus.

FDDI See *Fibre Distributed Data Interface*.

Fibre Channel A technology for transmitting data between computer devices at a data rate of up to 1 Gbps (one billion bits per second). (A data rate of 4 Gbps is proposed.) Fibre Channel is especially suited for connecting computer servers to shared storage devices and for interconnecting storage controllers and drives.

Fibre Distributed Data Interface (FDDI) Standard for computer connections on optical fibre cables at a rate of 100 Mbit. See also *Bandwidth*, *Ethernet*, *T-1*, *T-3*.

Field The smallest unit in a record in a database. Each field has a specific data type that contains, for example, text, dates, currencies, etc.

File Transfer Protocol (FTP) Internet protocol that allows the movement of files from one Internet site to another one. Public FTP servers allow the upload and download of files, creating public file archives.

Finger Tool to locate people on other UNIX servers. It helps to see if a certain person is online.

Firehunter A comprehensive solution for measuring, monitoring, and reporting on Internet services.

Firewall A tool to separate an intranet from the Internet by disallowing connections on certain ports, keeping the intranet very secure. See also *Intranet, Network*.

FireWire See *IEEE 1394*.

Firmware Commands stored in a ROM chip for controlling the hard disk. This data can usually be updated (known as flashing the ROM).

Flame A crude or witless comment on a newsgroup posting or e-mail. See also *Flame War*.

Flame War Instead of discussing positions in an online discussion, personal attacks (or flames) against the debators are exchanged. See also *Flame*.

Flat File A database in ASCII format that separates records by a special character. See also *American Standard Code for Information Interchange, Database*.

Flooding On IRC, when a person sends many messages in a very short period of time. You are normally limited to one line every second. So if you send 10 lines in three seconds, you are flooding. Bots in channels have the authority to remove users from the channel for flooding. See also *Bots*.

Font Typographic style, such as Times New Roman or Helvetica.

Forward Sending an e-mail on to a third person. See also *Electronic Mail*.

Frame Frames make it possible to divide the browser window into several sections and independently configure and control their contents. Thus, a fixed menu can be shown in one frame while scrolling text, images, or animations can be displayed in another. See also *Browser, HyperText Markup Language*.

Frame Relay A broadband, packet-based interface used to transmit bursts of data over a wide area network. Seldom used for voice.

Freenet Internet access provided on a nonprofit basis.

Freeware Software that is available to anyone without paying a fee, while the author retains the copyright.

Frequently Asked Question (FAQ) Many home pages and nearly all newsgroups offer FAQ lists to answer questions frequently asked by users. To save time, it is often sufficient to refer to the list of FAQs to determine whether specific questions have already been answered.

Front-end Refers to a part of a program that allows user to access the database. See also *Back-end*.

FTP See *File Transfer Protocol*.

Full-Duplex Transmission protocol for the simultaneous transfer of data and signals in both directions.

Full-Text Index Database containing every word of every document, including stop words. See *Stop Words*.

Functional Model A user's mental model that consists of the "how to use it" knowledge about an object. See also *Distributed Model, Structural Model*.

Fuzzy Search Finds matches even if the keyword is misspelled or only partially spelled.

FWIW Net language meaning "for what it's worth."

FYI Net language meaning "for your information."

Gateway Architecture for bridging between two networks that work with different protocols.

General Packet Radio Service (GPRS) Packet-based wireless communication service that promises data rates from 56 up to 114 Kbps and continuous connection to the Internet for mobile phone and computer users.

Geographic Information System (GIS) Enables you to envision the geographic aspects of a body of data. Basically, it lets you query or analyze a relational database and receive the results in the form of some kind of map.

Gigabyte 1,024 Megabytes, but some round it off to 1,000 Megabytes, because it is easier to calculate with. See also *Byte*, *Megabyte*.

GIS See *Geographic Information System*.

Glitch Small malfunction in the hardware or software that does not cause an interruption.

Global Positioning System (GPS) A series of 24 geosynchronous satellites that continuously transmit their position. Used in personal tracking, navigation, and automatic vehicle location technologies.

Global System for Mobile Communication (GSM) A digital mobile telephone system that is widely used in Europe and other parts of the world. GSM uses a variation of time division multiple access (TDMA) and is the most widely used of the three digital wireless telephone technologies (TDMA, GSM, and CDMA).

Glyph From a Greek word for "carving," a glyph is a graphic symbol that provides the appearance or form for a character. A glyph can be an alphabetic or numeric font or some other symbol that pictures an encoded character.

GPRS See *General Packet Radio Service*.

GPS See *Global Positioning System*.

Granularity The level of complexity of a content object. There are coarsely grained content objects (e.g., sites, databases, applications, collections) and finely grained content objects (e.g., documents, audio clips, drawings). More coarsely grained content objects contain more different types of content objects. Examples: (towards finer granularity) book—chapter—page—paragraph—sentence—word—letter; video—story—event—shot—frame.

Graphical User Interface (GUI) Allows users to navigate and interact with information on their computer screen by using a mouse to point, click, and drag icons and other data around on the screen, instead of typing words and phrases. The Windows and Macintosh operating systems are examples of GUIs. The World Wide Web is an example of a GUI designed to enhance navigation of the Internet, once done exclusively via terminal-based (typed command line) functions.

Grep UNIX command to scan files for patterns; also used as a synonym for fast manual searching.

GSM See *Global System for Mobile Communication*.

GUI See *Graphical User Interface*.

Guru Synonym for expert.

Hacker Skilled computer programmer or engineer who loves a challenge. Not synonymous with "computer criminal" or "security breaker."

Handheld Device Markup Language (HDML) Written to allow Internet access from wireless devices such as handheld personal computers and smart phones. Derived from *HyperText Markup Language*. See also *Wireless Markup Language*.

HCI See *Human-Computer Interaction*.

HDML See *Handheld Device Markup Language*.

HDSL See *High-data-rate DSL*.

Header Contains information about the type and/or meaning and/or structure of the subsequent data packet. The header forms the beginning of a data packet, so it can also be used to mark the end of the previous data structure.

Hello World! The program that every computer student learns first; program outputs "Hello World!"

Heuristic Usability principles or "rules of thumb", with which a system should be guided. See also *Heuristic evaluation*.

Heuristic Evaluation A method for evaluating a design if certain heuristics or usability criteria are violated. It is similar to the cognitive walkthrough in that it is carried out by an expert but is less structured. See also *Heuristic, Cognitive Walkthrough*.

High-data-rate DSL Transmission procedure capable of a transmission rate of 1,544 Kbps (T1) or with 2,048 Kbps (E1) with pulse-code modulation via dual copper wires.

Hit The download of an element on a Web page. If a Web page consists of HTML text, two images, and a sound file, then there have been four hits on the Web server. It is a way to measure the load of the server. See also *HyperText Markup Language*.

Home Page Starting page, i.e., page 1 of a Web site (WWW). It usually contains a table of contents and links to other areas or pages on the site.

Host See *Server*.

HTML See *HyperText Markup Language*.

HTTP See *HyperText Transfer Protocol*.

Human-Computer Interaction The study of how humans interact with computers, used to design computers that are easy for humans to use. A user interface, such as a GUI, is how a human interacts with a computer. HCI goes beyond designing screens and menus that are easier to use and studies the reasoning behind building specific functionality into computers and the long-term effects that systems will have on humans. See also *GUI*.

Human Factors The field that studies the role of humans in man-machine systems and how systems can be designed to work well with people, particularly in regard to safety and efficiency.

Hypertext Web documents that contain links to other documents.

HyperText Markup Language (HTML) The language for developing documents for the World Wide Web. See also *Client*, *Server*, *World Wide Web*.

Hypertext Taxonomy A taxonomy composed of hyperlinks that enable the non-sequential retrieval of related information, allowing users to follow associative trails within or between taxonomies in order to quickly locate specific resources.

HyperText Transfer Protocol (HTTP) The protocol for transporting files from a Web server to a Web browser. See also *Client*, *Server*, *World Wide Web*.

IBT See *Internet-Based Training*.

Icon Mnemonic convention to replace functional names by images. An icon can be a metaphor when such a metaphor is appropriate. When a metaphor cannot be found for an icon, the design of such an icon will take special effort in terms of user testing. See also *Metaphor*.

IDL See *Interface Definition Language*.

IEEE 1394 The P-1394 bus technology originally developed by Apple became the industry standard IEEE 1394/1995 in 1995, also known as "FireWire." The IEEE 1394 technology describes a serial interface for computer and video devices for transmitting digital data up 400 Mbps. In 1997, Sony introduced its "i.Link" logo for identifying standardized IEEE-1394 interfaces.

IMAP See *Internet Mail Access Protocol*.

IMHO Net language for "in my humble opinion."

Implementation The process of actually programming and testing a software system.

Incremental Prototyping An extensive form of prototyping in which the prototype is gradually developed into the product. Also known as evolutionary prototyping.

Index A searchable database of documents created automatically or manually by a search engine.

Information Architecture The design of information organization, labeling, navigation, and indexing systems to support both browsing and searching in order to minimize the time that users spend looking for information.

Information Management The application of information science principles to the administration of corporate information to ensure that information is captured, formatted, maintained, and disseminated across the organization to support decision-making and future use. See also *Information Science*.

Information Science Generally refers to the study of the production, collection, classification, storage, manipulation, retrieval, dissemination, use, and measurement of information. Distinct from Computer Science and Information Systems, which focus primarily on the study of technology and the design of hardware and software, Information Science examines the interaction among people, technology, and information.

Infranet Communication structure for networking equipment in the household or in other applications such as gas stations, restaurants, medical technology, or agriculture (a supplement to Internet and intranet).

Infrared Data Association (IrDA) An industry-sponsored organization set up in 1993 to create international standards for the hardware and software used in infrared communication links. In this special form of radio transmission, a focused ray of light in the infrared frequency spectrum, measured in terahertz, or trillions of hertz (cycles per second), is modulated with information and sent from a transmitter to a receiver over a relatively short distance.

Intelligent Agent A responsibility-accepting performer to whom you delegate and from whom you get desired results or exception reporting, usually possessing context, task knowledge, and knowledge-based means to bring about desired results under given constraints, e.g., an application that helps a customer by completing transactions, seeking information or prices, or communicating with other agents and customers.

Intelligent Appliance Any type of equipment, instrument, or machine that has its own computing capability. As computing technology becomes more advanced and less expensive, it can be built into an increasing number of devices of all kinds. In addition to personal and handheld computers, the almost infinite list of possible intelligent appliances includes cars, medical instruments, geological equipment, and home appliances. In the me-centric world, it is a device that uses intelligent agents to perform the work that needs to be done. See also *Intelligent Agent*.

Intelligent Home Control signals for building automation or transmitting multimedia signals. The forerunners of today's modern concepts: Professor Ken Sakamura's Tron house in Tokyo in the 1980s and Chriet Titulaer's Huis van de Toekomst in Rosmalen (Holland).

Interaction Reciprocal action between a human and a computer.

Interaction Design A systematic and iterative process for designing highly interactive user interfaces. Methodology includes research and discovery techniques such as requirements analysis, stakeholder analysis, task analysis, as well as prototyping, inspection, and evaluation methods.

Interface Definition Language (IDL) The prevalent language used for defining how components connect together. Beyond its use in CORBA systems, it has proven a popular way to describe platform and language-neutral connection interfaces, including the core API for XML—the Document Object Model (DOM). Even variations on IDL, such as that used by Component Object Model (COM), tend to be similar to IDL. Understanding IDL helps to bring about key insights to many of the techniques of component programming.

International Standards Organization (ISO) A federation of national standards bodies such as BSI and ANSI.

Internet Worldwide conglomeration of data networks. Initially intended for military use, the Internet was increasingly used for exchanging research data among universities and institutes. Today, online service providers and network providers have made the Internet available to everyone. It is the computer network for business and leisure based on the TCP/IP protocol. All other computer networks have become irrelevant. Evolved from ARPAnet. See also *Advanced Research Projects Agency Network, Network, Transmission Control Protocol / Internet Protocol*.

Internet-Based Training (IBT) Evolution of computer-based training; offers real-time learning over the Internet with a teacher. See also *Computer-Based Training*.

Internet Mail Access Protocol (IMAP) RFC 1730[-33] The IMAP4 protocol allows a client to access and manipulate electronic mail messages on a server. This should be viewed as a superset of the POP3. The IMAP4 server listens on TCP port 143. IMAP is definitely an emerging technology, and it completely outperforms the older POP environment functionally.

Internet Protocol (IP) See *Transmission Control Protocol / Internet Protocol*.

Internet Protocol Number Unique address for every computer connected to the Internet. Currently, each is composed of a series of four (IPv4) or six (IPv6) numbers, separated by dots. Example: 127.0.0.1. Domain names refer to IP numbers. See also *Domain Name, Internet, Transmission Control Protocol / Internet Protocol*.

Internet Relay Chat (IRC) Multiuser chat facility on the Internet. Many servers around the world are interconnected to allow hundreds of thousands of users to chat at the same time. Special IRC clients are necessary to connect.

Internet Service Provider (ISP) A company that provides individuals and other companies access to the Internet and other related services such as personal mail boxes. An ISP has the equipment and the telecommunication line access required to have points-of-presence on the Internet for the geographic area served.

Internet Society (ISOC) Nongovernmental international organization for global cooperation and coordination of the Internet and its technologies and applications.

Intranet Private network that is based on the same technologies as the Internet, but is restricted to a certain user group. See also *Internet, Network*.

IP See *Internet Protocol, TCP/IP*.

IP Address Address of a single computer in the Internet. The IP address consists of four numbers from 0 to 255, each separated by dots (example: 123.27.1.155). To make this system more practical for users, IP addresses are converted into alphanumeric names. IPv6 will extend the range from four numbers to six numbers, thus making many more IP addresses available for appliances.

IPv6 The latest level of the Internet protocol (IP), now included as part of IP support in many products, including the major computer operating systems.

IRC See *Internet Relay Chat*.

IRC-Op IRC operators who administrate the IRC servers on an international level. These operators have access to additional commands unavailable to normal users.

ISO See *International Standards Organization*.

ISOC See *Internet Society*.

ISP See *Internet Service Provider*.

JAR See *Java Archive*.

Java Programming language developed by Sun with cross-platform neutrality, object-orientation, and networking in mind. See also *Applet, Java Development Kit*.

Java Archive (JAR) A file format used to bundle all components required by a Java applet. JAR files simplify the downloading of applets because all the components (class files, images, sounds, etc.) can be packaged into a single file.

Java Development Kit (JDK) Basic development package from Sun distributed for free in order to write, test, and debug Java programs. See also *Applet, Java.*

Java Intelligent Network Infrastructure (JINI) Sun introduced JINI technology in the summer of 1998. It is based on Java and can "spontaneously" network connected devices. In other words, devices that are dynamically connected to the network are immediately detected throughout the entire network. JINI regulates the communication between computers and other devices in the network and allows peripherals to be connected to the network without special configurations and used immediately. The self-identifying devices transmit their technical specifications and eliminate the need the for "manual" driver selection. In contrast to Ethernet systems, JINI automatically allocates resources.

JavaScript Scripting language developed by Netscape that allows interaction within HTML pages. See also *HyperText Markup Language.*

JDK See *Java Development Kit.*

JetSend A device-to-device communications protocol that allows devices to intelligently negotiate information exchange. The protocol allows two devices to connect, negotiate the best possible data type, provide device status, and exchange information, without user intervention.

JINI See *Java Intelligent Network Infrastructure.*

JIT See *Just-In-Time.*

Jitter The deviation in or displacement of some aspect of the pulses in a high-frequency digital signal. As the name suggests, jitter can be thought of as shaky pulses. The deviation can be in terms of amplitude, phase timing, or the width of the signal pulse.

Joint Photographic Experts Group (JPEG) One of the most popular graphic formats. The JPEG format frequently used in digital photography compresses large or color-intensive pictures to a fraction of their original size. This reduces storage requirements and file transfer time (i.e., on the Internet).

JPEG Image format for the Internet using lossy compression algorithms. See also *Joint Photographic Experts Group*.

Just-In-Time (JIT) The concept of reducing inventories by working closely with suppliers to coordinate delivery of materials just before their use in the manufacturing or supply process.

Kilobyte 1,024 bytes, or sometimes 1,000 bytes. See also *Binary Digit*, *Byte*.

Knowbie Expert in computer networking.

Knowledge Facts or ideas acquired by study, investigation, observation, or experience. Within the framework of Information Science, knowledge results from the contextual analysis of information, which can be used repeatedly to inform decision making.

Knowledge Management The discipline of gathering, organizing, managing, and disseminating a corporation's structured and unstructured information resources in order to improve corporate decision making and maximize staff productivity. See also *Structured Information*, *Unstructured Information*.

Lag The delay caused by high traffic congestion or other overloading between IRC servers or Internet provider sites, resulting in slow communications.

LAN See *Local Area Network*.

Last-Mile Technology Any telecommunications technology, such as wireless radio, that carries signals from the broad telecommunication infrastructure along the relatively short distance (hence, the "last mile") to and from the home or business.

LDAP See *Lightweight Directory Access Protocol*.

Learning This refers to acquiring new concepts, new skills, and new knowledge to perform a job. In the HCI context, it refers to how users learn new interfaces in order to solve problems. The theory is that once an adult reaches a certain age, learning becomes very difficult. The HCI course offers several solutions to minimize learning difficulties.

Learning through Analogy The invoking of prior knowledge of an apparently similar object or system as a basis for interpreting new information.

Lightweight Directory Access Protocol A technology that provides access to X.500 for PCs.

Likert Scale A rating scale designed to measure user attitudes or reactions by quantifying subjective information. Participants indicate where along a continuum their attitude or reaction resides.

Link Allows the user to branch from one Web page to another. Links are usually displayed as underlined text on HTML pages. Clicking these links makes it possible to "surf" the World Wide Web.

Local Area Network (LAN) Computer network limited to a certain location. See also *Ethernet, Wide Area Network*.

Login Account name to gain access to a system. See also *Password*.

LOL Net language for "laughing out loud."

Look-up Service Also known as "spontaneous networking" because each device is detected immediately (as soon as it is connected to the network). A component of the JINI system architecture that registers every active JINI device in the network, together with its technical characteristics in a table, and makes it available to authorized users. Example: A handheld computer that has been registered in the look-up service detects available printers, free memory space on a hard disk in a desktop computer, or an Internet connection.

Mailing List A system to redistribute mail from one person to many other people who are interested in that mail. Mailing lists are used to create online discussions, similar to newsgroups; however, the mail is sent automatically, while newsgroups require the user to actively retrieve the information. See also *Electronic Mail, Newsgroups*.

Management by Exception A principle of management in which a management decision that cannot be made at one level is passed up to the next level for a decision; i.e., exceptional decisions are passed up the management tree.

Megabyte 1,024 Kilobytes, or sometimes 1,000 Kilobytes. See also *Binary Digit, Byte, Kilobyte*.

Man-Machine Interface (MMI) An old term for human-computer interface. It used to include automatic and semi-automatic machinery that is not necessarily a computer or is computer-controlled.

Me-centric Approach in computing that puts the human needs in the focus of the design. Instead of creating tools that help people doing their tasks, me-centric computing does the tasks on behalf of the people.

Mental model Humans establish mental models of how things work, or how they would behave in a particular situation. For example, having been a student at a university for a while, a student can establish a "mental model" of attending a university. That is, he goes to classes, talks to his classmates about how to accomplish certain homework assignments, knows how to interact with his professors, etc. Suppose now a virtual university is being offered to students for online courses, and a Web site is to be constructed for the virtual university. This Web site should understand and respect the "mental models" of targeted students in order to avoid confusion for the students in finding their way around at the virtual university.

Message Messages or private messages refer to messages sent to one or more IRC participants. These messages can only be read by the recipient and the sender.

Message Handling System X.400 series of recommendations of abstract services and protocols used to provide electronic mail services in an OSI networking environment. X.500 is a series of recommendations that provide a distributed, user-friendly subscriber directory to help users address X.400 messages. These services are called simply "the directory."

Message Transfer Agents (MTA) Part of the X.400 OSI stack. Responsible for the actual transport of the message between user agents. MTAs typically reside on separate machines.

Metadata Assigned information "tags" or key words that help index documents or resources by providing background information, such as creation date, author, and date of last update. Metadata is not necessarily visible to the user, but rather works in the background to ensure that documents are properly indexed for searching. It can be stored in fields in the document itself or in a relational database, which "fills" document fields with associated metadata when a particular document or resource is retrieved by a user.

Metaphor A figure of speech in which a word or phrase literally denoting one kind of object or idea is used in place of another to suggest a likeness or analogy between them. Designers of graphical user interfaces often use well-known objects as interface metaphors to give users an indication of how interface objects will behave. For example, an image of a trash can has been adopted to indicate the operation of deleting files.

Micropayments Payments that have a value between a fraction of a cent and roughly 10 dollars/euros.

Mirror Site Site that contains an exact copy of the original site. They are used to spread the load over several sites and to speed up the download for customers by placing the server nearer to them.

MMI See *Man-Machine Interface*.

Mobility The ability to use a device in any location and at any time.

Mock-up Another term for prototypes, usually referring to low-fidelity prototypes, such as paper illustrations, screenshots, or simple configurations of screens with limited interaction.

Modem See *Modulator / Demodulator*.

Modulator/Demodulator (Modem) Device between computer and phone line that converts computer signals to a form that can be used to transport the data over telephone networks.

Motion Picture Experts Group (MPEG) A common workgroup (Working Group 11, also known as the International MPEG Laboratory) of the International Standards Organization (ISO) and the International Electrotechnical Commission (IEC). MPEG was founded in 1988 by over 100 companies to negotiate proposals and define standards in specific expert groups (requirement or system groups).

Motivation The presence of some degree of necessity between the signified and signifier of a sign. Makes the sign proper, and complete motivation makes the sign lawful. For example, a painting may resemble its subject, making it a proper sign.

MPEG See *Motion Picture Experts Group*.

Multi-Mode Interfaces Use of multiple modes, such as voice and images, at the same time, to communicate with the user. A typical example is a car navigation system, which provides a map of the route and a voice that tells which is the next turn to take.

Netiquette Code of behavior on the Internet.

Netizen Responsible citizen on the Internet.

Network The connection of two or more computers in order to share resources.

Networked House House or apartment with a cabled or wireless intelligent network used to support the inhabitants. See also *Intelligent Home*.

Network News Transport Protocol (NNTP) Standard protocol for exchanging postings and newsgroups over the Internet.

Newsgroups The "blackboards" of the Internet. Includes thousands of public information and discussion forums sorted according to topic. Participants can read and submit messages. Discussion group on USENET. See also *USENET*.

Node A device connected to a network.

NNTP See *Network News Transport Protocol*.

Object-Oriented Programming (OOP) Art of programming independent pieces of code, which are then able to interact with each other. This program philosophy was made popular through Smalltalk, Object Pascal, and C++.

ODBC See *Open Database Connectivity*.

Offline Not connected to the Internet.

Online Connected to the Internet.

On-Screen Display (OSD) A screen menu providing user instructions and simplifying operation.

OOP See *Object-Oriented Programming*.

Open Database Connectivity (ODBC) Interface defined by Microsoft for database systems. With an ODBC driver installed on a PC, the user can access other formats such as dBase, Oracle, Paradox, or Access.

Operating System (OS) Software that is loaded right after the boot time. It provides the basic functionality to run applications, based on a single set of instructions. An operating system manages, for example, the resources and processes, input/output controls, file system, and the user interface.

Opportunistic Behavior Tendency for users to generate and pursue goals suggested by objects presented by the user interface (e.g., icons, menu choices, prompts, and error messages).

OS See *Operating System*.

OSD See *On-Screen Display*.

Output Device A device that converts information coming from an electronic, internal representation in a computer system into a form that can be perceived by users or used by actuators.

Packet The smallest unit for transmitting data over the Internet. Data is broken up into packets, sent over the network, and then reassembled at the other end.

Participatory Design A democratic approach to design that encourages participation in the design process by a wide variety of stakeholders, such as designers, developers, management, users, customers, salespeople, distributors, etc. The approach stresses making users not simply the subjects of user testing, but actually empowering them to be a part of the design and decision-making process. See also *Stakeholder Analysis*.

Password Secret code to identify a user when logging onto a system.

PCMCIA See *Personal Computer Memory Card Industry Association*.

Perception The process of becoming aware of objects by way of the sense organs.

Peer-to-Peer A communications model in which each party has the same capabilities and either party can initiate a communication session. Other models with which it might be contrasted include the client/server model and the master/slave model. In some cases, peer-to-peer communication is implemented by giving each communication node both server and client capabilities. In recent usage, peer-to-peer has come to describe applications in which users can use the Internet to exchange files with each other directly or through a mediating server.

Permission The ability to access (read, write, execute, traverse, etc.) a file, directory, service, or agent. The privileges are very important in a me-centric world, as everyone will interact with a great number of appliances that will require different types of information and services that can be pulled automatically by having the right permissions. This makes sure that privacy can be guaranteed.

Perl Powerful scripting language, often used to write CGI scripts.

Personal Computer Memory Card Industry Association (PC-MCIA) Originally designed as a memory expansion card for laptop computers, this interface is used today for miniature modems or for digital TV descrambling systems.

Personalization Personalization is the process of tailoring services to individual users' characteristics or preferences. Commonly used to enhance customer service or e-commerce sales, personalization is sometimes referred to as one-to-one marketing, because the enterprise's Web page is tailored to specifically target each individual consumer. Personalization is a means of meeting the customer's needs more effectively and efficiently, making interactions faster and easier and, consequently, increasing customer satisfaction and the likelihood of repeat visits.

PGP See *Pretty Good Privacy*.

Phidgets Short for "physical widget." A tangible interface platform that connects to a computer through a USB cable. They are building blocks for creating physical user interfaces or tangible interfaces, just as graphical widgets are building blocks for creating graphical user interfaces. Phidgets are wired devices that simplify the controlling of servomotors and other actuators and the reading of sensor data such as light/force feedback/sound/etc.

Phrase Search A search for documents on the Internet containing an exact sentence or phrase specified by a user.

Plug-ins Software that adds functionality to commercial applications, such as the Netscape browser or Adobe's Photoshop.

Plug and Play Procedure for automatically configuring computer expansion devices or cards.

Pluralistic Walkthrough A pluralistic walkthrough is a specialized usability group inspection method where users, developers, and usability specialists step through a scenario discussing each page element of the system/site.

Point of Presence (POP) Local access to the services of an ISP. See also *Internet Service Provider*.

POP See *Point of Presence*.

POP3 See *Post Office Protocol*.

Port Interface for accessing services on a server.

Portal Point of entry; Web site to the Internet.

Postmaster Administrator of the mail server. In case of problems, you can contact the postmaster. The postmaster of someone@foobar.org is postmaster@foobar.org, for example.

Post Office Protocol Protocol for receiving mail via a client.

Pretty Good Privacy Encryption algorithm developed by Phil Zimmerman.

Problem Solving Consists of setting up the objectives of a problem-solving act, planning a sequence of steps to achieve that objective, executing the actions in each of the steps as planned, and evaluating what has been achieved against the objective.

Process The sequence of activities, people, and systems involved in carrying out some business or achieving some desired result. E.g., software development process, project management process, configuration management process.

Procedural Knowledge Stored information that consists of knowledge of how to do things.

Process An instance of a program running in a computer. It is close in meaning to "task", a term used in some operating systems. In UNIX and some other operating systems, a process is started when a program is initiated (either by a user entering a shell command or by another program). Like a task, a process is a running program with which a particular set of data is associated so that the process can be tracked. See also *Task*.

Proof of Concept A prototype that shows that something can be implemented, but is not necessarily robust enough for a usable system. For example, a dull knife would prove that you can cut vegetables, but it is not something you would use in normal practice.

The difference between a proof of concept and its more complete incarnation is context-dependent.

Protocol Rules controlling how computers and applications interact.

Prototype An experimental design of the whole or part of a product used for illustration or testing purposes.

Proxy Server A proxy server retrieves documents on demand from a server and passes them to a client. The advantage with a proxy server is that it normally caches documents. It is considerably faster to retrieve documents from the proxy than directly from a Web server, especially if someone else has already downloaded that particular document.

PSTN See *Public Switched Telephone Network.*

Public Switched Telephone Network (PSTN) The worldwide voice telephone system, also called the Bell System in the US.

Push Technology Also referred to as "Web-casting" or "channel-casting," this technology broadcasts personalized information to subscribers.

Qualitative Data Data that can be categorized in some way but cannot be reduced to numerical measurements.

Quality of Service (QoS) The idea that transmission rates, error rates, and other characteristics can be measured, improved, and, to some extent, guaranteed in advance.

Quantitative Data Data that consists of numerical values.

Query Request for information from a database.

Query-by-Example Find search results similar to a search result the user finds particularly useful.

Queue Sequence of objects.

QoS See *Quality of Service.*

RAM See *Random Access Memory.*

Random Access Memory (RAM) Memory that is used for executing applications and storing documents while working on them.

Rapid Prototyping A form of simple, rapidly produced prototyping in which the prototype is used to collect information about both the requirements and the adequacy of possible designs; it is not developed into a final product.

Rational Unified Processes (RUP) An online mentor that provides guidelines, templates, and examples for all aspects and stages of program development. It is a comprehensive software engineering tool that combines the procedural aspects of development (such as defined stages, techniques, and practices) with other components of development (such as documents, models, manuals, code, and so on) within a unifying framework.

Readme A text file containing information on how to use the file you want to access.

RealAudio Software tool that supports transmissions of real-time, live, or prerecorded audio.

Relational Database A database that does not have a predefined link structure. This allows the user to create new relationships between tables dynamically, i.e., during the course of operation. For example, you can link customer names with invoices using the customer ID number.

Remote Login Logging into a computer system from a remote location, meaning from another system on the network.

Request for Comments (RFC) The process for creating an Internet standard. New standards are proposed and published in the form of a request for comments document. When a new standard has been established, it retains the acronym RFC and a number is added, such as RFC1029.

Requirements Analysis The investigation of a problem that focuses on what functionality is required but not on how to provide that functionality.

Requirements Animation A software prototype used to explore possible functions and elicit from users their requirements for functions in a system.

RFC See *Request for Comments*.

Robotics A branch of engineering that involves the conception, design, manufacture, and operation of robots. This field overlaps with electronics, computer science, artificial intelligence, mechatronics, nanotechnology, and bioengineering.

Root The administrator account that has super-user rights on a system. See also *Sysop*.

ROTFL Net language for "rolling on the floor laughing."

Router A device to handle the connection between two or more networks. See also *Network*.

RTFM Net language for "read the f*cking manual." Answer to a question that users could have answered themselves by reading the manual.

RUP See *Rational Unified Processes*.

Safety-Critical Systems Specialized systems, such as those used in power plants, aircraft cockpits, and air traffic control, in which human or environmental safety is of paramount concern. Also called "Mission-Critical Systems."

Scenario A narrative describing one or more users' interactions with a computer, including information about goals, expectations, actions, and reactions.

Search Engine Databases containing information about documents available on the world wide Web, i.e., the "reference works" or "indices" of the Internet. Search engines are created manually or automatically by computers.

Searching A method for finding information using keyword location systems (search engines) that index resources in an information repository. Common search types include known-item, exploratory, and comprehensive searches.

Secure Electronic Transaction (SET) Payments are encrypted and sent via a (trusted) third party—a bank, for example. Then they are checked, and the customer identity is verified.

Secure Sockets Layer (SSL) Protocol invented by Netscape to encrypt communication between Web browsers and servers. It provides privacy, authentication, and integrity.

Sensor An electronic device used to measure a physical quantity such as temperature, pressure, or loudness, and convert it into an electronic signal of some kind (e.g., a voltage). Sensors are normally components of some larger electronic system such as a computer control and/or measurement system.

Server A device that provides one or more services to several clients over a network. See also *Client, Network*.

Servlet A Java application that runs on a server. The term usually refers to a Java applet that runs within a Web server environment. This is analogous to a Java applet that runs within a Web browser environment.

SET See *Secure Electronic Transaction*.

Shareware Programs that can be copied for testing purposes. Users who decide to use the program are required to register the software and pay a fee to the author. Shareware programs can often be used without restriction—based on the presumption that users are honest. Sometimes, however, they are limited in function or expire after a certain period of time.

Shopping Cart Keeps track of all the items that a customer wants to buy, allowing the shopper to pay for the whole order at once.

Short Message Service (SMS) A feature of GSM phones that allows users to receive and sometimes transmit short text messages using their wireless phones.

Sign A deterministic, functional regularity or stability in a system, also sometimes called a sign-function. Something, the signifier, stands for something else, the signified, in virtue of the sign-function. May be either lawful, proper, or symbolic depending on the presence or absence of motivation.

Signified The part of a sign that is stood for by the signifier. Sometimes thought of as the meaning of the signifier.

Signifier The part of a sign that stands for the signified, for example, a word or DNA code.

Simple Mail Transfer Protocol (SMTP) The protocol to send electronic mail over the Internet. See also *Electronic Mail*.

Simple Network Management Protocol (SNMP) Protocol to manage and monitor devices connected to a network.

Simple Object Access Protocol (SOAP) A way for a program running in one kind of operating system (such as Windows NT) to communicate with a program in the same or another kind of an operating system (such as Linux) by using HyperText Transfer Protocol (HTTP) and eXtensible Markup Language (XML) as the mechanisms for information exchange.

Smart Card Plastic card of credit-card size with an embedded microchip. The chip can contain digital money and personal information about the owner.

Smiley See *Emoticon*.

SMS See *Short Message Service*.

SMTP See *Simple Mail Transport Protocol*.

SNMP See *Simple Network Management Protocol*.

SOAP See *Simple Object Access Protocol*.

Spam Inappropriate use of e-mail and postings by sending information and advertising to people who did not request them.

Spider See *Web Crawler*.

Speech Recognition Transformation of the spoken word into a computer-readable form, such as dictation software. Depending on the type of use, speech recognition should be either speaker independent (e.g., mail dictation) or speaker dependent (e.g., password entry).

SQL See *Structured Query Language*.

SSL See *Secure Sockets Layer*.

Stakeholder Analysis A technique used to identify and assess the priority, needs, goals, and requirements of key people that may significantly influence the success of the project. Common examples of stakeholders in Internet projects include the user, the site administrator, the site support employees, the business directors, etc.

Stop Words Conjunctions, prepositions, articles, and other words that appear often in documents yet alone may contain little meaning.

Stored Procedure A set of Structured Query Language (SQL) statements with an assigned name that's stored in the database in compiled form so that it can be shared by a number of programs. The use of stored procedures can be helpful in controlling access to data, preserving data integrity, and improving productivity.

Structured Information Pieces of information that are created and maintained in distinct and inflexible formats. Common examples include financial transaction records and operational databases.

Structured Query Language (SQL) One of the preferred programming languages for communication with databases.

Structural Model A user's mental model that represents the structure of an object and allows the user to reason about and to predict the object's actions in novel situations. See also *Functional Model*, *Distributed Model*, and *Surrogate Model*.

Successive Approximation Also known as "Iteration to Agreement", describes the process to run a two-way dialog to get to understanding.

Surrogate Model A user's mental model that appears to act like a replica of the physical object or world, using simulations that can be run in the mind. See also *Structural Model*.

Symbian Joint venture between Ericsson, Motorola, Nokia, and Psion to develop new operating systems based on Psion's EPOC32 platform for small mobile devices including wireless phones or handheld personal computers. See also *EPOC*.

Symbol A data block consisting of a defined number of bits (the most well-known example of a symbol is a byte consisting of eight bits).

Synchronization Update of two systems to the same level. This is often required for mobile devices that were untethered for a while.

Sysop See *System Operator*.

System Operator (Sysop) Person who is responsible for the operations of a computer system or network resource.

Table Combines identical records together in columns (fields) and rows (records).

Task A basic unit of programming that an operating system controls. Depending on how the operating system defines a task in its design, this unit of programming may be an entire program or each successive invocation of a program.

Task Analysis The process of investigating a problem by breaking down the tasks that potential users of a system would do; this provides information about how functionality should be provided.

Task-Action Mapping The functional mapping between a task arena and an action arena. Mapping refers to the association of one element from one set to another element from another set. In terms of the task-action mapping model, it refers to the mapping of existing knowledge about how to carry out a task onto the physical devices.

TCP/IP See *Transmission Control Protocol/Internet Protocol*.

Telematics The integration of wireless communications, vehicle monitoring systems, and location devices.

Telnet Program to perform a remote login to another computer.

Terabyte 1,024 or 1,000 Gigabytes. See also *Byte, Kilobyte, Megabyte, Gigabyte*.

Tethered Connected to a network.

Thick Client A high-end terminal with lots of processing power that enables the client to run all applications locally.

Thin Client A cut-down network terminal with no local processing power.

Tool Until today computers and computing devices have been built as tools, meaning that people use them. Computers in the future will not be used anymore like tools to support a process; they will be used to delegate work.

Transaction Ensures that any modification to a database is carried out either completely (i.e., for all records) or not at all.

Transmission Control Protocol/Internet Protocol (TCP/IP) A set of protocols that are the foundation of the Internet and that enable the communication between computers. Technical basis for transmitting data on the Internet. It divides the contents of a Web page into small packets and sends them along different paths, if necessary, to the receiver where TCP/IP then reassembles the packets in their original order.

Triggers A set of Structured Query Language (SQL) statements that automatically "fires off" an action when a specific operation, such as changing data in a table, occurs. A trigger consists of an event (an INSERT, DELETE, or UPDATE statement issued against an associated table) and an action (the related procedure).

Triple-dub Net language for "WWW."

Trojan Horse A program that seems to be harmless, but starts harmful functions after it has been installed.

Ubu Roi French for King Ubu, fictional hero in a drama of the same name by Alfred Jarry. This narrative predated and inspired the Dadaist and Surrealist movements. Ubu Roi is an inverted human being, carrying his deepest motives on the outside, and any semblance of civilized behavior on the inside. He is useful for imaginary user-testing, because he is extremely incautious, quickly bored, rude, infantile, and completely self-obsessed. In other words, he presents a reasonable average user.

UMTS See *Universal Mobile Telecommunications System*.

Unicode Text encoding scheme including international characters and alphabets.

Uniform Resource Locator (URL) Addressing scheme on the Internet to locate Internet resources. A URL consists of a server name, possibly a directory name or full pathname, and the document title (example: http://www.ebusinessrevolution.com/blgarski/).

Universal Mobile Telecommunications System (UMTS) Europe's approach to standardization for the third generation of cellular systems. Although not yet implemented, it has already received lots of publicity due to the high costs that telecommunication companies have setting up the networks.

Universal Plug and Play (UPnP) Windows 9x and Windows 2000 offer so-called "plug-and-play" technology for automatically detecting all compatible devices within a PC. Universal Plug and Play is designed to expand this technology to include devices in an external network. After devices are connected to a network supporting Universal Plug and Play, they automatically configure themselves, which eliminates the need for setup and configuration. UPnP detects the devices along with the relevant product characteristics including communication protocols. For example, a camera can automatically detect a printer in the network, determine its ability to print in color, and print a photo.

UNIX Operating system that was developed in the early 1970s.

Unstructured Information Information that is produced and stored in multiple, non-specified formats. Common examples include e-mail documents, memos, and reports.

Untethered Not connected to a network. This ability is important in a me-centric world where intelligent appliances should be able to work autonomously for a given time even if they cannot find a network.

UPnP See *Universal Plug and Play*.

URL See *Uniform Resource Locator*.

Usability The broad discipline of applying scientific principles to ensure that the system designed is easy to learn, easy to use, easy to remember, error tolerant, and subjectively pleasing. A figure of merit or qualitative judgment of ease of use or learning. Some methods of assessing usability may also express usability as a quantitative index. There is a set of international (ISO) standards on usability defining it as "the extent to which a product can be used by specified users to achieve specific goals with effectiveness, efficiency, and satisfaction in a specified context of use."

Usability Engineering An engineering approach to design in which the system's usability is specified quantitatively.

Usability Specification A specification quantifying target levels of usability for a system in terms of: learnability, effectiveness, efficiency, flexibility, and the positive attitude to be engendered in users. International standards (e.g., ISO 9241-11) attempt to formalize the process and format of usability specifications.

Usability Testing Testing whether a system meets a predetermined, quantifiable level of usability for specific types of users carrying out specific tasks. Several quantitative and qualitative usability testing methods exist and can include comprehensive video and audio protocols and statistical analysis.

USENET A decentralized worldwide system for newsgroups. See also *Newsgroups*.

User-Centered Approach An approach that views the interface of a system as a central concern. Users are not merely components of a system, but are valued in their own right with their capabilities and limitations viewed as the main criteria for design of an interface.

User-Centered Design A design approach in which the emphasis is on the user and through which a high level of usability can be achieved.

User-Friendly An over-worked term intended to imply a high degree of usability.

User Profiling Using data collected from a number of different sites, which can result in the creation a personalized Web page before the user has been formally registered.

Virtual Memory System (VMS) A multiuser, multitasking, virtual memory operating system for the VAX series from Digital Equipment.

Virtual Reality Modeling Language (VRML) A programming language for displaying 3-D spaces on the Internet. VRML allows the user to design virtual landscapes or 3-D games. Current browsers are capable of displaying such data. Numerous browser plug-ins offer 3-D functions.

Virus Malicious piece of code that can be hidden in programs to destroy data on a computer.

Visit A complete session of accesses to a certain Web site conducted by one person. A visit is concluded when the customer hasn't viewed any page for a certain period of time (60 seconds in most cases).

Visual Mapping Mapping is the relationship between controls and their movements and the results in the problem solving process. Visual mapping can be achieved via the use of metaphors (trash can, sliders, windows, etc.) and controls that have good affordances. Natural mapping use constraints and correspondences in the physical world.

Voice Mail Similar to e-mail, voice mail is a message sent or received within a network as audio data.

Voice Recognition The task of identifying the speaker. This authentication method is becoming more dominant in combination with a password. As voice can be easily recorded, it is important not to use it as the only authentication mechanism.

VoIP A term used in IP telephony for a set of facilities for managing the delivery of voice information using Internet Protocol (IP).

VoxML Voice Markup Language. A technology from Motorola for creating a voice dialog with a Web site in which a user can call a Web site by phone and interact with it through speech recognition and Web site responses.

VRML See *Virtual Reality Modeling Language*.

WAIS See *Wide Area Information Servers*.

WAN See *Wide Area Network*.

WAP See *Wireless Application Protocol*.

W-CDMA See *Wideband CDMA*.

Web See *World Wide Web*.

Web Crawler Service that scans Web documents and adds them to a database. After having indexed one page, it follows all links and indexes them as well. See also *Search Engine*.

Webmaster The person in charge of a Web server. Most Web servers will allow mail to be sent to the Webmaster. The Webmaster of http://www.foobar.org/ can be reached at Webmaster@foobar.org, for example. See also *Postmaster*.

WebQoS See *Web Quality of Service*.

Web Quality of Service (WebQoS) A product that assures consistent quality of service on shared systems by preventing surges in on-line customer demand from overloading the server. It also allows service providers to safely host multiple sites on a single system by preventing busy sites from impacting each other's performance.

Web Server A computer that provides World Wide Web services on the Internet (or intranet). It includes the hardware, operating system, Web server software, TCP/IP protocols, and the Web site content. The term may refer to just the software that performs

314 Glossary Appendix A

this service, which accepts requests from Web browsers to download HTML pages, other document, images, etc. It can also execute related server-side scripts that automate functions such as searching a database.

Web Service A software application identified by a URI, whose interfaces and binding are capable of being defined, described, and discovered by XML artifacts, and supports direct interactions with other software applications using XML-based messages via Internet-based protocols.

What You See Is What You Get (WYSIWYG) The promise that what you see on screen will also be what you get when you print out the document. Few software packages are able to fulfill this promise.

Wide Area Information Servers (WAIS) Software package that allows the indexing of large quantities of information. Uses a separate protocol from HTTP and is not used very much anymore. See also *HyperText Transfer Protocol*, *Search Engine*.

Wide Area Network (WAN) A network that is distributed over several locations. See also *Local Area Network*.

Wideband CDMA The third-generation standard offered to the International Telecommunication Union by GSM proponents.

Wide-SCSI Transmission protocol compliant with SCSI-2 that defines an extension of the bus width to 16 bit and thus requires special cables and plugs. Wide-SCSI is normally used with Fast-SCSI and is capable of data transmission of up to 20 Mbps.

Wintel The majority of computers today run the Wintel combination: the Windows operating system and an Intel processor.

Wireless Using the radio-frequency spectrum for transmitting and receiving voice, data, and video signals for communications.

Wireless Application Protocol (WAP) A specification for a set of communication protocols to standardize the way that wireless devices, such as cellular telephones and radio transceivers, can be used for Internet access, including e-mail, the World Wide Web, newsgroups, and Internet Relay Chat (IRC).

Wireless IP The packet data protocol standard for sending wireless data over the Internet.

Wireless LAN (WLAN) Local area network using wireless transmissions, such as radio or infrared instead of phone lines or fiber-optic cable to connect data devices.

Wireless Markup Language (WML) Formerly called HDML (Handheld Devices Markup Language), a language that allows the text portions of Web pages to be presented on cellular phones and personal digital assistants (PDAs) via wireless access.

WML See *Wireless Markup Language.*

World Wide Web (WWW) The part of the Internet that is accessible through a Web browser. The Web is not the Internet, but a subset.

Worm A program that is designed to replicate itself over a network. Although not all worms are designed to destroy, most of them will try to attack your resources.

WRT Net language for "with respect to."

WWW See *World Wide Web.*

WYSIWYG See *What You See Is What You Get.*

Xanadu Bill Gates's networked home uses a variety of methods for electronic house control. According to press reports, the house has over 100 PCs connected to thousands of sensors and activators used to regulate lighting, air, and temperature. They also use chip cards to identify the whereabouts of people in each room. After the person has been identified, his preselected music and video preferences can be played.

xDSL Designation for digital subscriber line technology enabling simultaneous two-way transmission of voice and high-speed data over ordinary copper phone lines.

XML See eXtensible Markup Language.

Yahoo! The original and most famous Web directory. The name Yahoo! is an acronym for "Yet Another Hierarchical Officious Oracle."

YMMV Net language for "your mileage may vary." A warning that not everything described in a manual will work exactly the way it is promised to.

Zooming Viewing a display at different levels of granularity by moving in and out of various aspects of a display. An important interface technique to hide complexity or to allow the user to reveal varying levels of information.

ME-CENTRIC WEB SITES

In this appendix, we have collected some Web sites that have drawn our attention. Please do not consider this list as complete or particularly up to date. As with all URLs, you need to take into account that they were available at the time of writing, but there is no guarantee that they will be available at the time of reading, nor that they will contain the information they used to contain. For up to date information, please go to an online directory such as DMOZ[1] or a search engine such as Google[2].

Smart Agents

http://www.agentland.com/ Portal providing information about software agents.

http://www.botspot.com/ Resource for agent and bot programming.

http://www.botknowledge.com/ A collection of Web pages on intelligent software agents, knowbots, and bots.

http://www.fipa.org/ A non-profit organization aimed at producing standards for the interoperation of heterogeneous software agents.

Smart Infrastructure

http://www.gridcomputingplanet.com/ News portal on grid technologies.

---

[1]http://www.dmoz.org/
[2]http://www.google.com/

http://www.hp.com/large/infrastructure/utilitydata/ HP's utility data center, which can provide CPU power and hard disk space (among other things) on demand.

http://www-1.ibm.com/services/ondemand/ IBM's e-business on demand.

Smart Appliances

http://www.allnetdevices.com/ Source of news and information about handhelds, smart phones, set-top boxes, and other devices that connect to the Internet.

http://www.corecom.com/ia/ A guide to the technology, features, and development of Internet appliances.

http://www.devicesworld.net/ Offers Internet gateway devices and software services that enable users to connect any existing appliance to the Internet for remote monitoring and control.

http://world.honda.com/robot/ Web site about Honda's Humanoid Robot ASIMO.

Usability

http://www.usability.gr.jp/ Usability site in Japan.

http://www.usability.ru/ Usability site in Russia.

http://www.usabilitysa.co.za/ Usability site in South Africa.

http://www.nooface.net/ Articles, news, and discussion on next-generation user interfaces.

http://www.useit.com/ Jakob Nielsen's alertbox, reports, and books on usable information technologies.

Futurology

http://www.framtiden-er-din.com/ Futuristic site on global ethics, Earth Charter, the future of science and religion, and the purpose of life.

http://www.human3.com/ Future human consciousness explored and found to be achievable now; also includes new economic model.

http://www.overmorgen.com/ Portal with links to future-oriented news stories, Web sites, and studies.

Ubiquitous Computing

http://www.disappearing-computer.net/ A EU-funded proactive initiative of the Future and Emerging Technologies (FET) activity of the Information Society Technologies (IST) research program.

http://www.ebiquity.org/ Information portal on ubiquitous computing.

http://www.viktoria.se/fal/ Swedish Future Application Lab.

http://www.pointservers.org/ Overview on point server technology.

http://www.smart-its.org/ Web site, providing a far-reaching vision of computation embedded in the world.

http://www.Webservices.org/ Portal on Web services technologies.

Wearables

http://www.redwoodhouse.com/wearable/ Commented link collection on wearable computers, software, hardware, research, commercial, communication, as well as clothes.

http://www.wearablegear.com/ Information on wearable computers, portable MP3 hardware, and other cutting-edge mobile technology.

http://wearables.blu.org/ Information and tools about building wearable computers.

BIBLIOGRAPHY

[1] Commodore-Amiga, Inc (1991). *Amiga User Interface Style Guide*. Reading, MA: Addison-Wesley.

[2] Amor, Daniel (2001). *Internet Future Strategies*. New York: Prentice Hall.

[3] Apple Computer, Inc (1992). *Macintosh Human Interface Guidelines*. Reading, MA: Addison-Wesley Publishing Co.

[4] Apple Computer, Inc (1992). *Guide to Macintosh Software Localization*. Reading, MA: Addison-Wesley Publishing Co.

[5] Benjafield, John G (1996). *The Developmental Point of View. A History of Psychology*. Needham Heights: Simon & Schuster Company.

[6] Bradshaw, Jeffrey (ed) (1996). *Software Agents. AAAI Press/MIT Press*. Menlo Park.

[7] Brooks, Rodney A (1990). "Elephants Don't Play Chess", In Pattie Maes (ed). *Designing Autonomous Agents*. Cambridge, MA: MIT Press.

[8] Cagan, Jonathan and Vogel, Craig M (2002). *Creating Breakthrough Products: Innovation from Product Planning to Program Approval*. New York: Financial Times - Prentice Hall Publishing.

[9] Copernicus, Nicolaus (1543). *De revolutionibus orbium coelestium*. Nuremberg.

[10] Cushman, William H. and Rosenberg, Daniel J (1991). *Human Factors in Product Design*. Series: Advances in Human Factors/Ergonomics, edited by Gavriel Salvendy. Amsterdam Holland: Elseview.

[11] Deely, John (1990). *Basics of Semiotics*. Bloomington, Indiana: Indiana University Press.

[12] Dix, Alan; Finlay, Janet; Abowd, Gregory; and Beale, Russell (1993). *Human-Computer Interaction*. Hillsdale: Prentice Hall.

[13] George B. Dyson (1998). *Darwin among the Machines: The Evolution of Global Intelligence*. Cambridge, MA: Perseus Publishing.

[14] Eco, Umberto (1976). *A Theory of Semiotics*. Bloomington, Indiana: Indiana University Press.

[15] Eco, Umberto (1984). *Semiotics and the Philosophy of Language*. Bloomington, Indiana: Indiana University Press.

[16] Goldstein, N., and Alger, J (1992). *Developing Object-Oriented Software for the Macintosh*. Reading, MA: Addison-Wesley.

[17] Hewett, Baecker, Card, Carey, Gasen, Mantei, Perlman, Strong, and Verplank (1996). *ACM SIGCHI Curricula for Human-Computer Interaction*.

[18] Hewlett-Packard, IBM, Sunsoft Inc. & USL (1993). *Common Desktop Environment: Functional Specification (Preliminary Draft)*. X/Open Company Ltd.

[19] Hix, Deborah and Hartson, H. Rex (1993). *Developing User Interfaces: Ensuring Usability Through Product and Process*. New York: John Wiley & Sons, Inc.

[20] Lansdale, Mark W. and Ormerod, Thomas C (1994). *Understanding Interfaces: A Handbook of Human-Computer Dialogue*. Computers and People Series, edited by B.R. Gaines and A. Monk. San Diego, CA: Academic Press.

[21] Laurel, Brenda (ed) (1990), *The Art of Human-Computer Interface Design*. Reading, MA: Addison-Wesley Publishing Co.

[22] Lewis, Clayton and Rieman, John (1993). *Task-Centered User Interface Design: A Practical Introduction*. University of Colorado, Boulder.

[23] Locke, John (1690). "Essay concerning human understanding". Dorset.

[24] Norman, Donald A (1988). *The Psychology of Everyday Things*. New York: Basic Books.

[25] Norman, Donald A (1990). *The Design of Everyday Things.* New York: Doubleday.

[26] Norman, Donald A (1999). *The Invisible Computer.* Cambridge, MA: MIT Press.

[27] Madell T.; Parsons C.; and Abegg J (1992). *Developing and Localizing International Software.* Englewood Cliffs: PTR Prentice Hall.

[28] Preece, Jenny (ed) (1994). *Human-Computer Interaction.* Menlo Park: Addison-Wesley.

[29] Proctor, Robert W. and Trisha Van Zandt (1994). *Human Factors in Simple and Complex Systems.* Boston, MA: Allyn and Bacon.

[30] Salvendy, Gavriel (ed) (1997). *Handbook of Human Factors (2nd edition).* New York: John Wiley & Sons.

[31] Shneiderman, Ben (2002). *Designing the User Interface (Third Edition).* Menlo Park: Addison Wesley.

[32] Watzlawick P.; Beavin J.H.; Jackson D.D (1967). *Pragmatic of Human Communication.* New York: W.W. Norton & Co.

SUBJECT INDEX

http://www.phptr.com/

Prentice Hall PTR   InformIT   InformIT Online Books   Financial Times Prentice Hall   ft.com   PTG Interactive   Reuters

TOMORROW'S SOLUTIONS FOR TODAY'S PROFESSIONALS

Prentice Hall **Professional Technical Reference**

| Browse | Book Series | What's New | User Groups | Alliances | Special Sales | Contact Us |

Search | Help | Home

Quick Search

PTR Favorites

Find a Bookstore

Book Series

Special Interests

Newsletters

Press Room

International

Best Sellers

Solutions Beyond the Book

Shopping Bag

Keep Up to Date with

PH PTR Online

We strive to stay on the cutting edge of what's happening in professional computer science and engineering. Here's a bit of what you'll find when you stop by www.phptr.com:

What's new at PHPTR? We don't just publish books for the professional community, we're a part of it. Check out our convention schedule, keep up with your favorite authors, and get the latest reviews and press releases on topics of interest to you.

Special interest areas offering our latest books, book series, features of the month, related links, and other useful information to help you get the job done.

User Groups Prentice Hall Professional Technical Reference's User Group Program helps volunteer, not-for-profit user groups provide their members with training and information about cutting-edge technology.

Companion Websites Our Companion Websites provide valuable solutions beyond the book. Here you can download the source code, get updates and corrections, chat with other users and the author about the book, or discover links to other websites on this topic.

Need to find a bookstore? Chances are, there's a book-seller near you that carries a broad selection of PTR titles. Locate a Magnet bookstore near you at www.phptr.com.

Subscribe today! Join PHPTR's monthly email newsletter! Want to be kept up-to-date on your area of interest? Choose a targeted category on our website, and we'll keep you informed of the latest PHPTR products, author events, reviews and conferences in your interest area.

Visit our mailroom to subscribe today! **http://www.phptr.com/mail_lists**